D0481877

PRAISE FOR *SAVING EACH OTHER*

"Sometimes we're given a physical or spiritual challenge that we have no idea how we're going to rise to. In this riveting account of a mother-daughter love story and their urgent search for a cure, we're made aware of the power that dwells inside utter necessity. By the end of this book, you'll laugh, cry, rage, and rejoice . . . and you'll feel that lovely connection to life that you only get when you pass through your dark night of the soul."

—Kathy Freston, New York Times *best-selling author of* Quantum Wellness and The Lean

"Any parent or child will be moved and inspired by this story of how love and dedication can conquer pain and fear; a vivid reminder that there is nothing more powerful or enduring than the bond of mother and daughter."

—Rob Lowe, New York Times *best-selling author*

"*Saving Each Other* is a love story, a medical mystery, and also the proof we badly need that cooperation beats competition every time. This is an irresistible book that inspires readers—and could reform experts."

—Gloria Steinem

"I once said that life is found in the dance between your deepest desire and your greatest fear. *Saving Each Other* is about a pathway where two women face their greatest fears and experience their deepest desires together as they take on an incurable disease. It's quickly obvious this disease is no match for the powerful combination of a mother's love and devotion with a child's hope, determination, and will. You will be moved and inspired as you go on a journey with these two extraordinary women and find newfound courage within yourself."

—Anthony Robbins, New York Times *best-selling author, internationally acclaimed speaker, and peak performance expert*

"This is a spectacular and gripping story of personal courage and entrepreneurial creativity involving a mother and daughter. It is a story of medical researchers and disease detectives working hard to cure a young woman's frightening disease. The saga is ongoing, exciting, and full of drama and hope."

—Larry Steinman MD, Professor of Neurology and Pediatrics
Stanford University and Chairman of Immunology 2002–2011

"As a woman, mother, and close friend of the authors, I find this story deeply moving on so many levels. The work that I've seen Victoria, Ali, and the foundation undertake has been extraordinary, especially in bringing doctors together to share ideas and create a dialogue that wasn't there before. As their experts grow closer to finding better, more effective treatments for this disease, they can open the door for solutions to many other diseases—and that's just incredible!"

—Reese Witherspoon

"The unstoppable power of these two extraordinary women is an unforgettable and inspirational experience you will carry in your heart forever."

—Dustin Hoffman

"I've made a career telling inspirational women's stories. This real-life story is a triumph. *Saving Each Other* is about a mother and daughter bonding over love, maturity, and survival. Victoria and Ali, two people I've admired for years, have written an incredibly moving and important story that must be shared."

—Garry Marshall

"*Saving Each Other* is a testament to a mother's incredible strength and a daughter's unshakable courage. However, it is so much more than that. The Guthy/Jackson family's journey in fighting Ali's disease—and their refusal to give up—is beyond inspirational; it is truly one of the greatest love stories I've ever read. This wonderful book will make you laugh and cry. But most of all, you will cheer for this amazing family's unfailing tenacity and hope in the face of enormous obstacles and fear. Their fight will ultimately help save countless other lives."

—Sherry Lansing, CEO, The Sherry Lansing Foundation

Saving Each Other

Saving Each Other

A Mystery Illness ~ A Search for the Cure
A Mother/Daughter Love Story

Victoria Jackson and *Ali Guthy*

with *Mim Eichler Rivas*

Afterword by *Brian Weinshenker*, MD,
Professor of Neurology, Mayo Clinic

GUTHY JACKSON®
Charitable Foundation

The Guthy-Jackson Charitable Foundation
Registered Trademark © 2012

Published by Vanguard Press
A Member of the Perseus Books Group

 Printed in the United States of America. For information and inquiries, address Vanguard Press, 250 W. 57th Street, 15th Floor, New York, NY 10107, or call (800) 343-4499.

Editorial production by Lori Hobkirk at the Book Factory
Designed by Cynthia Young at Sagecraft
Set in 11.75 point Adobe Garamond Pro

A CIP catalog record of this book is available from the Library of Congress.
ISBN: 978-1-59315-733-3 (hardcover)
ISBN: 978-1-59315-734-0 (e-book)

Vanguard Press books are available at special discounts for bulk purchases in the U.S. by corporations, institutions, and other organizations. For more information, please contact the Special Markets Department at the Perseus Books Group, 2300 Chestnut Street, Suite 200, Philadelphia, PA 19103, or call (800) 810-4145, ext. 5000, or e-mail special.markets@perseusbooks.com.

10 9 8 7 6 5 4 3 2 1

To my three blessings, Evan, Ali, and Jackson
—with love forever and always, Mom

and

For Survivors and Thrivers everywhere
—Ali Guthy

(from Victoria Jackson)

Perseverance is where the gods dwell.

—DIRECTOR WERNER HERZOG,
REPEATING AN OLD PERUVIAN SAYING

~

(from Ali Guthy)

Dreams, the way we planned them
If we work in tandem
There's no fight we cannot win.
Just you and I, defying gravity.

—TAKEN FROM "DEFYING GRAVITY,"
FROM WICKED

Contents

A Note from the Authors

From Victoria Jackson

You're standing in a bookstore, holding this in your hands.

Or, on second thought, you could be browsing titles online or on a digital device.

Wherever you are, you open to this page and learn that I'm the mom in this love story. Even though I may be best known as a makeup artist turned entrepreneur and philanthropist, truly, my most important role in life is that of mother to my three beloved children.

Oh, for the record, if you Googled me, you might come across another Victoria Jackson, the *SNL* comedienne turned right-wing darling.

That would NOT be me. I'm the Victoria Jackson of infomercial fame who challenged the status quo of the makeup world by honoring the natural beauty of all women. My foundation for the "no-makeup makeup" look became the crown jewel of my cosmetics company that today has sales of more than a half-billion dollars. But the focus of my work now has to do with a different foundation, one devoted to funding research to unravel a medical mystery that, up until four years ago, was seen as incurable and often fatal. My husband, Bill, and I created the Guthy-Jackson Charitable Foundation in 2008 when our otherwise perfectly healthy, gorgeous, extraordinary teenage daughter Ali was stricken with this rare autoimmune disorder that threatened to take her from us.

Living our worst nightmare, I began to write this book out of a desperate refusal to accept the unacceptable. Part of the process was to have an outlet, a confidante. Part of it was to keep track of the history we'd made by launching the foundation in record time. During most of that first year, Ali knew her affliction was scary but asked not to know the specifics of the diagnosis or prognosis. The pages I was writing in those early days then took on an even more meaningful purpose when I gave them the working title of *Saving My Daughter, Finding Myself: The Journey of a Fearful Warrior.*

Back then, the scope of the book was more of a memoir. More of a "momoir."

That first year my dark humor helped me cope as the pages started to become more of a Mom-*Noir*. That was the fearful voice talking.

Fear has been a recurring theme in my life. Fear is what has often motivated me and what I've battled at most turning points, past and present. That's probably not what you expected to hear from a woman whose rags-to-riches story has been as triumphant as mine has been—from starting a multimillion-dollar business in my garage with no start-up capital to becoming a pioneer of the infomercial industry and in countless other ways.

Still, the more I focused on confronting fear, the more I realized that the most dominant theme for me has been something else: survival. The survivor's instinct is what's allowed me to go further than I could have ever once imagined and to dig myself out of whatever hole that I found myself in, no matter how deep or how dark.

The moral is: you can't live in fear. You have to live like a warrior. You have to do more than survive—you have to thrive.

I learned that from the wisest, most courageous person I know, my beautiful daughter, Alexandra Rose Guthy.

Ali has miraculously defied many odds, coming into her own as a young woman and now as a leader in the work of our foundation, which helps develop new ways of raising awareness and accelerating the time in which groundbreaking discoveries have been made. To all of our astonishment, the findings today—after four short years—promise to shed light on a range of debilitating diseases.

And in the process this book that began as a solo effort for me has become a shared journey for the two of us, a true mother-daughter love story of *Saving Each Other*.

FROM ALI GUTHY

Four short years ago *if you Googled NMO, neuromyelitis optica, you would have found almost nothing other than a brief, terrifying account of a little-understood illness. Today, if you Google Ali Guthy, you'll most likely be led to an extensive definition of NMO. But that by no means defines me.*

So who am I?

I am a daughter, sister, friend, student, tennis champion, cupcake connoisseur, and a lover of all things chocolate. I am a leader, supporter, athlete, fan, and a fighter extraordinaire. I am a laugher, talker, listener, hugger, and supreme queen master of optimism in the universe. And I am also now an author.

I am all these things and more. But I am not a victim.

Four years ago I never would have agreed to write this book—not out of insecurity or spite or pure hatred for the disease I harbor but rather out of a deep-seated need to be ignorant. I was too young, too naïve, and too proud to confront the true nature of my disorder. I was a closet defeatist, too terror stricken to challenge myself and overcome the burdens of panic and anxiety this disease had embedded within me. But the lessons of Saving Each Other *are about how anyone can grapple with the most dire diagnosis and take action to transform reality positively.*

That was a story I wanted to tell.

Not in a self-help, how-to-cope-with-loss way but rather as a candid account of the deterioration of my erodible fears and my personal transition into adulthood. My mother and I had to agree to take the journey full-on, wherever it led, to scale the depths of despair and to rise to the summit of triumph together. We had to relive every moment from first being diagnosed with an incurable disease to initiating progress, change, and hope for the entire world of medicine.

SAVING EACH OTHER is not the story of the victims but rather the story of the activists, survivors, "thrivers," and the little foundation that could.

When your child, or anyone's child, is stricken with a parent's worst nightmare, or when you as a child know something's wrong but aren't ready for all the details just yet, you have a choice. You can fall apart and stick your head in the sand or you can face the truth and fight back!

We chose to fight.

SAVING EACH OTHER is our story, but it can be everyone's story.

You're standing in a bookstore. You turn the page and begin . . .

Prologue

Where It Begins

I have been through some terrible things in my life, some of which actually happened.

—Mark Twain

FIRE

Everything begins with fire.

Then me alone, age fourteen and a half, not used to being all on my own.

I'm in a dark place, a very dark place. Everything is burning around me, just burning.

I run.

I run so fast for the window that it's like I'm flying! But I don't seem to get there any faster. I see the tree—my escape, my only means of survival. My heart is pounding in my ears, throbbing repeatedly like the sound of bass drums.

Bum-bum-bum-bum!

The glass shatters and down I fall. But wait, where is everyone?

I turn to see all I hold dear burning, all that I love wasting away right before my eyes. The pain is too much to bear. I'm so helpless. How could I be so helpless? The tears begin to swell—with a pressure behind my eyes—fighting so hard to break down that dam I've built, to let the flood run through.

In the dream I can't stop the force and finally give in, breaking as the steady flow of giant-sized tears make their way down my face.

In my safe and secure life I shake myself awake, slowly lifting my head off my "Sweet Dreams" pillowcase, as I reach for the ready box of tissues at my bedside.

The bewildering part is that this isn't the first time I've had this nightmare. But it is the first time I let the feeling of loss coax the tears from my eye sockets, opening the floodgates I've been so desperately holding back for days.

JUST A BAD DREAM, I tell myself, catching my breath.

JUST A BAD DREAM.

Of course. But then why do I keep dreaming about fire? And why does it seem so real, like a serious warning—a symbol of looming danger, a sign of impending doom?

I mean, dreams rarely come true in real life, right?

They rarely, if ever, come true, that's fair to say.

Except in our family, apparently. For better and for worse.

—ALI GUTHY

~

Valentine's Day, 2008 (plus a week or so)

Everything begins with the imagined sound of a phone ringing.

A return phone call from a specialist is scheduled to come in just after dinner. The phantom ring sound is unfamiliar, unsettling.

My husband, Bill, and I get up from the table, watch the kids bolt off to their rooms, and then make our way up the stairs to his office.

In the main foyer a leftover, scented holiday candle is burning—a reminder of the festive atmosphere enjoyed over the previous Christmas break that has managed to linger in the air. Well, that is, until recently.

If that seems incongruous with the odd sense of foreboding that I can't shake, it's only because I'm personally trying to hold onto the seasonal spirit—always bucking the odds, rule-breaker that I am—because nothing makes me happier than whenever all three kids are under the same roof with me. Forget the rituals and festivities. All that matters is when I can hear their laughter and the music of their three distinct personalities in multiphonic surround sound. Then, all is well in the world.

In Bill's office I'm greeted by a family photo, our most recent holiday card, shot a couple months ago at the beach. There I am in it, clearly cracking up about something someone just said. There's Bill in the middle, tall and athletic, blue eyes twinkling, hair graying but looking otherwise ridiculously youthful for his early fifties.

Next to me is my strapping, seriously handsome, almost twenty-three-year-old son, Evan (born to me and Joe, my former husband). Evan, always my soulful child, stands slightly at a distance from me, something I can't change, as much as I try, as more and more he needs to navigate his own way into the world.

On the other side of me, also standing next to Bill, is Ali Rose, four teen and a half. Athletic, incredibly self-possessed yet fiercely private, she has this rarest of rare kinds of beauty—one that is both girl-next-door and otherworldly—as she looks deeply into the camera lens, pulling on your heartstrings. Without even trying.

And then next to his big sister is our youngest, twelve-year-old Jackson (tall and lanky in Guthy tradition), irresistibly cute, unbelievably sweet, and sometimes too brilliant for his own good. Or ours.

Bill, noticing the photo, insists that it's a great shot of me too. But then, knowing that's not the issue, he gives me a look that says "don't worry."

"Don't worry." It's a phrase that has not played well in my life, given the circumstances.

To give that some context, I should mention some salient facts about my somewhat worrisome start in life.

Fact #1: I wasn't planned; my parents were very young.

Fact #2: I was a preemie, born three months early, weighing all of three pounds, and I had to stay in the hospital three months before they let me go home.

Fact #3: There was still a little discussion required about what my name should be. I'm pretty sure that I came out early just to get a head start on worrying.

If you talk to my father—which I don't anymore—he'll say, "Your mother never visited you in the hospital." And my mom, who now refers to my father as "you and your sister's sperm donor," always says, "That man never visited you in the hospital." There was also this story my parents both seemed to recall about trudging through the snow to visit me. Really? Snow in Long Island at the end of August?

A part of me was resentful. They didn't even bother to get their stories straight! But then again, they were young, ultimately incompatible, and nowhere near ready to have kids. Hence the delay in coming up with a name—Vicki Ellen. Strangely, the birth certificate has somehow vanished. No wonder I felt lost most of my young life.

All I knew was that when I had children, they would be celebrated and welcomed into the world, secure in the knowledge of being wanted, loved, and adored. So maybe I was compensating for the feeling of not belonging that I had when I was growing up.

My mom recalls that when I did come home from the hospital, the nurses had spoiled me so much that I wasn't an easy baby. I had a host of medical problems. At age four I had to have tubes in my ears because there was something wrong with my hearing. Then there was stomach trouble too. Most of the health stuff was outgrown once I started school. Even so, I had already become what I later learned in therapy is known as the "identified patient." The therapist explained that one child usually winds up at the center of the family dynamics. That was me.

Fact #4: My parents divorced when I was about nine years old, after we moved from New York to Los Angeles, which didn't help my feelings of insecurity. No sooner had Mom remarried when Dad called to say he was giving me and my sister up for adoption.

We weren't orphans—how could he do that? Adoption?

"You bastard!" were the first words that flew from my nine-year-old lips.

He didn't see why Mom's new husband, Mort, couldn't adopt us. "Look, these kids"—his new wife's kids—"they don't have anyone. You at least have Mort." He paused and said, "Some day you'll understand."

Oh, right. Years later, during one of the few awful visits I had with him, I had to say, "Uh, no, I'm a parent now, and I still don't understand."

Those facts set the stage for me, the identified patient in the family, to become hyperaware of possible threats to my safety but also to be seen as the girl who cried wolf.

"Mom? Mommy? Is there someone in the house? I think there's someone in the house—" I knew that something or somebody was coming to get me. It became the family joke. The older kids would tease, "Why would they want to get you? What's so special about you?" Translation? "Don't worry."

Fact #5: One night, when I was seventeen, with the rest of the household asleep upstairs, my stepbrother waited in my bedroom for me to come home. It was one in the morning when I sat down on my bed to watch TV and spotted his reflection in a mirror. He was wearing a ski mask, holding a pillowcase, and I was instantly terrified but caught myself, figuring it was only a mean prank.

What I remember next for some reason is realizing that *Highway Patrol* was on. Then he touched me. The smell, the size, the sound as he spoke—they all told me I was wrong.

Not my brother. Not a prank. A robber? Was the pillowcase for carrying whatever he stole? No, it turned out that the pillowcase was for me. In Los Angeles at the time a man was running around, breaking into women's homes, and putting a pillowcase over the heads before he raped them. And now I was one of those women.

That trauma and its aftereffects, plus the foregoing facts, are important to the backstory of how I became prone to having irrational fears. But clearly they're not always irrational. I believe that somewhere back in that incubator I developed this survival mechanism—call it a highly developed protective instinct, a Voice, that warns me of actual threats or helps me be attuned to real opportunities. Kind of like a sixth sense. Complete with premonitions.

Sometimes I'll have a flash of something that could happen and it may take weeks or years. It's that feeling of waiting for the other shoe to drop. Usually it does. For better and for worse.

There are no rules for when to trust that vibe, that feeling.

Although there is my Rule of 2%. Basically, whenever the odds of something happening are really low—say not impossible but about 2% likely—turns out in my life they're going to happen.

I started referring to premonitions about rare occurrences when I went in for a root canal some years back. The dentist was telling me what to expect, saying that most of the time people recuperate well. But then he added, "There's always that 2%." Some of us, it seems, have an extra canal, which can make things difficult.

The dentist laughed when I told him that was going to be me. Sure enough, during the procedure, he remarked, "You know, you're right. You have the extra canal."

My Rule of 2%.

That's why I'm worrying on this evening in question in February 2008, even though the doctor who ordered the most recent test actually said he had never even ordered it before, much less read a positive report. The odds were even more impossible—one in many million. That's how rare and unheard of it is, whatever the thing is they're testing for.

It's also why when Bill takes a seat in an inviting armchair behind his desk, I perch myself nervously on the edge of the small straight-backed chair across from him. In between us a telephone with a speaker sits on the desk, poised to ring any minute.

A series of phone calls have come in over the past few evenings. Each were to rule out possible causes for Ali's sudden onset of unusual, debilitating symptoms. Most of the doctors say that not knowing what she has but having the tests turn out negative could be a positive—medical language that confirms somehow that my world is about to be turned upside down. But other doctors say that a positive test wouldn't necessarily be bad because it means they can then do something about it—you know, treat it or fix it or remove it. Well, except in cases like some of the really unheard of diseases like this one. Which the doctor only ordered as an afterthought. Just to rule it out. Like you would in a criminal lineup, when you include the least likely suspect.

I find it unnerving how medical terminology likes to turn positives into negatives and vice versa. My only earlier frame of reference for all this comes from the many years of doing volunteer work with women in hospitals and in other settings—doing beauty makeovers for patients—and hearing doctors speak of the "positive makeup sign." When a woman battling cancer or recovering from a devastating illness or injury or combating depression is making strides toward healing, one of the indications of that is when she takes an interest in how she looks. The positive makeup sign, when she asks for makeup or puts it on, indicates that a corner has been turned in her physical and/or spiritual healing. Well, at least that's one aspect of medical language I can speak.

Calming myself with these thoughts, if only to convince Bill that I too agree that there's nothing to worry about, I summon one of my own mantras (or, if you prefer, a Momtra): Fake It Until You Make It.

Besides, as Bill might have argued, being the most logical, 2% cuts both ways. It's the Rule that wins the jackpot, that helps you turn crazy pipedream ideas into ways of revolutionizing the marketplace, and that once empowered a scared, insecure, but determined teenager like me to eventually build a cosmetics empire. That enabled a young, single, struggling mom to become a global Good Will Ambassador for mascara. Obviously, I tell myself, Ali's symptoms are some kind of bizarre virus and thank God other worst-case scenarios have been ruled out. Whatever this NMO-IgG test is all about, there's no point in worrying.

Like a snap of the fingers, I've banished the worry. Not bad.

And that's when the phone actually rings.

~

In a household like ours, *talk of my mom's Rule of 2% isn't your common dinner-table conversation.*

I don't mean to say that it's taboo, but to go into all the kinds of rare, unusual, coincidental, or magical occurrences that occur with unusual frequency would be seen as, well, tempting fate. Besides, compared to a lot of people, I've found that we're one of the most normal, everyday families around. (Note: my big brother, Evan, and I are the deputies of keeping it normal. Everybody else, not so much.)

Here's the hitch: not really normal things do happen to all of us, all the time, including us kids. Not just because we're the offspring of self-made parents and we live in "rarified air." Like Mom says, she's lived most of her life without money, so that's not the issue. But from what I've heard of both my parents' lives, each has had their share of flukes, coincidences, and big-time overcoming the odds.

Some would say it's all about luck, the generous sprinkling of fairy dust. Magic. A Midas touch.

The problem with that is when you get into the dark spectrum of rare occurrences. There are those freakish, unlikely coincidences, for example, when you hear on the news that there's been a tragic accident and the victim turns out to be one of your best friends. Some would say that you've been marked by misfortune, that you are cursed.

There is no rhyme or reason. So that's why, in our family, when good things happen, we talk about how lucky and grateful we are—and how all the hard work paid off, how all the steps along the way were taken. When the fluke of fate causes something not good or terrible to happen, then it's even worse to credit any kind of strange system of odds for having your number come up. (Hint: my mother couldn't bring herself to fly for something like thirty-four years.)

Oh, and one more thing—you don't get to choose 2% or not. It chooses you.

~

The sound of the phone's ring seems to go on forever, piercing the quiet.

Dr. K., our ophthalmologist/neurologist, who referred us to the doctor's office where the test was ordered, begins speaking in a soothing tone, apologizing for the delay, explaining something about how this test works, why it had to be sent out to a special lab. His calm manner suggests, yet again, a negative test result is about to send us back to the drawing board. And who knows—by then, we might have the entire matter behind us.

Though it sounds very convincing to me, that Voice I've known ever since Ali was born begs to differ. In my mind's eye I'm seeing her in my arms for the first time. She was translucent—this pure, tiny angel. She had a vein that went from eyebrow to eyebrow, right across her nose. She had a sweetness about her, a gentleness. A transparency. Just different, I felt that right away. With Evan there was colic, sleepless nights. Not Ali. She was so easy. But I had the haunting sense there was going to be some challenge for Ali, that all would not be so easy up ahead.

There was nothing to base it on, and my worries did seem irrational. I never told anyone that because I didn't want to make it real. And who wants to be right about something like that? I thought . . . well, maybe I'm projecting my own fears and anxieties. I had enough for us both! But it stuck with me: the more she blossomed, the more extraordinary she was in almost every way, the more I began to wait for the other shoe to drop.

And that's really what's so crazy about my Rule of 2%. It's not that your intuitive sense makes you so special, that you are directing the traffic of your universe or that of your loved ones. Sometimes you just know it's going to be different. Sometimes you just know that when somebody's number comes up, good or bad, it belongs to your daughter.

Dr. K., in the midst of what shall heretofore be remembered as The Phone Call, announces on the speaker phone in Bill's office that the test results have come in as positive for something, something, something I-gG. Or is it Eye-gG?

Thinking I haven't heard correctly, I'm about to ask what that means when he continues, describing the little he knows, then says a few more things, none of which I hear except, "Your daughter has a fatal illness."

Bill? Bill? Did you hear what he—?

"Did you say—was that . . . those three letters before the gG were what?" (That would be Bill, because my vocal cords have ceased to work.)

The doctor explains that's the name of the test. He says more about something, something, something, being the initials for a longer Latin-sounding name only recently coined because the disease was originally named for the French neurologist who first identified the affliction over a century ago after treating patients with its more prevalent symptoms, "blindness and paralysis."

Bill, stop him, tell him to stop, make him—

" . . . very rare. If she were my daughter, I'd . . . "

I don't remember much that was said after those words or much of anything in the days that followed. (Sometimes, I still don't.) I didn't sleep for weeks. (Still can't.) Some nights I'd leave the house and wander the streets at 4 a.m. in slippers and a robe. Couldn't stop crying. Couldn't stop trying to understand how this had happened.

But I wasn't going to fall apart either. Because I had no choice, because I had an almost fifteen-year-old angel of a daughter who needed me to be there for her in the fight of her life. Falling apart was a non-starter.

My mother used to tell me, "Wash your face, put on your makeup, and go out there." That was the mantra, her Momtra for me. It had served me well all my life, and now it was going to serve Ali.

But as I'm thinking about this one night a short while after that Valentine's Day massacre of a phone call, out in my robe in the unseasonable balmy night air, I realize it's not about makeup anymore. It's about war paint.

I'm remembering me in my garage way back when, like a mad scientist, mixing my own foundation for my work as a makeup artist, playing with color and consistency in pots and pans, not realizing that the labors there were going to yield my own version of finding gold. It occurs to me that somewhere in some garage, some hospital, some lab, a real scientist, mad or sane, could be at this very moment working on discovering the cause and cure for the killer that's loose and after my child.

That was when the journey began, when it became clear that I knew enough about the Rule to know I had a fighting chance. If my 2% got us into this, then my 2% could get us out.

PART I

It would be so nice if something made sense for a change.

—ALICE, FROM *ALICE IN WONDERLAND*, BY LEWIS CARROLL

1

The Eyeball Headache

MONTHS EARLIER, IN THE LAND AND TIME OF PREDIAGNOSIS.

The beginning, of course, *came long before the phone call. But where does it begin? It's difficult to recount a lifetime when it hasn't really begun.*

I was fourteen when things started to change, when my world began to twist and turn on this tornado of a journey we call life.

Stomachaches and vomiting are not necessarily the first things you would think of in terms of symptoms that would lead to a life-changing illness, but in my case they certainly triggered the avalanche of symptoms in the years to come.

I don't remember exactly how or when it started; I just remember that around Christmas one year I began to feel very ill. The holidays are supposed to be a time of joy and merriment and family, but the Christmas of 2007 was quite the opposite. Instead of singing the "Twelve Days of Christmas" or setting out cookies for Santa, I spent most of my winter vacation staring down the basin of an empty toilet bowl, trying to settle my never-ending nauseous stomach and expel any substance I had consumed earlier that day.

Overall, this entire four-week period—and I mean the ENTIRE *four-week period—could be summarized in a three-step process: eat, puke, try to eat some more.*

For a tall, skinny, beanpole like me, it's not difficult to imagine how my parents began to suspect a sort of body-image problem. After all, middle school is an awkward time in development, when puberty is in full swing, and young girls are more likely to fall prey to media-portrayed stereotypes and other influences. Therefore, it's not surprising at all (especially as the five or six doctors I visited during this time couldn't find anything wrong with me) that my parents were driven to the conclusion that I might be anorexic.

The other favorite theory among my concerned relatives was that I was suffering from anxiety due to the annual holiday departure of our beloved family friend and major influence in my life, Raquel.

Of course, to me none of this made sense. "I'm not anorexic—I'm sick!" was my mantra of choice when I was bombarded with words of reassurance.

"You look great, honey! If you ever have anything you want to talk to me about, I'm here for you. You know that, right?"

"Yes, I know that, but there's nothing to talk about because I'm not doing this on purpose!"

I remember one particularly nasty adventure to the G.I. (gastro-intestinal) doctor, during which they forced me to drink this utterly repulsive liquid that smelled like glue and tasted just the same. The nurse added a packet of Nesquik to the concoction, as if a little chocolate powder would make the drink even the slightest bit more appealing. The entire procedure, which resulted again in inconclusive evidence that did not help my claim that I was not anorexic, scarred me. And to this day I sometimes gag at the thought of Nesquik.

After a month of suffering and absolutely no conclusive idea whatsoever as to what had caused this sudden and bizarre strand of vomiting, everything went back to normal. As quickly as the ordeal began, it went away and all seemed to be right as rain.

That is, until a year later.

Was I still mad at my parents? Well, let me say that I don't necessarily consider myself to be a very forgiving person. I remember one time in the fourth *grade I was very good friends with this girl. Let's call her Rachel. My friend Rachel and I had started a club together to raise money for charitable organizations (I think our biggest donation was about $75 to my school's library). Well, one day Rachel decided to tell everyone to quit the club and join another club that she made up herself; oh, and she also told everyone to stop talking to me. For an entire day no one in my class would talk to me—until I told my teacher and everything went back to normal. I haven't spoken to Rachel since. Now I know it was the fourth grade, and I think it's safe to say things have changed since then, but I still hold a grudge against Rachel for what she did.*

That being said, you would think I would hold a pretty decent grudge against my parents for believing for a solid year that I had been anorexic. I mean I'm still mad at a girl who messed up a day of my life in fourth grade!

But I could never be mad at my parents, not even for a second, even if that did mean being the only one who knew the truth about that winter break: I wasn't doing this to myself. Something else was.

~

Early February 2008

If you drive east on Sunset on any given day, leaving Beverly Hills behind as you head toward Hollywood, just before Doheny Drive there is a particularly graceful, arching stretch in the road as it rises and bends to the left. For years whenever I returned from our Beverly Hills offices to the San Fernando Valley where we used to live, I sometimes would go out of my way to drive this stretch of Sunset toward Laurel Canyon and would slow down while driving past the familiar landmarks, not out of caution but just to savor the ride. Even when we moved closer to our offices—feeling somewhat starry eyed, a little like the Beverly Hillbillies—I loved to drive east on Sunset and especially along that turn in the road.

That is, until one night when I happened to luck into two tickets to a Hollywood premiere of a movie described as a fairy tale about a young heiress born with a curse. In hindsight that would not be exactly the storyline I'd want to embrace. But this being in the days of innocence, before The Phone Call, Ali and I are nothing but thrilled to have an excuse to get all dressed up and step out together for a mother-daughter night on the town. It's a chance to talk without brothers and Dad, to catch up on how everything's going with school and tennis and everything else that Ali does—everything that she does, I should add, at a level of peak performance and with A-type-personality perfection, always injecting humor, intelligence, and a sense of adventure into everything.

Ironically, though Ali loves film and television, it seems that, for her age, she's unusually aloof from the show-business whirl or the gossip that makes up so much of the media these days. Instead—and it's actually kind of bizarre—she's obsessed with medical dramas and documentaries, digesting such shows as *Mystery Diagnosis* on the Discovery Channel with a pronounced attention to detail.

It's as though unraveling the cause of a patient's symptoms—a stranger—is a matter of grave, personal importance to her. Over the past year, after a series of stomach ailments and some sort of allergic skin reaction, Ali has been led to extensive self-diagnosis and frequent announcements that she has developed the latest, obscure new disease.

"Mom, I think I have Ryder's Syndrome!"

Say what?

Then the next day it would be, "You don't understand—it's textbook porphyria!"

It's at the point that she's taken to diagnosing us. "Mom," she'll start, "I don't want you to worry, because there is treatment. But I know what you have. It's Munchausen by proxy!"

Besides the humor in these exchanges, I can't help but feel the tiniest bit pleased that my daughter might be leaning toward the medical field as a potential profession. Or maybe it's my past as a high school dropout who never went to college—and my desire for Ali Rose to know there is nothing she can't do or be. Ever.

The other thing about her and the medical dramas is that on those few occasions when the team discovers the diagnosis and treatment too late and the patient doesn't make it, Ali is predictably livid.

That's another irony about her watching the medical shows—the fact that my almost fifteen-year-old is a true romantic, a connoisseur of love stories and endings when they all live happily ever after. Whenever any plot takes a dark turn, Ali is not one to want to travel down those roads.

She's a lot like her dad in that way. This is a man, after all, whose family literally sings their favorite song from *The Sound of Music* when they say goodbye! The first time I saw it happen—as his vibrantly beautiful mother (a former model) and equally lovely aunt were leaving after a dinner visit and they suddenly broke into "So long, farewell, Auf Wiedershen, adieu . . . " and Bill belted out the lines right along with them, "to yieu, and yieu, and yieu . . . "—I thought it was the sweetest, funniest thing ever.

But after a while—after almost a decade and a half of their insistence on singing that same song every single time a member of the family is leaving—I'm starting not to be as delighted as in the past.

Maybe that's just the realist in me. Maybe it's just that I know not every story concludes with all's well that ends well.

Pleasantville's a nice place to visit, really. But it's not somewhere to live. Some endings aren't happy, as much as we would like for them to be otherwise. Some good-byes aren't easy. Some break your heart.

Don't get me wrong. There's a romantic in me too. I have obviously been Cinderella who has gotten to go to the ball, thanks to the magic wand of mascara and the power of believing that, regardless of circumstances, we can all make up our lives. Seriously. As the thought occurs to me, I have to admit that, yes, in fact, *Make Up Your Life* was the title of my beauty/self-help bestseller, my second book. No plug intended—although I should credit Collette Dowling's *The Cinderella Complex*, a book that I read back in the 1980s and found to be life changing, leaving me with the conviction that the only fairy tales that come true are the ones you create for yourself.

Of course, growing up in the home that I did, marked as less likely to succeed, I figured out that eventually I needed to write a better story for myself than the one that I'd been living. My sister Audrey, younger than me by two and a half years, was the one with potential. Mom sent her to the Lycée, and Audrey skipped so many grades that she was in college studying psychology when I was still in high school (I attended a few of them), pursuing a degree in Rebellion.

Let's just say I took the "Rebel without a Cause" class, failing in "rebel" but doing well in "without a cause." Ditching was my forte. One year I was truant for 176 days. How do you even do that? I was the girl who had low self-esteem before they even called it low self-esteem. That's me—always the pioneer.

Senior year at Beverly Hills High School (we lied and said we lived in the district) I was starting to come around and do well in my studies. But then came the trauma of the Pillowcase Rapist, who, as with his other victims, had put a pillowcase over my head to make sure I couldn't identify him later.

After that unfortunate incident, I didn't want to be known as a victim. I dropped out a few months shy of graduation and began a major reinvention. A few apartments of my own later, I decided that although juggling various waitressing and odd jobs was paying the bills, I wanted and needed to find my true passion.

So I sat at home and moved my finger down the career list until it stopped at Makeup Artist. My first thought was, *Hey, I could do that.*

I'd been doing makeovers on friends since I was a teenager. What an incredible feeling to witness that look, the dancing lights in my friends' eyes while they stared in the mirror and studied their transformation. Those young women made me feel like a magician. Aha. An early taste of the Power of Mascara.

And don't forget the Momtra: "Wash your face, put on your makeup, and get out there."

Off I went: a $2,000 scholarship to the Marinello School of Beauty. A booming career as a top Hollywood makeup artist followed, as did a second calling teaching the art of my craft at the university level. From there it was only a couple more steps to launching my own cosmetics line and eventually coming into my own as an infomercial pioneer.

Yep, from high school dropout to the woman who climbed on her blush-covered wagon and, with the help of a few courageous celebrities, crossed the wild frontier of Televisionland to stake a claim for Victoria Jackson Cosmetics. When Bill and I met, each of us being divorced at the time, his company, Guthy-Renker—best known today for bringing the world Proactiv™—was the main competitor to the company that represented me.

How 'bout that for a reinvention? No, I didn't go to my high school prom, but Bill and I were crowned King and Queen of Infomercial homecoming instead. Ah, the love I have for the possibilities of a life makeover—or any other kind—can't be overstated.

And that, as it happens, is the heartwarming thought that comes to mind as our car winds its way east on Sunset, right as I'm signing off from a phone call, when I look over at my beautiful, smiling daughter: that we really do have what anyone—including me—would consider to be a charmed life.

And in this very same split-second of reality-based enchantment, just as we come around the bend and arrive at my favorite stretch, just as I'm glancing over at Ali, feeling practically giddy, I notice her wince.

Not a big thing. Just a little ouch kind of wince. Or an involuntary wince over a fearful thought that comes into your head.

"What's wrong, honey?"

At first, Ali shrugs, not able to explain. She doesn't say, "Nothing." But that's what she's going for.

An eerie chill shoots through my veins. The old taunting, warning Voice clears its throat. *It's not nothing*, the Voice tries to say, only it's talking in a foreign tongue. The Voice seems to be hinting that this is the something that's been in the works for a very long time, from the moment I first held her in my arms.

Mark this spot, here on Sunset Boulevard right before Doheny as we veer left and as the grade rises, as when it all changes. As the dividing line between our past and present. Between everything that used to be solid, certain, and predictable and all that is none of that anymore.

~

So it was a Saturday, *and my mom and I had been invited to attend the screening of the new movie PENELOPE. I was so excited to go, I had my hair done up and everything just for that special night. But most of* *all I was just looking forward to spending time with my mom, because no matter what we're doing or where we're going I know we'll always have fun.*

We got in the car and began our drive down Sunset Boulevard toward the theater. My mom was on the phone talking to our close family friend, Dr. Katja Van Herle, who just so happens also to be sort of our family doctor. Bored, I turned to the window.

Outside, I was not drawn to the mirage of passing storefronts or the cascade of cars piling down the road beside me; rather, my eye was drawn to the sky or, more specifically, the full moon that was emerging from behind a big marshmallow-shaped cloud. I remember thinking how splendid it all was: the stars, the night sky, and that perfect full moon that (being the foodie that I am) reminded me of the creamy filling of an overstuffed Oreo.

In that very moment of utter bliss and contentment, I felt something. My left eye began to twitch as a sudden, piercing sensation swept over the top of my eyelid. It was as though someone had dropped a weight on the top of my eyeball and I didn't know where it came from or how to get it off. In a matter of seconds it began to register that this wasn't a feeling I was going to shake easily and may be something worth discussing with a doctor, who so conveniently remained on the phone with my mom just next to me.

I motioned for my mom to let me talk to Katja, and after we exchanged a few words and I waited for her to pass me the phone, I couldn't shake this sense of eeriness.

You know that feeling you get when something happens, even the smallest thing, and you automatically draw the worst conclusion imaginable about what might happen? I did that. I spoke to Katja, who, after hearing my symptoms, restored me to a place of calm and told me not to worry "unless," she said, "the vision becomes fuzzy. Now go enjoy the movie!"

I sat through the entire film very uncomfortably as I tried to focus on the plot and forget that my eye continued to burn furiously at every blink. At home my mom prescribed me a few drops of Visine, and I was off to bed. DON'T WORRY, *I thought as I tucked myself beneath my covers,* IT'LL BE GONE IN THE MORNING.

I could not have been more wrong.

And after that, I keep replaying and replaying the moment in the car, how everything happens at once: the curve in the road that suddenly sharpens while I'm looking up to see an incredibly full moon, which is beautiful but also weird—because it's sort of blurry, like an Impressionist painting of a big creamy white full moon on the night of a Hollywood premiere. In those instants the blinking doesn't clear my vision. The moon is still creamy white and the night dark and misty. And then, wow, the pressure intensifies, there right before Doheny, adding a new sensation into the mix that makes me wince again.

~

I also replay an exchange in the car that night.

"Honey?"

Ali nods and then says, groping for the words—not like her—that it feels like something heavy has suddenly been placed in her left eye. That's exactly what she says: "placed." She exhales, punctuating the accurate assessment she has made before adding, "It's really inconvenient."

Nothing just goes to something and back to nothing fast enough for me to get whiplash. Even though she's had close to perfect health and very few injuries—Extra Strength Tylenol may be the toughest medication I've probably ever given her—I always have to pay extra attention because Ali can be funny in that deadpan way, even if something's serious. And she hates when anyone worries—about anything.

"You know what it is, Mom? Sort of like an eyeball headache."

An eyeball headache? It is nothing or almost nothing. I have the solution, and it's to ward off the ominous presence of the Voice and the eerie cold in my veins. With relief, I announce, "We'll get some Visine."

Visine is a not well-kept secret for most makeup artists. A must-have in every bag of tricks. For unknown reasons I've left my little bottle at home. Still, I'm wondering if she might need some more potent drops. Antibiotic drops. That can be a hassle for a kid. Besides, it'll require a visit to the doctor. Really inconvenient.

But if it gets worse, that's what Katja Van Herle said to do, and that's what we'll do.

Those are my next set of thoughts as we cross the imaginary line that intersects the stretch of Sunset Boulevard that I have always loved. But do not anymore.

~

The next week is a blur of doctors' appointments.

Dr. S., Ali's regular eye doctor, determines after an exam that "There's inflammation along the nerve." But as to its causes, Dr. S. explains in her no-nonsense, right-to-the-point way, "This is out of my league."

So Dr. S. sends us to see Dr. K., an ophthalmologist/neurologist. Short but with a commanding, almost Napoleonic air, not big on bedside manner but clearly an excellent clinician, he orders a series of tests, including an MRI.

The extreme claustrophobic that I am, the mere thought of Ali having to lie still in an airless, metal tube for all that time sets off a mini-panic attack—which I do my best to cover up. In an overly cheerful voice I ask Ali, "Honey, you want me to rub your feet while you're in there? Stay in the room and talk to you—you know, to make the time go faster?"

This makes Ali laugh. "I'll be fine, Mom. You can wait for me in the waiting room." Seeing my hesitation, Ali puts her hand on my shoulder, comforting me, as if to say, *IT'S JUST AN EYE THING, REMEMBER*?

Relieved, as much for myself as I am for Ali, I return to the waiting area and fend off thoughts of brain tumors and other dire diagnoses. Finally, with findings in hand, Doc K. tells Ali she can go out to the waiting room as he calls me into his office and says, "Well, she's got optic neuritis."

The MRI shows a long lesion on the optic nerve. Not a brain tumor. Not any of those dreaded diseases. A weight lifts. How bad can this be? Optic neuritis just means it's swollen, inflamed. He'll give her a prescription for some anti-inflammatory drops, and we'll be good to go.

But still looking at Ali's MRI of the optic nerve and the brain, Dr. K. says, "No . . . this isn't . . . she shouldn't be having this." It's like he's confused or something.

Now I'm confused. Her regular eye doctor, Dr. S., sees inflammation. Dr. K. is the ophthalmologist/neurologist who says it's "optic neuritis," and now we treat for that, right? What's the problem?

The problem, he explains, is that "We need to know why."

~

Let me take this back a few steps.

Asking "what if" is like a nightmare. You close your eyes and you pray and you pray that when they open, the "what ifs" are not true. The moment my pain began I started to wonder "what if?" What if the pain never stops? What if this isn't just an ordinary pain, what if it's a tumor, or a vein bursting or something worse? What if I wake up and can't see anymore and I never get better? What if these "what ifs" come true?

My brain teased me from the moment the pain began, setting off a terrifying spiral of fear and anxiety, the likes of which I had never experienced to this extent before. I truly believe something within me knew this was no ordinary pain, because I certainly worried about it more than I should. Right?

The morning after the movie premiere I woke to find my "what ifs" were now looming in reality. The pain had not ceased, and the vision in my left eye did seem off.

Still in denial, I told myself, YOUR VISION IS FINE ALI, YOU'RE JUST SEEING THINGS BECAUSE YOU'RE THINKING ABOUT WHAT DR. KATJA SAID ON THE PHONE. THERE'S NOTHING WRONG. IT'S JUST A PAIN.

But I couldn't persuade myself entirely that nothing was wrong. Otherwise I wouldn't have told Mom that the pain was still there.

Being the worried, overprotective, on-the-ball mom that she is (a trait that has earned her our affectionate term "Smother Mother" and could sometimes be a bit of a nuisance growing up, though now I am very grateful and appreciative of it), I was immediately routed to Dr. S., who examined me thoroughly. I aced every test, and the doctor, I could tell, was a bit skeptical of my reasons for being there. Maybe she thought I was trying to skip school or get out of doing homework by pretending to have an eye problem. We breezed through the first portion of tests without even the slightest glitch during the entire process. Then it was time for the physical examination.

I sat down in the retractable, plastic-covered chair and tried to make myself comfortable. Not easy, I might add, due to the irritating squeaking sound that penetrated the otherwise silent room every time I tried to move. I leaned back, and like a fly swarming around my head with the brightness of car headlights, Dr. S. gazed into my eyes with her ophthalmoscope. Swerving from one eye to the next, she seemed to be either perplexed or very intrigued by what she saw.

Once she was satisfied with her observation—and the vision in both my eyes was even more blurred by the piercing light of her examination tools—Dr. S. spoke to Mom and made a dramatic claim: "The optic nerve in her left eye seems to be inflamed, but I'm not an expert on this matter. Let me refer you to a specialist."

A specialist? I needed a specialist for this? No, this is just a simple, ordinary eye pain. There's no need for a specialist to see this!

A storm of "what if" thoughts began to flood my mind, as the eerie feeling that things were going to get worse suddenly reared its ugly head again. I sulked back in my chair as my mom reassuringly told me to wait so she could speak to the doctor alone for a moment.

Here was my brain's inner battle: another doctor? Something must really be wrong with me. But there can't be anything wrong, there just can't be!

With that thought, I started getting to know doctors by initials. Why bother learning their names when I wasn't going to ever see them again. So next came Dr. K. Or Whatever.

On the way to the appointment, we passed several shops, but one in particular caught my eye: 7-Eleven. That probably seems strange: of all the stores and streets and signs we passed on our drive to Dr. What's-His-Name's office, the 7-Eleven seemed to be the most important. I think it's because when I was seven, I was playing one night in the garage with our golden retriever, Sandy. I was running around in a pair of yellow, fuzzy socks while Sandy chased me from behind, and suddenly I collapsed face forward and smashed my chin on the cold, hard, cement flooring. On the panicked drive to the emergency room, while my parents scrambled to find an available plastic surgeon on call, I remained sobbing in the backseat, staring out my window into oblivion as if something out there would come put me out of this misery. And that's when I saw it: a big, shiny, green-and-orange 7-Eleven sign, directly across from the hospital driveway we were now entering. After I received all my stitches and an "okay" from my doctor, I was allowed to get my favorite Coke Slurpee, and I returned home in one piece, quite content with my delicious feel-good treat.

Ah, the power of association. My one big medical trauma to date had a happy ending. In the stories I embrace, the ending always has to be "and they all lived happily ever after." Surely there was a Slurpee waiting for me after this not-such-a-big-deal visit.

We entered the waiting room, and I took my seat in the same style chair I sat in before, and stared at the month-old magazines I'd already read. As my mom checked us in with a pink-smocked nurse behind the counter, I took to people gazing as my entertainment of choice. I was off put by my initial observation that I was the youngest person in the room—by a lot. I was probably the only person in the room under fifty, and everyone seemed to be staring aimlessly into space. Well, this was some kind of an optical-neurological office so that would make sense. But I clearly didn't belong. They were sick with something serious. But not me.

"Alexandra Guthy?" A nurse announced.

As usual, it took a second for me to register that by "Alexandra," she meant me.

Yes, Alexandra is my full name, but no one ever calls me that. Since as long as I can remember I've always just been "Ali." The story of how I got my nickname is a matter of debate in my family. My dad claims that if you watch videos of me growing up, they used to call me "Alex" until I was about three, and then they just suddenly stopped. The story I tell people is that in kindergarten I met a boy named Alex. Being the idiosyncratic child that I was, I didn't like sharing my name with someone else, especially a boy! From that moment on the name "Ali" was born, and no one ever called me Alex or Alexandra again. I like this story better because it has a purpose. My name was not just some arbitrary happening of fate that is suggested by the claim that it "just happened." I like to think that my nickname came from somewhere or someone. When things don't make sense, I still try to make them make sense.

Then, after Mom and I were led to an exam room, Dr. K. entered and began to do similar tests as those done by Dr. S. The difference was that my vision was worse. Letters on screens that I made out the day earlier were now fuzzy. OH NO, *I began to panic,* THIS REALLY IS BAD. WHAT THE HELL? *The next test, involving a larger machine that looked like a big freeze ray, made me feel like a villain's prisoner in a Batman movie. I leaned back as the doctor drew nearer and nearer to my eyes. The bright light was so piercing that I instinctually shut my eyes, though I was constantly reminded to keep my eyes open throughout the entire procedure.*

That's when Dr. K gave us the diagnosis of optic neuritis. A left eye nerve was inflamed. Didn't sound too terrible. But then came the need to find the cause. Another series of eye tests followed. The conclusion? My left eye was definitely weaker than my right eye. Optic neuritis, whatever the cause that no one was telling me, was clearly a bad thing.

Dr. K. and Mom were exchanging worried expressions and both muttering rather than talking normally to each other. All of it went over my head.

Maybe that was because I chose to let it not invade the private sanctum of my conscious awareness. If that seems strange, I can only use the example of how it feels when you walk into a room and you get that uncomfortable sense that everyone was just talking about you. I've experienced it before, but not like this. They were talking about something bad, I just knew it, and I was struggling to decide whether I wanted to know what this "optic neuritis" thing was or just pretend I never heard it. This was a decision to understand what I was facing and how I needed to deal with it or simply ignore its existence. I chose the latter.

The decision to uphold the "ignorance is bliss" mantra carried me over the next many chapters of this journey in which I would remain mostly clueless as to what I really had or the severity of its consequences.

~

When Dr. K. hands me a card with the name of one of his colleagues, Dr. O., a top neurologist, he is confident that this expert will be able to identify the cause of the optic neuritis. Oh and, by the way, he gestures, using a slight thrust of his chin, just to make sure I get the seriousness of the uncertainty—Run, don't walk.

In the meantime, even though he's in the dark about why this is happening to Ali, Dr. K. does prescribe steroids to control the "inflammatory cascade." Jotting down notes, he thinks aloud about another test he wants to order, saying, "We should do a spinal tap."

Loved the movie! Not so wild about the procedure.

Dr. K. gathers up paperwork, ready to hand it over for my approval.

I dig in. "A spinal tap—why? I mean, it's an eye thing." The timing is not good either. "Can't we just wait for the steroids to take effect?"

Glowering, Dr. K. is not happy. I'm being really inconvenient. But rather than lecture me, he leaves it to Dr. O. to explain the necessity.

In the midst of this clinical blur, over the period of forty-eight hours, the headache in Ali's left eye has escalated into pain that's off the charts. At the same time her vision in that eye is totally going south. Color is fading. She is losing depth perception. Everything looks blurry, Ali admits, finally giving in to a flicker of worry.

She confesses that her big concern is not being able to play tennis.

My big concern, I don't confess, is that I'm worried she's going blind. But I talk myself off that ledge, aware that there are all kinds of logical explanations, ones that have treatments that can banish all these concerns immediately.

While I calm myself and decide to wait for enlightenment from Dr. O., Ali tells me and Bill that she doesn't want to hear the medical details. If that's okay with us. Whatever the cause of the temporary symptoms, she just wants to find out whatever she has to do to get rid of the inflammation and pain.

Makes sense to me. Whatever the appropriate equivalent of Visine is, we'll find out and clear up the problem. Preparing to argue against the spinal tap, I feel sure that the prednisone will do the trick.

Almost sure. No, not enough to dispense worrying about as-of-yet undetected causes of optic neuritis. But sure enough to co-opt the idea that inflammation of the optic nerve is no big deal.

~

My mom had to pry me from my bed *to get me to go to the next appointment. I was done. Three doctors in a week! This is ridiculous!*

After five minutes of coaxing me from my resting place, Mom finally managed to get me ready. Still recovering from my deep stupor, it took me a moment to realize my vision had not returned to normal; in fact, it looked as though (no, it couldn't possibly!) my sight had gotten worse. Suddenly more eager to see the doctor, we both scrambled to the car and made our way through the crowded LA traffic to our appointment.

We arrived at the medical center not knowing what to expect. Who was this doctor, and why was it so important that we see him? What could he possibly know that the past two doctors did not? As we entered the waiting room (with the same furniture, carpet, and wallpapering as I've now seen twice before), I sat anxiously in the far corner. My mom signed us in, which unfortunately now started to seem routine, and then she joined me, lovingly stroking my leg in reassurance. When we were finally called into the examination room, my stomach suddenly lurched in excitement or fear, most likely a combination of both.

I rose and followed the nurse into a cluttered office. The room was very antiquated, with furniture that seemed to be taken directly off the set of the TV series MAD MEN. I scanned the chaotic bookshelves stuffed to the brim with a mounting pile of medical journals. The walls were outfitted with a display of awards and diplomas from various degrees of academic achievement. My mom and I sat in silence, waiting for the doctor to arrive. It seemed as though we were waiting in the lair of a mad scientist, like Dr. Frankenstein.

Then, sure enough, he arrived.

His white lab coat and freshly polished black Italian loafers gave him an air of dignity, definitely not the mad-scientist type. He strolled into the room, eyes fixed on me as my mother rose to give him a handshake. He was an elderly man with slicked-back silver hair and a pair of cool, blue eyes. He had a very reassuring grin about him and instantly made me feel better in his presence. As I shook his hand, the more I thought about it, the more he reminded me of a character in one of my favorite movies: THE WIZARD OF OZ.

It's no secret that I'm a big fan of happily-ever-afters. I guess it comes from my happy-go-lucky nature I was fortunate enough to inherit from my dad's side of the family. It's also no big secret that I'm a big fan of Broadway musicals, my favorite being WICKED.

So I couldn't help but picture Dr. O. as none other than the Wizard himself, and it was then that I knew he could help me. I mean the Wizard gave the Tin Man a heart, the Scarecrow a brain, and the Lion his courage, so why couldn't Dr. O., my Wizard, give me some answers?

After our brief introduction, the doctor led us into the neighboring exam room, in which he proceeded to probe and prod me—reflex test on my knees, bending over to feel my spine, walking up and down the halls in a straight line while touching my nose with alternating left and right hands. At first I didn't understand why this was necessary.

I continued to question his every move until he began to look into my eyes with his ophthalmoscope, the part of the exam I was oh too familiar with. He raised his head silently and began to speak: "We're going to need to do some blood work."

Uh-oh. I've never liked needles. The thought of a needle piercing my veins makes my stomach drop and my heart go numb.

The nurse directed me to a blood-drawing station (which, if you've never had your blood drawn, isn't really a station at all, but rather just a chair with a little armrest). She motioned for me to put my arm down so the torture could commence. I reluctantly relinquished control and my arm collapsed like a lead weight onto the chair. Obviously sensing my discomfort, the nurse assured me that everything would be fine and she'd done this many times before. Somehow that didn't make me feel better, but before I had any more time to think, the needle began to puncture the skin. The force of this foreign entity entering my body made my veins turn sour. I saw my blood, thick and scarlet red, oozing slowly into the compact vile. I continued to sit still as humanly possible. I don't know where it came from, but I've always had this fear that if I moved while getting my blood drawn, the needle would irreparably puncture my vein and I would suddenly die from blood loss. Crazy, I know, but anything seemed possible to me at this point.

After a few long, painful minutes, my time was up. I winced as the nurse steadily removed the needle from my arm and wrapped the wound in gauze. My mom and I were escorted back to Dr. O.'s office, where we reviewed the discoveries of today's investigation. So far, I had passed every inspection. Other than the fact that I could barely see out of my left eye, I was perfectly normal. Dr. O. began explaining the purpose of the various blood tests he ordered and what he hoped to rule out with each or rule in.

My mom listened intently; I stared into space. Besides the whole 2% premonition thing, Mom and I have mother-daughter ESP. We're so connected that we can basically tell what the other is thinking. Through many years of practice and another sort of natural motherly instinct, my mom could clearly tell I was not in the mood to participate in this conversation. She told me I could wait in the hall and play a game on my phone while she finished talking to the doctor. In the hallway my mind was far from focusing on my current game of BrickBreaker. What did they have to order tests for? What were they looking to find? What if I never get better? What if . . .

I stopped. These kinds of questions can lead to a lot of trouble. These are the kinds of questions that are prohibited by my "ignorance is bliss" mantra. These are the kind of "what if" questions that will take me away from my happy place, my place of calmness, serenity, placidity. I was not yet willing to give all that up for speculation. No. I was going to let my mom handle this one. If something was really wrong and she felt I needed to know, she'd tell me. What did I have to worry about? I have her to protect me; I don't have to think about "what if."

Several minutes later my mom emerged. Her eyes were a bit glassy and she seemed a bit hazy. I wondered if everything's okay. I wondered if . . .

STOP. STOP WONDERING, I reminded myself. THOSE ARE THE KINDS OF QUESTIONS THAT WILL TAKE YOU OFF YOUR COURSE OF IGNORANCE. HEAVEN FORBID.

~

"NO SPINAL TAP" is what I first say to Dr. O., a charming absent-minded-professor type with a cluttered desk and a warm smile, nowhere near as stern as Dr. K. After listening to my update on the symptoms that are actually starting to diminish with the power of heavy-duty steroids, Dr. O. says, "Sure, we can put off the tap—but let's get a lot of blood."

I'm relieved, or I imagine I am. Holding the paperwork afterward, I review it very carefully, though only to distract myself. Because I'm trembling. There's that déjà vu feeling of cold running through my veins that's now taken root down in my stomach. It has no name yet, but I'm getting the message that it's not leaving anytime soon.

Dr. O. orders this series of blood tests, one of which is called NMO-IgG, which I notice (not by the first three letters but by the chemistry major sound of the last part) and ask, for reasons I can't explain, "What's that?"

Weird that I even see it, and weirder still that I bother to ask about that one in particular. Because I'm definitely not thinking—I'm just stressing.

Dr. O., as if to himself but out loud, says, "It's nothing. She won't have that." Then he says, "That wouldn't be good. We're not even going to think about that."

And this is most of the back story of the week leading up to The Phone Call from Dr. K. that takes place at home in Bill's office.

There's one more delay. When Ali Rose tests positive for this mystery disease, before I can even ask what it means, the doctors want to retest.

Dr. O.: "The lab must have made a mistake."

Dr. K.: "That has to be wrong."

Lab technician: "Someone else screwed up."

Dr. O.: "We'll test her again."

They're positive it's negative, and negative it's positive.

Which means that before we get The Phone Call after the second test, we must be seeing a false positive. This isn't so uncommon for the more uncommon diseases. Retesting to confirm a dire diagnosis is usually recommended.

Up until now it seems that everyone's in denial but me. At least so far.

~

The "ignorance is bliss" decision *held sway, even though I was having an inner meltdown from the moment we returned home after the visit to Dr. O. Making such a pivotal decision in the first place probably has a lot to do with my family history.*

I love both sides of my family. My dad's side, the "walk on the sunny side of the street only" side, is the one I take after. It's easy to be distraught and overwhelmed by the sudden presence of fear, anger, and sadness. It's easy to be brought down by the encroachment of unwanted things in life, like, oh, coming down with mystery symptoms that could be nothing or something so scary nobody understands it.

I think we all can agree that it's very difficult to remain positive, upbeat, and optimistic in the face of most kinds of adversity. However, it does not take a special kind of strength or courage to choose to pursue the path of positivity but rather only a desire and a will to overcome. I am a true believer of this philosophy. My dad, being the genuine, confident, intelligent, exceptionally positive, and understatedly brave man that he is, continues to be my model, my guide in terms of how I chose (and continue to choose) to rise above the fray of whatever's thrown at me.

My mom's side of the family—the rational, logical, and, above all, the "face reality and don't pretend otherwise because dreaming won't help" side of the family—could not be more opposite. Being practical is a good thing—I'm not saying it's not—but being practical does not need to come at the loss of optimism.

All of that said, the dueling influences tormented my next few days.

I wanted to know what was wrong, but then again I didn't. What if it's really bad? What if I can't be fixed? What if I'm doomed to live like this forever, wandering from one doctor to the next? What if I can't play tennis? What if I have to drop out of school? What will my friends think? How will I tell them?

My parents seemed weighted by real concern, though they tried to be upbeat. Mom asked practical questions, holding her two fingers in front of my eyes to check my eyesight as the days clicked by. On a hopeful note, I thought it was getting slightly better. Then again, I had a knot in my stomach that was especially pronounced as I hurried downstairs to dinner at the end of the week and sat at my usual seat as though nothing was wrong. Even though I had no appetite, I ate like I was starving, and although I was in no mood to talk, I participated in every conversation. Part of my "ignorance is bliss" mantra demands not only that I think positively but I act that way as well. Not so different from my mom's approach to conquering things new to her: "Act-as-if."

I would just like to take this moment to say this approach is not the best for everyone. Some people do well to express their feelings vocally or write them down or share them with close friends or relatives. For me, the best way to deal with a crisis has always been to internalize the problem and process it over time. I'm Daddy's girl that way.

Don't get me wrong—the denial was no bliss. Not that night or for many nights to follow.

~

So here we are back at where this officially begins with The Phone Call, the scene that we'll replay again and again in some crazy fantasy of thinking the more we replay, the more the tape will thin and sever and cease to be true.

Dr. O. has received the test results and has reported back to Dr. K., who has decided that instead of calling us into his office and speaking directly to me and Bill, he'll use an evening phone call to give us a crash course in the reality of the disease identified by the antibody marker NMO-IgG.

Neuromyelitis optica. NMO. Also known as Devic's Disease.

Hardly able to breathe, heart hurtling against my chest, I hear my words race.

Bill tries to be my interpreter. We understand NMO is bad, but not all cases are, right? And what are the treatments? What steps can be taken to prevent that worst-case scenario from happening for our Ali Rose, God forbid? For all the reality that Dr. K. is attempting to offer, it turns out that he doesn't have many answers.

For example, when we ask if maybe, just maybe, the test was wrong twice, he doubts it but admits there are other tests that will need to happen to expose whether there's another autoimmune complication masking or connected to NMO, and this would further confirm the diagnosis that the MRI and the blood test have established almost conclusively.

This is the crazy thing about NMO. It's so rare and so little known, Dr. K. concedes, there aren't many who can answer questions about treatment. For a moment I actually catch my breath and navigate the wreck of myself back to a hopeful thought, built on a lifeboat of possible reality. If they know so little, there is no reason to speculate on any dire prognosis, right? So what do we do? What would *you* do, if this were *your* daughter?

A long pause. The kind of pause that can kill you with a thousand cuts of silence. Then, the same ophthalmologist/neurologist who hardly knows me, my husband, or our daughter decides somehow that if I'm looking for hope with respect to Ali's prognosis, he has little to give.

In a crisp, deliberate way of speaking, he states, "She could have four years. She could have six. Now is the time to go into denial." Another pause. "In my opinion, it would be best for everyone to go into denial, and," he softens a bit as he adds, "just enjoy the time you have left with her."

Then it was our turn for silence. Bill and I didn't even look at each other. We both stared at the phone sitting on the desk between us as if it had been placed there in error or like the voice coming out of the speaker really meant to call someone else's number.

The world crashed around me.

All I could see, and I don't know why, was a never-ending hospital corridor—lonely, cold, and antiseptic—and then a series of countless waiting rooms. One after the other. Each with different furniture, different artwork, but the same magazines, the same suspicious smell. In my imagination I saw Ali Rose, my angel, walking slowly with effort down the hall, as the other patients in the waiting rooms craned their necks and followed her with watchful eyes.

Whatever else was said on the phone call with Dr. K. after he answered the question as to what he would do if this were his daughter, I don't remember.

Let me amend that. I remember thinking that he clearly didn't know me and that he was going to be wrong. That, in fact, those were fighting words. What I also remember thinking—right before I stood up and steadied myself enough to be able to walk down the few stairs and into our hallway—was how much I hate waiting rooms.

~

EARLY MARCH 2008

***"Except for whatever this eye** inflammation thing is—and by the way, it's getting better—I can confidently say that everything's going pretty peachy in my world."*

After almost a month since the onset of the Eyeball Headache, this is a line that I enthusiastically write in my journal one night, making up for the few weeks when I hadn't written much.

I know, journal writing must sound quaint to people my own age. But keeping a record of the days was a concept that sort of landed in my lap back when I was in the second grade, and I really grew to like my nonjudgmental friend, "Journal."

So this night, as I close the journal without rereading my notes, I contemplate how well everything is going. Freshman year is more than halfway finished, and between my classes, my friends, a fantastic varsity tennis season, and my wonderful, loving family, life is beautiful.

For a minute there I was worried. Not because of the Eyeball Headache or the blurry vision. And the eyesight is close to normal, by the way. But Mom and Dad, as much as they tried not to show concern, were overcompensating so much I thought that there was something really serious in the works. That's one of the reasons I just made it very clear that I didn't want to know—whatever it was. Besides, Mom has the worry bases covered. Not just the bases—she's got the bleachers, the dugout, the entire field covered.

Dad lacks the worry gene entirely. But for a couple weeks I notice his brow's more furrowed than usual when he's looking in my direction.

With spring break coming up though and my eyesight improving, nobody's acting all overprotective anymore—anymore than usual, that is, as far as Mom is concerned.

As many times a day as is humanly/logistically possible, she does that thing she does: waves her hand a foot in front of my eyes to ask how many fingers she's holding up.

For a while there, if I covered my right eye, I couldn't tell. But now I can make out the blurry outlines of however many fingers she's holding up.

She doesn't want me to see how relieved my improvements have allowed her to be, because that would be admitting that she wasn't so sure. And, well, I'm not going there on that kind of speculation.

So all is close to being no big deal as possible when one night I stop in to say goodnight and spot her with a panic-stricken face as she's reads some print out that she's downloaded from the Internet. Panic stricken in any conjunction with my mother is not just a figure of speech.

"Mom, are you okay?"

My mother looks up in shock, and the minute she sees me, flips the paper over like I've caught her with top-secret files. OOOH, CONTRABAND! *Catching herself, she explains, "Oh, this is . . . ummm . . ."*

"Mom stuff . . ." I smile, and blow her a kiss good night, heading back down the hall. Part of me suspects there is a worry-about-my-daughter factor going on. The other part still really, absolutely, totally doesn't want to know.

~

During the early months of 2008 anyone who happened to have the misfortune of meeting up with the term "NMO" would have found next to nothing about it by Googling or surfing the Internet. Like me, they would have found some anecdotal nightmare stories and possibly some scientific abstracts and the like. Or, as I did, they may have dug up the scant information that existed for most of the preceding century—a gothic horror tale that dated back to 1894.

In that year a thirty-four-year-old French neurologist by the name of Eugène Devic, a native of Lyon, sat down with his medical student, Fernard Gault, to describe a rare nervous condition the two had been studying in a series of stricken patients. The condition that they had been studying—a syndrome that resembled multiple sclerosis and affected the spinal cord and optic nerves—had so stunned them in its refusal to follow any kind of predictable pattern that Devic realized he was uncovering a disease that had never been studied before. It was a true orphan disease in that sense. He adopted it and named the disorder for himself—Devic's Disease, much later known as neuromyelitis optica (NMO).

This is not what Ali has. There has to have been a mistake.

~

Walking back to my room that night*, the image of my mother holding that paperwork felt scorched in my brain. What did she know that was so horrible she would panic over me possibly seeing? Was it definitive? Was it crazy wrong? The only way to not fret over the NOT KNOWING was to go to the drawer in my bedroom and pull out the journal, flip to the entry for that day, and add a P.S.: "Dear Journal, Remember always to be good to Mom. She does so much for all of us."*

That's all I have to do to exhale and flop back on my bed to appreciate happier thoughts. I think it's because Mom absorbs the worry, fear, and uncertainty that inevitably impact most people's lives at least to a certain extent, she hopes to spare us the pain. The motivation is 100 percent loving. By the same token, she spares no effort in giving us opportunities to have the ultimate charmed life. Both my parents grew up without much, so they make a point of trying to keep us grounded in the values that shaped them: hard work, ingenuity, vision.

When people ask me, "What do your parents do?" I usually respond with "They're entrepreneurs." It's hard really to encompass all that they do into one job description. It's easier for my dad, because his focus is mainly in infomercials, but my mom is another story. She has these amazing abilities that she takes for granted, like she's always great with words and titles. And when you look at what she's created in her life and how she can change the most boring, humdrum occasion into an enchanting, unforgettable celebration, it's easy to start to think of her as being magical, sprinkling the fairy dust on everyone around her.

There is no job description out there in this entire universe to really define all the things Victoria Jackson is able to accomplish. I'd say the closest job title out there would be superhero. But I had no idea at the time just how incredible a superhero she'd turn out to be.

~

When I tell myself this can't be happening, not again, not in defiance of all mathematical odds, I have to go back to 2006, when Bill's facialist noticed a lump in his neck and said, "You oughta get that checked out, Mr. Guthy."

From years of marketing products like Principal Secret and Proactiv™, not to mention being around me, Bill usually maintained an excellent skin-care regimen, which included the occasional facial. But somehow he didn't make time to have the lump checked out.

And not because it was a facialist instead of a doctor who brought it to his attention—my husband's anything but a snob. Bill didn't follow up because it just wouldn't have occurred to him that something might be wrong. (Remember, he is the guy who sings the good-bye song from *The Sound of Music*. Even the kids know that too much Pleasantville can be a problem.)

So now we cut to the facial salon, six months later.

Bill's in the chair again with the same facialist who first noticed The Lump.

FACIALIST (casual): So, Mr. Guthy . . . ever have that thing on your neck checked out?

BILL (casual): Uhm, what thing was that?

This time, Bill came home and showed me. I said whoa. The Voice knew it was serious. Some things you just know.

Having been upstaged by Bill's facialist, I swung into high-gear in terms of medical options for his treatment plan. He was my husband, and goddammit, I wasn't going to sit there while recommendations for the perfect surgeon rolled in from Bill's tailor or a trainer at his gym. Besides, this was supposed to be my turf. I wasn't just any old wife; I was a 2% wife, and in the Land of 2%, the hills were alive—with the sound of second opinions.

Hell, yeah.

I began to do my thing: researching, networking, talking to friends. I kept hearing the name Dr. Katja Van Herle and how amazing she was. Van Herle . . . was that like von Trapp? From *The Sound of Music*? People kept saying I had to meet her. Had to. I mean, they really said it, until I was certain Bill's life depended on it. "You'll love her," they said.

"She's this incredible concierge doctor—"

What did that mean? She worked at the Four Seasons?

We got together, and I liked her right away. She was stunning, sophisticated, and Belgian. Aside from her great looks and all of her honors and degrees, she was apparently superhuman. Not only did Katja commute a few times a week from her home in San Diego to a private practice in Beverly Hills, but she was also a professor of medicine, full-time faculty at Scripps, on the Clinical Faculty at UCLA, had three young sons and a husband who was the captain of a ship that traveled the Seven Seas—wait a minute! George von Trapp! The widower in *The Sound of Music* who was captain of a ship! . . .

Though I can jest now, at the time I needed these magical details because otherwise I sort of had to pinch myself that she was real. The bonus was that she had the gift of really listening. Katja looked warm and friendly—which she was—but her ability to focus was almost brutally intense. It forced me to be more articulate than usual, yet somehow with less effort. I found she had that effect on anyone who was in the room—be at the top of your game, or else. To this day I seriously think she's the one person who may actually get less sleep than I do.

Katja and Bill's surgeon reassured us. I don't remember it being so comforting at the time, but a consulting doctor did say that of all the cancers, thyroid was probably "the best." If you caught it early (which we did), you could pretty much wipe it out forever.

When Bill got sick, I thought we would bond around the pain. It didn't work out that way. He never talked about it. His way of dealing was private. Quiet and introspective. I admired that. I needed to respect it, but I also expected he might need to seek comfort, to not be so dysfunctionally healthy for a change. That the two of us could have the elusive emotional intimacy that would normally accompany a crisis, right? Wrong.

For a while I fretted in thinking about what might have happened if he hadn't gone back to the same facialist! The whole thing was a little surreal. The night before his surgery Bill danced his ass off. He was so into it.

The image glows permanently in my mind: dusk at the beach house, he and Ali, dancing together. The pure, shining sun of my little girl and the sunny enigma of my husband. Watching from a distance, I envied them both just a little, the two of them so tall and beautiful, so easy together. So much life.

He danced, and then he had surgery. He came, he chemo'd, he conquered. Ali would later remind me how he had to stay at a hotel while he was recovering from having radiation. We all went to the hotel and stood outside in the street and waved to him on his balcony.

That weekend he came home and rode his horse with happy abandon. By the way, his horse's name is Happy. I watched from a distance and knew I'd never have what he has.

The Ides of March, Give or Take

The steroids have worked their magic.

An eerie calm settles over the household. It's the feeling you have after an earthquake when you wonder if that was all there was or if it was the main jolt and if aftershocks are coming, or if it was only a precursor to something of a much larger and more devastating magnitude. Whether it's before or after, I recognize that we're all in various stages of shock and denial and that my job, now that I've gone into warrior mode, is to remain on high alert.

Let me rephrase. Now that I've gone into warrior mode, I really have two jobs. First and forever foremost, I have to protect Ali and surround my little girl in powerful white light and pure, positive, undiluted love. And secondly, even though I'm holding out for the big old cosmic "ooops, didn't mean that," I need to beef up on the science of what the doctors are all talking about. Not because I'm suited for the job (lest we forget that I never graduated from high school), but only because that's what you do in survival mode; you don't completely hand off the job.

And on this front, as good fortune—and another quirk of 2%—would have it, I have Dr. Katja Van Herle to help me navigate my/our shock and disbelief with dispatches from the immunological front, where only a handful of docs in the world have any inkling about how this Devic's Disease works. We were blessed that she had become like family in the period leading up to the Eyeball Headache and that Ali already adored her.

Katja is the first to tell me not to be overly confident that we've seen the last of the NMO.

"But her sight is coming back. That's a really good sign, isn't it?"

"It is. This is exactly what we were hoping for." With NMO, she goes on to explain, symptoms can yield either temporary or permanent damage.

My fearful/hopeful fantasy that we're still dealing with a mistake is shot down by a new MRI that still shows a lesion on the optic nerve. Katja points it out to me and Bill, noting, "Her eyesight is getting much better, but you see the inflammation here?" Like smoldering embers, they can be lit up anytime.

"If we could prevent any other attacks from happening, would that be the end of it?" I'm trying to fake it here, trying to believe that you can control the uncontrollable. Although, technically, without attacks, we would be dealing with a one-off situation. The trick, of course, is preventing other attacks. For that, Katja advises, I need to go to Rochester and meet the Wizards of NMO.

Bill and I have heard this before, actually, right before we hung up with Dr. K., who did say, in a resigned tone, "If she were my daughter, I'd bring her to the Mayo"—as in, it'll probably be a waste, but at least you'll get it out of your system.

From February through the middle of March, that's really all I've been hearing: "You have to get her to the Mayo."

Now Katja Van Herle is joining in the chorus.

Not only is the Mayo where the original NMO-IgG was sent and returned positive—and where Ali's blood was retested too—but they also shared some of that second sample with Oxford, to be extra thorough.

Weighing the choices, I would much rather go on our planned family vacation, as would Ali, I know. I would much rather keep clinging to the slim chance that this has been some bizarre statistical blunder on the part of the universe or medical science. But I would much rather go to see the lead medical authorities and have them do their magic for us and make it all better. To cover all the bases. Yes, and the bleachers in the stands and the rest of the field.

We are out of false hopes.

Because I'm not versed on the whereabouts of any major medical Meccas and definitely not the Mayo, I'm thinking it's in New York because everyone keeps saying Rochester.

This Rochester, it turns out, is in Minnesota.

Minnesota? In March? Scratch the former thinking.

I mean, now that the steroids have taken down the inflammation and Ali's improving, what with my theory about preventing further attacks as a way to let us be done with this ordeal, I'm feeling like we should postpone. By summer she'll be out of school, so we can do the Mayo then.

Her doctors, Katja included, press the issue.

Funny thing. When Dr. K. first said, "It's time to just go into denial," I remember being outraged. But it seemed that by late March, in that regard, I was getting ready to follow his advice to the letter after all.

~

If you ask me what one of the worst days *of the Eyeball Headache was, hands down nothing quite throws me like the afternoon when I come home from school, right before our vacation, and find Mom and Dr. Van Herle sitting outside under the palm trees, next to the fountain, chit-chatting away with excessive pleasantries.*

It's one of those "what's wrong with this picture?" moments. A sunny afternoon, a leap out of the car, and a sprint up the driveway, books cradled in arms, a dash behind and around the hedges toward the kitchen, and spotting my mother and our family doctor luxuriating over afternoon ice tea and baked goods, like two women of leisure?

I stand there in my gray pleated skirt, knee socks, sneakers, white blouse, and navy blue cardigan, deliberating over whether my eyesight is really getting better or whether I'm starting to hallucinate.

Something is up. Clearly, as I'm not stupid. I know something is coming. This moment has been staged.

Together or overlapping, Mom and Katja then inform me that instead of the usual family fun trip over Spring Break, we're all going to go to the Mayo Clinic.

Mom's face is sad and worried, even though she's trying to play down the seriousness of it.

Katja is more matter-of-fact about it. You know, everyone goes to the Mayo to check out too much inflammation. Why not?

I don't know anything about that or anything other than this is NOT COOL. *Bursting into tears, I run up to my bedroom and, before I know it, am talking and cussing out loud to myself. Have I ever uttered a swear word in my life? Not at the volume that others could hear, not that I can remember. But when I go into the bathroom to throw water on my face and try to calm down, all I can do is yell over the water: "This is a bunch of bullshit and I don't want to go to the* FUCKING *Mayo Clinic!"*

That was the beginning of my deciding that I can reserve the right to cuss when the occasion warrants.

Later, I come down for dinner and announce to my parents that I will agree to go. But I remind them that if the facts of my condition are only offered on a need-to-know basis, I don't fucking need to know them!

~

March 25, 2008, Los Angeles

Figuring there is strength in numbers, Bill and I arrange for most of the family, as well as Katja, to travel to Minnesota with Ali.

As we drive to the airport, I look back at my daughter staring out the window of the car. Whatever she's thinking or feeling, it's buried somewhere below her everyday sunny demeanor.

It's a beautiful day in Southern California: everything in bloom already, everything green and lush, thanks to the winter storms. The weather outlook for Rochester, snow in the forecast, is not so encouraging. The flight might be bumpy.

How ironic that there was once a time when the possibility of turbulence would have me refusing to take a flight. In recent years, after not flying for most of my adult life, I have started to travel by air again, in spite of the debilitating waves of panic brought on by claustrophobia. But not an inkling of fear makes itself known as we board the jet or, a short time later, when we take off. I have no bandwidth left for anymore dread or fear. Somehow, I've convinced myself, I need to reserve my strength for the bigger battles ahead.

The Voice chastises me. Why would I expect the worst? Habit, no doubt. After all, we're going to the Emerald City, where the real Wizards will teach us how to click our heels together and wave the magic wand of whatever it is you do to banish rare orphan diseases.

Then it hits me how much I do not like the association of "orphans"—sad, lonely waifs who nobody wants like the kid that I was—with a malevolent, killer disease. A flashback follows of that day when I got the call from my father the wallpaper salesman (from whom I inherited an eye for design and color) to say he was giving us up for adoption. Ever since that moment I've always had to fight feeling like an orphan, a misbegotten urchin trying to find out who and where she was—never really being able to find my way home.

These memories, long lost, come rushing back to me now as we fly into stormy skies over the Mayo, with one in particular coming into focus. Once, probably when I was around Ali's age, someone asked me what I wanted to be when I grew up, and without hesitation, I answered very seriously, "Someone else."

2

Stuck in the Snow Globe

MARCH 26, 2008, EN ROUTE TO THE MAYO

The sting of having to go to *wintry Minnesota over Spring Break was lessened once Mom announced that the whole family, just about, was going to go too. Vacation at the Mayo? Not my idea of a top destination of choice. But, then again, I convince myself, the trip might be educational in terms of widening my exposure to places off the beaten track.*

See, the thing about travel with us is that we go ALL IN. *Even our regular family vacations are not really family vacations, as they include friends, friends of friends, therapists, business partners, doctors, and the occasional yoga instructor. We go big or we stay home.*

The reason? Mom's panic and claustrophobia used to be so bad that she couldn't join us if we were going to fly anywhere. Dad is a travel devotee, and I think that Mom wanted so badly to share that with him and us kids that she came up with a way to handle her issues about being away from home. In the early years that meant wherever we went on vacation, it was by car. For Mom there seemed to be greater safety in numbers, hence the entourage. And of course trekking to different destinations in a caravan is absolutely more fun.

So then, when Mom began to fly, we stayed with the "more the merrier" approach.

I'm not suggesting that anyone is pretending to be in a superfestive mood on the flight to Rochester. But I have to say that there is an atmosphere of normalcy, like we do this all the time—doesn't everyone? Or else there is a lot of Acting-as-if, or something, on the part of most of my family members. Even Katja Van Herle has the demeanor of being used to little out-of-town jaunts for second opinions.

Not that I'm complaining. I could never complain about my group of loved ones.

Mom never ceases to amaze, and Dad, as a father, has his own superhero qualities. Besides being a mentor and cultivating the competitiveness in me that is such a part of him, he has a kind of intelligence that is galvanizing. Sometimes he can come up with some pretty bad puns—humor so bad that it's funny. His gift, in my view, is his supportiveness. When he is behind you and when he believes in you, there's nothing you can't and won't do.

I'm thankful that my older brother, Evan, is on the trip with us. He is another one who cares on such a deep level that there aren't always words to go along with it. Evan could be like the Tom Hanks character in CAST AWAY*—the guy who can survive by himself forever in the wilderness. I love that about Evan, how self-reliant he is and how his identity isn't connected to the trappings of success or material possessions that so many people use to measure their self-worth. Evan and I have always had a strong big brother–little sister bond.*

The decision for Jackson not to come on this trip was based on the fact that he goes to a different school and didn't have time off. There may have been other reasons I don't know about but can only suppose. Jackson is passionate and creative and has the appetite for attention that goes along with his talent, which will serve him in the long run, I hope. Some of that can drive me crazy at times, but I do know, bottom line, how sensitive and caring he is.

Nanny, or Barbara, my mom's mom, is my card-playing partner and always great to have on the trip. Nanny is a font of wisdom. We call her

411. Seriously. That's her nickname. Obscure Information is her a.k.a. For years my dad has never won a bet with her over any kind of fact-based questions that come up in conversation—and they've been making bets nightly at the dinner table for as long as I can remember.

Nanny is a listener who gives no-nonsense advice. Really grounded. She gets it. Nanny is also tough, strong, and supportive. (Plus, whenever I want to hang out in the guest house with her, I can watch her TV and dip into the stash of chocolate-covered raisins she keeps on hand for me.) Not many of my friends have grandmothers who are even an ounce as fantastic. Sometimes, if you don't know how to handle her zingers, she might take you off guard, but I think her advice almost always turns out to be right on the money. Look at the "Momtras" she gave to my mother that helped her build a career.

Because Jackson's not on this trip, Grandma, Dad's mom, Elaine, stayed to hold down the fort. She is the most loving human being, always with an abundance of unconditional love to give. She's uplifting and encouraging, there for me in every way, sending me hopeful and positive e-mails all the time. As different as they are, Grandma and Nanny have interesting traits in common. Both modeled when they were younger, and both are still head-turners. Both were single working moms who raised ultra-entrepreneurial kids. Both have ex-husbands who wound up working as security guards. Go figure on that one.

All of this is a roundabout way of confessing that even with the company of people I love, I really wish that instead of heading north into a snowstorm, we were on our way south to the same vacation spot we visited right after the New Year: Cuixmala, Mexico.

Closing my eyes, I can summon the images of the rustic resort where we usually visit once a year—especially the driveway that goes on for miles, winding its way through what seems to be an endless field of trees and grass, with feral zebras running wildly alongside the cars as we caravan to the resort. The Mexican jungle always reminds me of what I would imagine an African safari to look like. With my binoculars, I can spend hours roaming around the resort, trying to spot wild animals as they run in and out of view on the distant plains. The sea salt pool makes the fact that you can't go in the ocean more tolerable, and the light breeze that whisks through the beams of the shady palapas is always welcoming, crisp, and refreshing.

Every year as we return home I long to go back once more to our Mexican getaway. And just as on this trip I continue to look forward to the day when I would again get to sit back under the shade and walk on the beach under the pink halo of a Mexican sunset.

That wistful longing is the way that I remember flying into Rochester, little knowing that in the coming years a disastrous hurricane would all but destroy the resort.

For that as well as other reasons, we haven't been back there since before the Eyeball Headache. And I doubt we ever will.

~

It's already dark when we check into our hotel across the street from the Mayo Clinic, connected by a skyway.

"Clinic" is a misnomer. The Mayo is a basically a country populated by more than fifty thousand people working in more compartmented areas of specialty than can be counted. We've come here as a delegation from another place in time, from back in the land of the pre-NMO charmed life where we once resided.

The first thing that Ali does as we gather together in our hotel room to discuss dinner plans is to open the curtains to reveal a picturesque scene of the Mayo at night. We join her at the window as if beholding the Emerald City.

For a moment it conjures an image that I'll hold onto: a mental snapshot of us in miniature, Ali and her posse, tiny, helpless figures at the bottom of a snow globe, everyone gazing over at the huge glass building lit from within by myriad twinkling lights, all seen through the snow flurries.

Scraps of things I've heard about the Mayo Clinic all my life compare and contrast to the view. As part of Americana, up until now I've always pictured it as a cross between the Smithsonian and Lourdes—a sacred destination where the sick arrive after making long pilgrimages on foot and where the blind go to see again. A legendary place where the crippled throw away their crutches. Where Arabian sheiks and Hollywood royalty are reported as being treated there for some "undisclosed illness." In my sketch it was more of a World's Fair installation than a hospital, my layperson's explanation for why it was called a "clinic" and not a hospital. At the clinic, I supposed, visitors could ride through the secret inner workings of the amazing human body, journeying back to a quaint and charming time in yesteryear—a time belonging to *Reader's Digest* and Norman Rockwell.

Despite the inaccuracies of some of those old fragments, I can't help but feel proud that America has created this place where we have come for answers. The thought also distracts me from feeling incredibly sad.

Out of the corner of my eye I look at Ali studying the snowfall, peering across to the offices where researchers and doctors review findings in their glassed-in cubicles. I have no idea what she's thinking.

Ali, I will mention now, is not or has not ever been the identified patient who dominates family dynamics in our world. Ali has always been the Supergirl who lives next door, not needing to be the center of attention but doing everything and anything extraordinarily, effortlessly. Evan—who also rejected the role of the identified patient, no doubt rebelling against my mothering excesses that attempted to make him the center of the universe—therefore understands Ali's need for normalcy possibly better than anyone. Which is partly why he agreed to come and lend his calming presence on this trip. That and his love for his sister.

And as for Nanny, she has the ability to keep everything on an even keel. In fact, we already have a system in place for the serious doctor visits. Whenever Bill and I are called into the doctor's office, Ali and Nanny, both crazy competitive card players, will go out to the waiting room and engross themselves in a game.

Yep, that's us, in our snow globe, armed with a deck of cards, all catching a first glimpse of the Mayo at night under the falling snow. The denial that has been working for me goes on the blink, leaving me to feel dark, lost, and heartbroken for Ali.

This is where we're going to live now, I think, not wanting to cross the border, wishing to be denied a passport or a visa. Once we go there, I fear, our lives will be stuck on skyways and pushed along on people-movers that will keep Ali from the life she was supposed to have.

Sticking with the Oz theme, the next morning we all enter the main reception area where we wait to meet the Real Wiz, Dr. Brian Weinshenker, reputedly one of the foremost authorities in the world on NMO.

At the Mayo all things neuromyelitis optica at this point in time go through the MS Center—NMO still being an *hors d'oeuvre* to the MS *entrée*—and some of the patients waiting to be seen are not in such great shape. Wheelchairs, crutches, sight-impaired, people in pain, young and old.

Ali watches them.

I watch Ali watching them, descending below the calm surface. Run silent, run deep. It's what she does sometimes, going somewhere else. Then she struggles to find her game-face, to come back from underwater.

Nanny takes out the cards, but Ali doesn't respond. Not this time. She leans on my shoulder and looks up into my eyes. *I know, honey*, my eyes tell her. I know she hates the dark roads and that she feels cornered, here in this place I've brought her to, where those long, beautiful legs aren't enough to pull off an escape.

To see her pretend to be cool, putting on a mask to hide her terror, that just does me in. Kills me. This is not what I wanted for you, I want to tell her. But she knows. And she expresses it by asking the obvious, finally, "Why are we here?"

"To find out what's wrong."

"I mean here, why are we here? Do I have MS?"

"No, Ali. You do not have MS."

At least I can say it forcefully, because it happens to be true. What else can I say? "Sweetie? You don't have those two letters. You have the thing with three letters." Besides, it feels good to sound definitive—to be able to answer one goddamn question with any kind of certainty.

Ali shakes her head, returning to her refrain of, "I don't want to know." The idea that it's an autoimmune disease connected to excessive inflammation is enough. She doesn't want to know the name or the prognosis because, in her own logic, any negativity will prevent her from staying positive. And then she adds, "I don't need to know because whatever it is, you're going to fix it. I know you, Mom."

Yeah, me and my "no-makeup makeup" foundation, sure. No pressure. But you know, the germ of the idea for a foundation—a much different kind, of course—suddenly seems like a place to start.

Ali continues to watch the comings and goings in the waiting area.

In addition to patients and their loved ones, the other predominant sight is that of serious-looking medical personnel in white and blue frocks as they bound in and out, pausing now and then to check their watches, like the rabbit late for an important date in *Alice in Wonderland*. Or should I say *Ali in Wonderland*.

When they call her name, Ali instantly regains composure, flashing her gorgeous, almost sardonic smile, like—*OMG, why's everyone so serious?* But I know she's just doing it to put us at ease. Ali rejects anyone feeling sorry for her as much as she has no room for self-pity.

By the time Dr. Weinshenker comes in, her guard's up. Her vision isn't a hundred percent back from the whole Eyeball Headache deal of a month ago, but it's so much better. At the start, she was unable to see my three fingers held up close to her left eye. Now she can make out how many fingers there are. Colors are coming back too.

As mentioned, this is why I'm able to cultivate the hope that we're experiencing some kind of anomalous NMO one-off, and I don't want anything to happen in the room to take us off course. Plus, I need for Dr. Weinshenker to live up to his reputation and get us through the storm. So nothing can happen to indicate that he is less than all-NMO-knowing. Or, worse, nothing can happen, as the fearful warrior must anticipate, that might endanger him in his own right. Therefore, in addition to sending all the protective white light to Ali, I've got it working on Dr. Weinshenker—a man I've only just met. Logic being absent in this equation, my reason is that if something—anything—bad, awful, or unforeseen was to happen to the one man with the knowledge vital to Ali's well-being, well, frankly, we would be fucked. Ali would be through the looking glass with nobody able to help her get back to yesterday.

If it's hard to follow the mixed-up Wonderland and Oz metaphors, it's only to evoke the NMO altered state of reality in which everything is jumbled. It's like MS but not, an autoimmune cousin to lupus or a counterpart to it, a completely unpredictable tornado of symptoms that can be either temporary or permanent. Nothing makes any sense, as if we *did* fall down the rabbit hole and land in Oz, Alice/Ali as Dorothy, with the support team trying on the role of the Good Witch, and all the while I'm feeling more like the Lion, the Scarecrow, *and* the Tin Man, in need of heart, brains, and courage.

Literary metaphor mash-up break now over. Back to sobering reality.

After the exam Ali and Nanny go out to the waiting room to play cards with Evan. Bill and I, accompanied by Katja, are led by Dr. Brian Weinshenker into his office. There really is a magical, super-powered quality about Dr. Weinshenker that I can't quite find the essence of. Maybe it's something elfin that I associate with his shorter stature, his light Nordic coloring, and the superserious focus behind his glasses. But the true magic lies in his kindness and his wisdom, I am sure.

Temporarily put at ease by this quality, after Bill, Katja, and I take our seats, I don't expect to see the expression of sadness on Dr. Weinshenker's face as he goes behind his desk, sits, and says definitely, "Textbook NMO."

Unable to breathe, I go out of body. Bill hangs in, dying inside, I imagine.

For our benefit Katja asks, "What do you describe as textbook?"

Trying to peel myself off the ceiling, I hear Dr. Weinshenker explain, "The optic nerve is the first to come under attack—"

We know this part. The next part is the shocker, the part that you read about when you make the mistake of Googling NMO. To put any hope to rest that we're going to skip the next phase, he predicts, "It will probably be just a matter of months before she has the transverse myelitis portion—the spinal cord attacks."

Panic kicks in, full blown. I can go out of body and stick to the ceiling or I can leave the room. Choosing the latter, I step outside into the hall and run into the bathroom, throw water on my face, and then race back into his office to take my seat, as if I've been there all along.

It seems like the most inappropriate moment to float my "one attack" theory, but as I've called attention to myself already, I figure it's only going to get worse. Why not run it by the Wiz while I've got his ear?

"I was wondering," I begin, my voice shaky and breathy, "her recovery is excellent. I mean, she's only had the one attack, and her vision's almost totally back. Her depth! Her color! Maybe she just has some version of the condition. Maybe it's something you don't even know about or you've never even seen before. Maybe with whatever she has, she's not going to have the spine attacks."

He nods. Bill leans in. Katja shrugs. She wants my point to be well received, I can tell. But an exceptional physician in her own right, with a specialization as an endocrinologist, she knows what I do—that it is only wishful thinking dressed up with a mother's desperation.

Dr. Weinshenker says something to appease the angry gods in me, something like, "Well, we can hope, but it's not likely."

You can't negotiate with NMO. I get that now, and it's close to crippling. But not enough to keep me from going back and forth between being out of body and up on the ceiling—or compulsively racing between Dr. Weinshenker's office and the restroom and my chair. Each time I leave, Bill picks up the thread of the conversation so I can jump back in upon my return.

Dr. Weinshenker recommends a "very aggressive approach to treatment." Chemo drugs. Painkillers. Immunosuppressant steroids.

Which makes sense because with NMO, like other autoimmune diseases, the immune system has gone overboard in doing its job warding off infection and other cellular miscreants and it starts attacking good cells, disrupting necessary life systems and mainly the myelin sheath that coats the nerves.

But I don't know. Bill looks equally unsure. Even Katja seems worried. Suppress her immune system? What happens when she gets a cold and it becomes pneumonia?

Dr. Weinshenker admits there are no guarantees to an aggressive approach and that the treatments have downsides. However, if Ali was his daughter, he says, he would consider hospitalizing her here at the Mayo, right away, and starting an IV infusion of a chemo medication—the "A" drug that we have discussed. Or, he tells us, there is one doctor at another hospital whose studies of the use of the "R" drug have shown promising results in preventing attacks. For the "R" drug, another trip to another city with this one doctor—let's call him Dr. R.—will be required.

In time, I'll become more familiar to references that come up to the one doctor somewhere else who might offer a second opinion or an alternate approach to the one doctor you've already come to see. But in that moment, "R" was the only straw to grasp, the only thing standing between Ali and immediate hospitalization.

I'm on the ceiling again, stuck to the glass of the snow globe, with a freaking blizzard coming.

Between the years of the late nineteenth century and the early twenty-first century, Devic's Disease had managed to elude capture by most clinicians and researchers, retaining its orphan status at every turn. It was, of course, eventually given the more scientific name of neuromyelitis optica (NMO). Then in 2004 work at the Mayo Clinic had finally paved the way for the test that would be used to diagnose the spectrum of NMO, as it is now more widely understood to be.

Therefore, it was not unreasonable that when I began thinking about starting a foundation to come up with desperately needed, life-saving research, treatment, and a cure for my daughter, my first partner and the first institution I would fund would be the Mayo Clinic. Before we had even left Dr. Weinshenker's office, the framework for the Guthy-Jackson Charitable Foundation had already crystallized in my mind. Or as I told Brian Weinshenker after he alerted me to the scant research being done at the time, "You don't know me, but I have a checkbook and we will be working together closely."

In hindsight I can acknowledge that was a most presumptuous statement on my part because I knew nothing about launching or running a foundation, especially one that would be devoted to an under-researched orphan disease and would turn out to be the only organization doing so! Nor did I know, until I started the process, that the institutions already studying NMO (usually as an offshoot of work focused on MS and other more prevalent autoimmune diseases) had the same policy: Don't Ask, Don't Share.

Though shocking to me, a lot of folks were all too familiar with why the nonsharing policies exist—partly to serve funders of research who are invested in owning the patents for drugs that might come from studies and partly for the physicians, scientists, and institutions who have proprietary claims to the findings that they want to publish with their names attached. That's how the game was played, I was told, not only in rare disease research but also across the medical field.

With little private funding and not enough of a statistical impact to qualify for government grants, NMO research was all but languishing back in the day of Devic. There was barely anything on the Internet except some obscure published studies and anecdotal accounts of individuals with histories of perfect health who were then suddenly cut down in their prime, blinded, crippled, and led to early graves. There was no central database for physicians and scientists to access. No national registry. No way of locating patients for testing when funds for research might become available. No conferences or free-flowing exchange of information and ideas. No easy way to get answers (or at least start the conversation) to the most basic questions: How many people had it? How many had been misdiagnosed with MS? Had anyone considered the number of us who were walking around with the NMO-IgG antibody?

If answers were known, they weren't generally available.

What happens in the Mayo stays in the Mayo? Sort of. Or Johns Hopkins, or Scripps, or Stanford, or wherever—each being an exclusive, gated community with strict, traditional by-laws for cutting-edge research.

Though I was the least likely candidate to undertake the job, I recognized that a major medical makeover was in order.

With my own mental antibodies forming against the acceptance that Ali really had this thing, I had to find some crack in the snow globe.

While Mom, Ali, and Evan headed back to the hotel, I huddled over coffee with Bill and Katja, the three of us talking frankly about the kind of resources and the amount of catalytic energy needed even to begin what was the equivalent of marching off to the North Pole. Without a map.

Whatever we were going to discover in terms of Ali's condition (who me, still in denial?), I could only believe this was how we were supposed to fight. Of that I was sure.

No grand hope of busting out of the snow globe existed. But at least the idea of a research-driven foundation was a start. And in the meantime I must say again for the record that I still hadn't signed on to the inevitability of another attack—desperately fearful of it though I was.

~

***Alone in my room**, back from the Mayo, I'm trying not to think of the past few days but am having trouble.*

Honestly, the trip wasn't easy. Everything was so surreal, as if all the medical experts were like Keebler Elves bustling around and working at their cobbler benches/lab stations. Everyone was so very kind, but they all wore expressions of such pity that I almost wanted to tell them just to lighten up. Like, really? Anyway, the trip confirmed for me, yet again, that the less I know, the better.

Here's the thing though: more needles! I mean, is there some kind of vampire tendency among doctors these days? They just can't get enough.

Before the Eyeball Headache, I didn't like needles, but I didn't cry or get upset every time I got blood drawn. And I always thought that the more you do something difficult, the easier it gets. Not with needles. So far my experience has been that the more someone needs to stick me with a needle, the more scared I get and the more I cry.

My remedy, now that I'm home, is listening to the music from my absolute favorite show on this planet—yes, the previously mentioned WICKED. *Lately nothing helps put everything into perspective more than that soundtrack. I mean, not only is the singing incredible, but the story is really inspiring for me. The main character, Elphaba, is constantly discriminated against due to the color of her skin, yet she still perseveres and does not let anything get in her way of fighting for what is right.*

She can overcome her entire world hating her and thinking she's evil, yet she is still able to find the courage to fight continuously for what she believes in. She can do all that, and I'm crying over a silly needle every once in a while?

With that encouraging thought, I head down to dinner and greet members of our extended family, who are joining us tonight. First the discussion touches on a difficult situation of someone else's, and I mention my hope there will be a silver lining to those problems. Because I really hope that for them. Then one of my relatives begins to speculate on the plethora of medical tests I've undergone. Dad and Mom both look ready to change the subject, but because I'm the one being discussed, I'm just about to pipe up and say that I don't want to talk about it when my relative interjects, "You know, Ali, there doesn't always have to be a silver lining."

I freeze.

WHAT DO YOU MEAN THERE'S NO SILVER LINING? I shout in my brain, with strenuous effort to make sure those words do not stray past the thin barrier of my lips.

I want a silver lining. I need a silver lining!

That's exactly how I felt then in my state of ignorance, unaware of the ordeals ahead of me. But it's how I would continue to feel, even in my less-ignorant days to come.

~

As Bill, Katja, and I continue to consider and debate the various aggressive treatment methods Dr. Weinshenker recommended, the next diagnostic step is taken when Katja orders an MRI of the spine to assess where we are with the transverse myelitis part of the equation. Though I'm still a holdout for my theory that Ali may be dodging a bullet, we are about six weeks down the road since her initial attack, and I just want to be prepared. Much to our overwhelming relief, the MRI of the spine comes back pristine—not one lesion, not one hint of inflammation.

For about a second I start to rethink the aggressive, preventative approach to treatment. But the Voice—yes that one!—bursts my balloon of magical thinking with a few scientific reminders. The main point is that Ali's blood tests have consistently shown high titers, measures for the antibodies detected by the biomarker NMO IgG, a protein targeting aquaporin-4, the water-carrying molecular protein needed to fend off demyelinating inflammatory diseases.

Where the Voice got its medical training, I have no idea, but even a lay-person like me can see that something bad is laying in wait. I also know now from doing my homework that one way to try to stop the attacks, other than through the immune-suppressant power of the steroids, is with the B-cell inhibitors such as the "A" or the "R" drugs. In the immune system both B-cells and T-cells are responsible for making the antibodies that, unfortunately, are causing and targeting the destruction of the myelin. So the theory is that by lowering the population of B-cells with "A" or "R"—pick your poison—we can lower the antibodies and the chance of the disease recurring.

Bill and I soon conclude that taking Ali to be seen by Dr. R. to discuss whether she is a candidate for the "R" drug needs to happen—and soon. Despite the perfect MRI of the spine, despite the fact Ali has no symptoms whatsoever and even looks healthier, more glowing, and more vibrant than she has for a long time, we assemble the team and take another flight to another city to another MS center to meet the one doctor who might or might not know something that the Wizards at the Mayo don't.

Let me just say, if the Voice was to have an actual persona to accompany its doom and gloom, Dr. R. turns out to be that guy. So much for sending white light in his direction.

Even before meeting him, the atmosphere of his waiting room exudes darkness. Ali starts a hand of cards with Nanny, and Bill reads a magazine, while I try unsuccessfully to avoid looking around at a postcard of despair—patients, some blind, some with canes, in wheelchairs or walkers, partially or fully paralyzed.

"Alexandra Guthy?"

When the receptionist calls for Ali, Bill, Katja, and I accompany her to a family-sized meeting/exam room. Katja has asked Dr. R.'s nurse if she can have a few words with him out in the hall before he comes in—

just to make sure he doesn't mention the name NMO or, please, any dire prognosis that would upset anyone, let alone a fourteen-year-old girl.

Without being obvious, I step into the hallway, letting my now-supersonic Mom ears pick up on any problems. Dr. R., I can hear, doesn't think much of our approach. He tells Katja, "I don't *not* tell patients what they have. She's almost fifteen, correct? I think she should know."

"Yes, but she's asked not to know."

Releasing a begrudging puff of exasperation, Dr. R. agrees to the request. When he enters the room, I swear that it noticeably darkens, especially when he looks at me.

Dr. Katja Van Herle, a slender blonde with sparkling blue eyes and a bright white light unto herself, stands and starts to present the case. She begins by mentioning the trip Ali made to Mexico that preceded the Eyeball Headache back in February, at which point he cuts her off, saying, "I just want to talk to my patient."

Awkward. Worse than awkward.

Katja sits. Bill shifts his weight in his seat, and I look over at Ali, who simply nods and proceeds to answer questions. No matter what she says that's hopeful or attempts to downplay the drama or any lightness that any of us interject, Dr. R. either dismisses it or interrupts, not letting her finish her answers or allow us to talk.

Even when I bring up the results of Ali's last MRI, he shoots down the mere possibility that anything could bode well. Dr. R. is all about bad boding, about seeing boogey men reflected in mirrors. Emotional claustrophobia pushes me further into a dark, narrow place, unbearable except for the fact that I'm not alone it. We're all there.

After Ali goes out to the waiting area to resume her card game with Mom, Dr. R. ushers us into his office and, in brutal fashion, tells us that we need to act and we need to act immediately or Ali will have another attack. Imminently. If she doesn't start the "R" drug—and he is recommending putting her in the hospital then and there for seven days to administer it by IV—we may just as well write her death sentence, or at least expect to see her blind and completely paralyzed in the near future.

"But what about her MRI?" I ask, shaking, choking.

Well, he says, you can postpone taking action if you want to roll the dice with your daughter's life. He directs this not at Katja or Bill, but at me. Dr. R. clearly doesn't like me. No—he hates me, he really hates me.

Bill leans in my direction, trying to play good cop, asking in a low, unemotional voice, "What do you think? Maybe we should check her into the hospital here for the first IV."

Everyone turns to me, the identified patient, the problem child in the bunch, and I say, "No, I need to think about this. I'm not ready. We should go home and take a few days to consider the ramifications, discuss what's best for Ali. This is sudden, and I need to gather my thoughts." The fact is that the "R" drug can be given on an out-patient basis at a hospital near to where we live. This is me in I-wanna-go-home! mode, thinking if I'm on my own turf, we can sort it out, it'll all go away, and Dr. R. will be proven wrong.

But then again. The Voice disagrees. Maybe Dr. R. is right. Maybe there is no right move for Ali and we should err on the side of vigilance.

Torture.

We agree that we'll return to LA and sort things out and, within the week, be in touch and probably make arrangements to begin the "R" drug.

Upon leaving, I expect to have some warmth, some light, some crumb or morsel of hope tossed in Ali's direction.

But Dr. R. doesn't do that.

The whole freaking "rolling the dice" image messes with my head.

On the one hand, it's the end of April and, whether it's just all been a crap shoot or it's the uber-strength prednisone fighting inflammation, we've passed the two-month mark and Ali has been attack-free. On the other hand, knowing that an attack can come at any minute and imagining the feeling of not having done more to preempt it, we schedule the first IV infusion in Los Angeles. It could have been random, but in the literature there were case studies of NMO patients regaining their sight and their mobility after having been on downward spirals. If we could get out in front of further attacks, why wouldn't we? The only thing I ask is if we can avoid anything before her fifteenth birthday, May 15. For the sake of her already-stolen childhood, I beg to wait until after her birthday. With a puff of exasperation, Dr. R. agrees.

Counting down the days, I'm not sleeping. Neither is Bill. All I can do is pray that the intuitive powers helping guide our decision have some clarity of vision in the midst of fear bombardment.

Then, the night before the first scheduled IV infusion, Dr. R. calls to say that he has done some thinking and believes we should wait thirty days.

Say what?

If Ali was his daughter, he begins again, even though he doesn't have children, but if he had our resources, he would wait a month, and in this thirty-day period, wean her off the steroids so that her blood could eventually be collected for future testing. The "R" drug was going to change her blood chemistry, so without a pure blood sample taken after thirty days to use as a baseline for comparison, the impact of the B-cell inhibitor would not be known or measured, and this would lessen the likelihood of finding a cure for Ali.

Wait. First I'm rolling the dice if I don't get her started right away, and now I'm playing with her life if I don't postpone treatment for thirty days and take her off all steroids? The night before the first treatment he is calling and arguing against everything he said before?

Not because there are any guarantees but because he has been thinking, and this is what he would do if Ali were his daughter.

What do we do? What the fuck do we do? That's my prayer to God, who benevolently looks past my language in this instance. The answer comes. We go with what Dr. R. would do if he had our resources. We begin slowly tapering off the prednisone. We keep praying.

June 1, Two Weeks Later, Cedars-Sinai Hospital

Ali comes down with severe lower abdominal pains. Whether this has anything to do with NMO, we don't know. However, because we have eighteen more days to go to get her weaned off everything, we can't treat with any steroids. The solution, we decide, is to check into Cedars for observation. Thank God, she starts to feel better around dinnertime.

Ali and I both have our trays, and we're doing what we do—using humor, changing the subject, just in the middle of chatting—when a White Coat Battalion marches in, or, should I say, invades.

We will call them Dr. Clipboard and the Lookieloos. (That's what happens when you outgrow people pleasing and Dr. R. has gotten on your very last nerve—you get to call it like you see it.) So Clipboard, smiling like an undertaker, ignores me—just as he has ignored the ***big, bold*** printed note in the chart that says *DO NOT DISCUSS DIAGNOSIS WITH PATIENT.* Obviously Ali is not an adult, and I'm the Mom. But to this doctor, I just as well might be her personal assistant.

"Miss Guthy?" he begins. "We've never seen anyone with NMO before. Mind if we talk?"

Ali stares at him and the entourage.

Hoping against hope that she hasn't heard those three letters, NMO, because she doesn't want to know, I jump out of my chair, saying, "I'd love to!"

Appearing more annoyed than startled, Clipboard maintains his smile—to be read by his underlings as a demonstration of patience when dealing with family. "Are you the mother?"

"Yes!" Am I ever.

Before he knows it, my hand is on his arm, brusquely steering him into the hall. I keep my smile too—not wanting Ali to pick up on anything—and as we leave the room, my fingers apply more pressure.

Clipboard gets the hint. In fairness, although his disregard has given me every right to be pissed, he is not the enemy. He's more like a minor character from one of those medical shows that probably inspired him to become a doctor in the first place.

Still, when I tear into him, man, does it feel good. And to his credit, he accepts responsibility, even though he doesn't really understand why a fifteen-year-old might not want to know the details of the dreaded disease that picked her at random.

The tirade I have just delivered makes me feel great. That is, until I go back in Ali's room.

"What did he mean?"

"Nothing. He didn't know what he was talking about."

"Right, Mom, sure." I can see her processing the three letters, NMO, mentally turning them up and down, not sure what to do with them yet.

I watch her disappear—the way she was at the Mayo, how she can go under. Run silent, run deep. But for now she will maintain deniability. Hear no NMO, speak no NMO.

And later when an attack does come, and there are more needles, and doctors' visits and tests and MRIs and overly eager strangers with clipboards, Ali has ostensibly buried that which dare not speak its name.

Before we leave Cedars, Ali makes me promise her again, reminding me not to forget: "Whatever I have, Mom, I don't want to know the name. Don't let them accidentally tell me."

3

Leaving Paradise

Faith Healers, Dromedary Cures, and Sweet Sixteens

Knowledge is knowing a tomato is a fruit.
Wisdom is not putting it in a fruit salad.

(ATTRIBUTION UNKNOWN)

June 7-ish, 2008, Beverly Hills

My friend's husband, one of the dearest human beings I know, calls to express his concern.

Like so many of our close friends who have heard about Ali and want to offer support, many of them with suggestions for little-known yet promising treatments, he says that he knows this is a dark time but that he has something important to tell me that could offer hope.

"Yes, really? Oh, thank you . . . " I love these calls. I live for these calls. Anything to combat the dark and doom and the bad boding. Candles, prayer rooms, affirmations, holistic or folk remedies, whatever. We have to cover the bases, after all, especially during this period when Ali is off all meds.

Covering bases is not new. Spiritually, I've always been open-minded, a searcher, not a follower of only one faith or doctrine or approach to healing. Whenever I'm asked to specify religious affiliation, I usually write down, "Yes." I love all rituals that honor a greater power in the universe. In fact, in both my weddings and blessing ceremonies for my children, I drew from multiple faiths.

That probably started with my first marriage, which happened not long after I left home and crossed paths with a handsome, big guy I'd known in high school whose last name was Jackson (a last name I kept, even though he and I were married less than one year). Actually, there was nothing at all religious about it. It took place in a chapel that seemed like a mellow, quaint place to get married, and I wore this hippie halter dress. The ceremony was very laid back with a nondenominational minister presiding. We all went back to the house afterward for a small gathering. No big deal. . . .

When I married Joe, Evan's father, because he was raised Catholic and I was raised Jewish (culturally at least), we held our ceremony at the interdenominational Wayfarer's Chapel, part of the Swedenborgian Church. When Evan was born, I didn't see why we should limit ourselves to blessing him in one faith, so I arranged for a couple different denominational ceremonies. The more blessings the better, right?

Bill, who was raised Christian in the Worldwide Church of God, knew more about Jewish laws and holidays than I ever would. He even started out as a theology major when he attended the church's college. He eventually left the church, but growing up with structure and this big, loving extended family at the church had a positive influence. As he put it: "I absorbed the good stuff. Character, faith, family, the Old testament and the New."

When Ali and Jackson were born, just as with Evan, I made sure that they too were blessed in several faiths. My feeling is not that every form of religious observation has the universe all figured out. Far from it. I just know that *I* don't have it figured out. So why not be open-minded?

So as far as healing practices go, why on earth would I not be open to potential cures that someone I know and respect wants to recommend?

My friend's husband knows this about me and proceeds to tell me about a woman whose child with a rare autoimmune disease was saved by a homeopathic remedy that he has researched. Then he describes foreign news reports he has seen and scientific literature he has read about this particular, extraordinary, natural cure found in Israel that can combat other insidious and rare diseases. He knows people who can get their hands on this cure, but it will probably require a trip to Israel.

A natural remedy? I love natural.

My wheels spin. How do we get to the beloved Holy Land with the family? God knows I hate to fly, particularly for that many hours, but if it's going to save Ali, why not? Then I think to ask what this miracle medicine is.

"Camel's milk." No, it's not a certain species of Israeli camels. It's the milk of this certain one-humped camel. Oh, a dromedary cure. It's come to this, has it?

I'm imagining what Ali's doctors will say if I ask how the one-humped camel's milk will work in conjunction with other treatments. Then again, so what?—they already think I'm nuts. Besides, it's natural!

There is a slight concern. For the milk to be effective, it can't be pasteurized, which means there is a risk that it carries tuberculosis. "But," my friend's husband says, "TB probably wouldn't be as bad as this NMO."

Actually, he has a point. I jot down more details on how to locate said camel's milk and ship it to our shores without spoiling, then I dash downstairs to greet the new healer who has come to take a look at Ali.

The family is used to these people coming out of the woodwork, and they know I'll talk to anyone.

The healer says she needs to see my daughter and look at her eyes. "Wait right here," I say to the woman, who exudes a wellness vibe, after offering her a seat in the living room and something to drink. I race up the stairs to knock on Ali's door, thinking that this new healer really does have a therapeutic aura.

"Ali," I say after a quick knock, not wanting to intrude on her homework, "can you come down and meet a friend of mine?"

Silence.

I walk in and see my industrious child with books spread on her bed. "Ali, come say hello. She's really cool."

Shaking her head, Ali Rose is not buying this at all. "Mom," she nods, "It's a healer, isn't it?"

Uhmm. "You can meet her—she's downstairs!"

Ali looks at me as if to say, *yeah, I knew it.* And then she won't even come out of her room.

Fine. Trying a new tactic, as my daughter is an athlete, I connect with a guy who specializes in helping people overcome major health challenges with exercise and nutrition. Better yet, he is married to someone on *So You Think You Can Dance*—one of Ali's favorite shows. How can she say no to coming downstairs when he stops by?

Somehow Ali manages to say no.

A psychic who comes highly recommended then suggests that instead of trying to engage Ali in a process that's upsetting her, why not keep the focus on exorcizing my own demons?

Gosh, that makes sense. I bring in a top energy-clearing expert—who turns out to be a kindly looking woman with matted hair and tattered sneakers—who holds a big branch of burning sage and walks through the house waving the smoke around, then puts sea salt in the corners of our bedrooms. She finishes up by throwing rice everywhere, and Jackson comes running in a panic. "Mom, why is there a lady in my bedroom throwing rice at my door?"

Ali calls from upstairs, "It's in my room too!"

When I explain that the rice is left to break up and absorb any negative energy clumps that the sage and salt missed, my kids say nothing as each of them returns to other tasks at hand.

No, I know it's not going to make everything all better, but none of this can hurt. Besides, a few days after the energy-clearing woman leaves, when I hold my fingers up in front of Ali's eyes, she can see them perfectly and says so with the same relief and joy I feel.

The Voice that's been telling me a big attack is right around the corner suddenly goes quiet. Maybe, just maybe, the doctors really are wrong.

~

JUNE 10, 2008

Since Mom started flying again *in recent years, we've been taking an annual family trip to New York City that is so much fun. This year I'm really ready to get there, to get all this focus on me behind us, maybe go see a great show, and go fit in as many museums as is humanly possible.*

File all this under our "Go Big or Go Home" banner.

Lately, maybe it's just the amusement of the "woo-woo" healers, but it seems like everyone isn't as on edge as they were before. Or maybe just being annoyed by the weirdness helps me feel less vulnerable.

Because I'm feeling fine and almost back to seeing perfectly fine, I've psyched myself into a way of playing offense—rather than just being on the receiving end of anything upsetting. Call it a sports thing, a strategy.

Tennis is a mental game, as anyone can tell you. It's been a passion for me since the fifth grade when I couldn't wait to play for the Buckley team, which required waiting until the seventh grade. In middle school, match play is very different than it is in high school. Instead of playing three rounds, one set each, you play one pro-set match (or one eight-game set). The first singles match I played was against this boy who was insanely good! I think he might have been ranked in the US Tennis Association or something. For real. He beat me 8–0 in about a half hour.

Embarrassed beyond words, I stormed off the court crying and left the match early. We ended up tying with the other team, and I needed to replay this kid again for a shot for our team to win, but because I was nowhere to be found, my team forfeited that match. Although I probably would have lost to that kid anyway, I was even more embarrassed and ashamed for not being there for my team. I made a very clear promise to myself that from that day forward I would never lose my cool like that again, that I would remain calm in the face of a challenge whenever I played tennis.

That one very bad experience is the key reason why I've been able to maintain such mental toughness in my games. That was a crash course in conquering the mental game and knowing that if I wanted to win, I had to beat myself first.

Other lessons came along in the ninth grade, when joining the Varsity team required tryouts. On the first day of tryouts we had been running a couple laps, just a couple, and I had to sit down for twenty minutes. I was THAT *out of breath! My coach, Sherm, would often recall how she looked at me that day and thought,* OH BOY! WHAT AM I GONNA BE ABLE TO DO WITH HER?

Sue Sherman was a godsend. My coach and mentor since that freshman year, she was always there to support me, teach me, and help me grow as a person in more ways than I can ever describe. Her dedication to the team and her passion for the sport has always been and will continue to be an inspiration to me in everything I do. The success of my team—and myself personally—would not be possible without the guiding hand of Sherm.

After a strong ninth-grade season and getting back into shape for next year, I've become even more convinced of the importance of strategy. Yes, I'm very strong, I have my good shots, and I'm a solid net player, but time and again I come back to the fact that tennis really is a thinking person's sport. People assume it's all about power and how hard you hit the ball, but that is so not true. My winning percentage is on the way to being 90 percent, and I know it could be at 99 percent with strategy and finesse because it's all about where you put the ball—how you read your opponent, how you follow through on your strengths, and how you hit as you see your opponent unraveling.

Strategy is about reading people, studying their reactions, reading their mistakes, and just nailing them on their weaknesses. My strength has been exploiting those weaknesses, which I am competitive enough to do 'til the very end.

The person who really taught me that has been my father. Playing tennis with Dad over the years made me have to study him and read him, simply because that's what he was doing when he was playing me. Part of the strategy I learned was never to show weakness, never to show fear, never allow myself to be intimidated.

Which brings me back around to my strategy to avoid too much information about too much inflammation. I figured it was enough to know my opponent at a distance and not get all friendly and on speaking terms by knowing its name, not letting myself admit or show how freaked out I really was.

My strategy right now, because everything is as normal as can be and I'm doing great, is just to avoid the conversation. Mom knows that.

She knows I'm not going to ask how her day was. Because she might have found out something medical and won't tell me because she knows I don't want to be asked something medical.

Nope, not going to happen. That's me. When I don't want to know something, I don't want to know it, and I will just do everything in my power not to know it.

~

Aside from the organizational requirements of getting a foundation up and running, our initial focus has been scouring the globe for experts in autoimmune diseases who also happen to have touched on Devic's/NMO in their research. We're clear that even obscure, long-shot studies should be considered.

I'm taking pages from what I learned in my career journey. Even if it's only the confidence to believe in myself, I have this hunch that something of value can be borrowed from whatever audacity of purpose allowed me to transition from waitress to makeup artist, UCLA instructor, and, eventually, CEO.

Could the history of the creation of the "no-makeup makeup" foundation really help me now? Why not? All I know is that from the time I decided to rewrite my story, I defied the odds by being three things that weren't so difficult—Professional, Passionate, and a Problem Solver.

While multitasking at various jobs before going to beauty school, I forgot my mother's second-most-repeated Momtra: "If you don't figure it out yourself, a man won't do it for you."

I relearned that quickly in my brief first marriage, a mismatch from the start. Although, again, I did get a great last name. I'd already dropped my biological father's last name, and my stepfather Mort's last name always felt temporary. The new last name was a smart choice. The name Vicki Jackson proved to be memorable to clients.

While building up a clientele, I worked in retail at a department store, developing an expertise in makeovers. As a budding Good Will Ambassador for Mascara, my eventual job description, my focus on the Before's and After's was using makeup to get women to emphasize what they liked about themselves as opposed to focusing on what they didn't—about making others feel good about themselves and their intrinsic beauty. That was my true passion.

Before long, cosmetic problem solving evolved into a series of forty-four solution cards that I'd give to my clients so they could achieve the same look on their own. The anti-elitist in me refused to accept that there were secrets only the beauty geniuses could give you. And nobody had to give me permission to have a strong point of view or to be generous in spreading my nonsecrets for natural beauty.

At first, I focused on texture and careful blending of foundation as important to getting that natural look. Eventually, I called that approach "no-makeup makeup." With that concept, the magic dust—or iridescent powder, to be more factual—was sprinkled as my career took off and my agents could boast that Vicki Jackson was the go-to gal for making everyone look incredible yet natural. From haute couture fashion models to punk rockers. One day it might be a call to do a cover for *People* magazine, doing hair and makeup for Tom Selleck or Morgan Fairchild, and the next job could be a *Rolling Stone* cover for James Taylor or Tom Petty. All in a week I might do editorial fashion work for *Glamour* or *GQ* magazines mixed in with a movie ad for *Romancing the Stone* or a promotional campaign for *Dynasty* or a For Members Only commercial or a Levi Strauss print ad job or any one of the more than two hundred music album covers that I eventually did.

Working with iconic celebrities like Bette Davis and Tom Hanks or superstar athletes like Joe Montana or comedians like George Carlin or public figures like Arianna Huffington, I never felt intimidated or out of my comfort zone professionally. Eight years into that career, right before my thirtieth birthday, I decided to graduate to the name Victoria, as many of my clients called me that anyway. Along with that graduation came another decision to spread the gospel of no-makeup makeup by teaching a class at UCLA.

My goal was to demystify the process for young makeup artists trying to develop their skills. After all, the fundamentals were simply the fundamentals. To get my students to relax, forget what so-called experts said, and trust their own instincts, I would often say, "Look, it's not like we're curing cancer or anything." (That phrase would later have ironic resonance.)

In the meantime, as far as breaking into the business, the updated Momtra was, "Look, if I can do it, anyone can. So get your make-up supplies in order and go on and get out there." Have lip gloss, will travel.

Oh, except, which lip gloss was best?

For a while, I'd send my students to the two top Los Angeles beauty supply stores with a comprehensive list of essentials they'd need to be the well-stocked makeup artist. As for the question as to which professional makeup lines made a versatile foundation, I was hard-pressed to make a recommendation for a particular brand.

Most of the foundation being used in those days still had that overly orange or too pink of a tint. The textures either had too much grease-paint or had a dry pancake consistency that sat on the skin and didn't move with it. The old-fashioned painted mask. To get the no-makeup makeup look from a base that blended beautifully to give the look of natural, perfect skin, I'd gotten used to mixing up my own blend, combining base from one professional line with tint and then adding base from another line and whipping it up in pots and pans at home in my kitchen—a.k.a. laboratory—until the desired texture was achieved.

Before the thought of creating my own cosmetics line had ever occurred to me, I came up with the idea of doing my own foundation specifically for clients who requested it and for my students to buy when they went to purchase the other makeup items on their list. The operation became too big for the kitchen, so I moved it into the garage with more pots and pans, more product lines and tints, and expanded my concoctions to include more yellow undertones and beigey top tones and more shades in general.

The next step was finding a cosmetic chemist, a formulator, who could translate my handmade mixtures of fourteen distinct shades into a product line. The odds that I'd find not only the best formulator in the business but also one willing to take me on without any money to pay upfront were definitely low. (Can we say 2%?)

So, yep, crazy odds and all, I was referred to that very formulator. Before I knew it, I was in business, supplying a handful of local stores with my foundation and then building a loyal following. Word-of-mouth was incredible, almost like marketing a street drug. Frantic actresses would call me up to say, "I'm shooting a film tomorrow and I have to have the base!" Beauty supply store managers were calling to let me know they were sold out of my foundation and "How soon can you restock us?"

Long story somewhat shortened, the next stages of my journey as an entrepreneur continued to flow from my one overriding belief that whenever trying to venture into a new arena—like, say, infomercials—do not to be afraid to try. I learned that after developing a whole cosmetics line that I was marketing on my own and agreed to take a meeting that one of my students suggested.

Apparently this new infomercial company was looking for investment opportunities. There were many reasons why my line wasn't suited to the kind of television marketing that was being done in those days. The conventional wisdom was that women bought cosmetics at retail because they wanted to touch, feel, and sample the makeup in person.

Well, my feeling was that, even if nothing came from the meeting, it couldn't hurt to go. All things being equal, I stood as good a chance as anyone else.

Such is the backdrop to the new story of a very different kind of foundation I'm in the middle of trying to get up and running, but without the cushion of time that I had before. We can't go in thinking that we have as good a chance as anyone else at unraveling the mystery of NMO. We have to make sure our chances are much, much better than that.

Which is why, to echo our previously described intentions, we have to gather a team of medical sleuths from across the world and the healing spectrum. Whatever is or isn't happening with Ali—and we can't predict the course of the illness—we have to get ready to go to war.

Forget no-makeup makeup. It's time to put on war paint.

~

Whatever is or isn't going on *with me really seems to have subsided. Because of some treatments that I have to do when we get back from New York, I'm not taking anything at the moment, which is not just a relief physically but also mentally.*

If only my parents could be less on edge, I could relax. That's really the toughest part of all this. I'm okay. I'm choosing not to know anything. They don't have the luxury of a choice. This just got dropped on them like a nuclear bomb.

I can't ignore how freaked out they've been, all the while trying to protect me from being freaked out too. They continue to manage the news, or lack thereof, in different ways.

Dad has become even more introverted than usual, spending longer hours at the office and appearing to be almost excessive in his level of calm, like someone bracing for a hit of some kind. He has been wearing this very brave face lately, but somehow it's not quite convincing. If I'm paying close attention—which I'm trying not to do, I should add—his face lapses at times to a sort of shell-shocked glare. Oh, it's only in passing, as if the active effort to convince everyone that everything's fine becomes too much. At times I've caught a glimpse of myself in the mirror with a similar expression on my face.

So Mom, as we now know, can't even try to wear a pretend "everything's okay" mask. Not in her nature, not in her no-makeup makeup kit. She's authentically expressive, always open with her feelings, and never attempts to act any other way. For a while there she was retreating to her bedroom whenever she had a chance to lie down, reading medical stuff at all hours of the night, wearing sweat pants practically every day, one pocket full of used tissues like someone with a bad cold. Obviously there was something wrong and she wasn't telling me, which meant that I really needed to worry—except I had asked not to be told so that I didn't have to worry.

The past few weeks have seen an improvement. Mom and Dad have been looking over paperwork together, and I did hear something about different roles they would be playing in getting the foundation going.

Well, that made me happy for a few reasons, not the least of which is that I'm hoping that this means we won't have anymore weirdos sprinkling salt throughout our house.

How 'bout that for a silver lining?

~

June 15, 2008, New York City

Any last shred of hope that Ali will somehow be saved from the transverse myelitis stage of NMO is ground to dust during the family vacation in New York.

We're still within the "matter of months," which Dr. Brian Weinshenker estimated it might be before the first spinal attack. Some patients could go much longer before a second assault, and others not very long at all, he also said.

As of June 15, a hot, muggy day in New York City, Ali is three days away from the thirty-day mark that will allow the final blood collection to take place so that we can start her on the "R" drug. She's been doing so well without steroids that when the decision about whether or not we should travel came up, Bill and I, after deliberating at length, decided maintaining normalcy and sticking to the annual vacation plan was the right thing to do.

See, here's another example of how 2% can really mess with you.

I mean, if best- and worst-case scenarios happen to you 2% of the time, that still doesn't help you know when you're going to get which of those. That is, unless, you're listening to the Voice that's sending you fairly accurate weather reports. And there's the rub: because there's a point in which your fear uses some sort of molecular mimicry to pose as the Voice, and in your effort to sort the two out, you stop listening.

Therefore, there is no warning or sense of foreboding when Ali and I go for a fun walk in Central Park on that hot afternoon. When I see her hand go to her right thigh, the gesture is so subtle I don't want to jump to conclusions and make more out of what could be as normal as overexertion on the tennis court.

Ali shrugs it off too, saying it's only a little tingling, maybe a cramp. She feels better in moments and we walk on, stopping to buy a couple bottles of cold water from a vendor.

Instead of opening it, Ali holds it to her cheek to cool off, then places it on her thigh, almost like an ice pack for a cramping muscle. This is a child who has been a superlative athlete since she started out as the only girl in Little League baseball, who could out-pitch and out-hit and, especially, out-run all the competition. The only girl on the team who played all the way to Majors, Ali knows about applying cold packs to muscles in spasm. And so on this blazing hot summer New York day in Central Park, she touches her icy bottle of water to her leg and says, "That's weird."

Now all my sensors are on alert. "What's weird?"

"I can't feel the cold on my leg." The numbness has a sensation, she says, of having her leg full of sand, like an appendage of a Beanie Baby that's gone limp.

Not wanting to feed into any kind of alarm, I say, "You want to sit down or try walking it off?"

We hobble together for several minutes. By the time we stop, she says, "Oh, yeah, must have been one of those things when your leg goes to sleep. The tingling stopped."

Everything goes right back to normal. All's well. For a day and a half.

~

At the top of the list of reasons *why ignorance is not bliss I would have to put waking up in the middle of the night convinced that some malevolent force had broken in and was stabbing me up and down my spine with piercing, flaming knives. Bewildered and probably in the worst pain of my life, I had an equal and opposite bizarre sensation of going numb in my lower extremities, the right leg more than the left, and that inability to feel cold, all the way from my feet up to my belly button.*

This being one of those occasions when permission to swear ought to be granted—I mean, what the fuck?

~

We confer with Katja and the rest of Ali's doctors in the middle of the night, and they advise us to fly home immediately and whisk her to a setting where she can have her blood drawn (this being the thirtieth day off of steroids), have an MRI to confirm that the attack is what we know it is, and, after that, mercifully administer the steroids intravenously.

A million what-ifs cloud my mind on the flight home. What if we hadn't weaned her off the prednisone and hadn't left her unarmed for this episode? What if we had gone ahead with the "R" drug and had said no to waiting for her blood to purify? What if we had done the "A" drug at the Mayo? What if there was another treatment not yet known?

On the plane home, watching Ali try to stare out the window to distract herself—from the pain, from having to wait for relief, from not knowing where the roller coaster is going next—I turn to look at Bill and see, for the first time, a crack in his armor. He has hung in through the trips to the Mayo and to meet Dr. R., maintaining his positive, even keel, agreeing with the more aggressive forms of treatment, not showing the anguish he's feeling inside. But with the reality of this attack, he sees the new hell we're approaching—so alien to Pleasantville good-byes that are only farewells and adieus to you and you and you—and he makes a decision to stay on the sunny side of the street.

Henceforth, he will be there to hold Ali's hand when blood is being drawn and whenever she needs him at her side, and he will fund the research that's going to be essential to finding a cure. We have settled on our divide-and-conquer roles. He'll be the funder and I'll be the finder.

But I think on this flight home he decides that he can't go to the clinics and sit with the doctors in the rooms and be tortured, forced to spend hours listening to a pitch for some crazy, horrible, overlooked disease in need of tending that not only has no profit potential but also may actually cripple and kill the light of his life.

Finding or creating the promising research to fund, understanding the real science that can save Ali, sitting in those rooms and seeing the future if we don't demand that medicine catch up to our reality—those are going to be my jobs.

When we touched down again in LA, I realized for the first time ever that we weren't going to wake up and have another reality. This was NMO. There was no going back.

~

I have to confess that I didn't enjoy *having to get an MRI the moment we returned, only to confirm what we already knew: that there was inflammation in my spinal cord. The broad strokes were also starting to emerge that apparently I did have this stupid antibody that my cells were making—so stupid that the antibody was attacking me instead of doing the job of warding off infection and whatnot.*

Then the vampire nurse drew a lot of blood. I don't think that the process will ever become easier. But afterward I was given an IV steroid, and thankfully they were able to do it at the house while I watched TV. It took about an hour, so it wasn't that bad, except for the needles. The IV infusion was to be given every night for five nights. But on the fourth night the needles would not go in. The nurse tried it twice, and all my coping mechanisms failed. There is no explanation for how much I screamed. It wasn't the nurse's fault, but I was weary and just felt like crying.

Mom looked so helpless standing by, and I couldn't do anything to make her worry less. She has been suggesting lately that I should probably tell a friend what's been going on with me and all this medical stuff. But I'm honestly content with my journal. Even Nanny has tried to convince me to see a psychiatrist.

"Not necessary," I have tried to say, diplomatically. Besides being a very happy and upbeat person, I've never liked the idea of telling problems to a complete stranger. Why on earth would I talk to a complete stranger when I can talk to one of the most amazing listeners in the world—my mom?

And why should I have to tell my friends what's going on? It would just make me feel uncomfortable. Besides, telling people about it isn't going to make it go away. People keep saying to "let it all out" and "don't hold it in." But don't hold WHAT *in?*

There's another way to look at the stupid antibodies: don't give them any power they don't deserve. As long as I have a choice, I don't want my whole life focused around what is the equivalent to a bump in the road, but now everyone just keeps bringing it up, which makes it worse.

What I love about my journal is that it lets me vent. I always sign off the same way: "Thanks for listening!"

And then I'm back in action, good as new. Or close to it.

~

We were already moving at warp speed, but the first spinal attack accelerated the effort at bringing the best and the brightest experts together. Questions remained about whether a start-up foundation could really do that. Usually, even with the best of intentions, as I learned at the start, the "global coming-together party" rarely happens. Often organizations committed to charitable research wind up in the business of raising money to keep their lights on and their staffs paid, or they inadvertently become invested in not finding a cure for their disease because, after all, that would put them out of business.

Those were the pitfalls of the nonprofit world that Bill and I were determined to avoid. We recognized that our family had been cursed by NMO, but we were blessed to have the financial resources to do something about it. Or at least try.

Bill and I, as funder and finder, maintained those separate challenges that we had decided would work for us at the start: me running the foundation, him making sure the money was there to support it. To complicate that concern, this so happened to be at the start of the global economic collapse that was definitely not leaving us unscathed. "Old school" wasn't going to cut it. Even the usual approach of throwing a fundraiser to tap the wallets of our friends and associates wasn't for us. Did anyone really want another black-tie gala or another silent auction of sports memorabilia and gift certificates for dermabrasion? Telethons were fantastic, but the market for selling worthy causes to the masses seemed to be cornered.

Besides, America loves big, scary numbers, and with NMO, they just don't exist. Welcome to the sideshow of orphan diseases—seven thousand and counting in diagnosed cases, at least back in those days.

Around half a million people were then estimated to have MS. If you dug deep, experts said you might find someone dusting off a number—four thousand—of those estimated newly diagnosed to be NMO. It's higher because there's a whole new group with the NMO-IgG antibody still misdiagnosed with MS and yet to be documented.

But really, tell me: in marketing, headline-shouting, fund-snaring terms, how sexy is ten to fifteen thousand (thinking big, we were looking at maybe twenty thousand, tops) suffering from the "Say What? Syndrome"?

Most nonprofits of the scope we had in mind could take a year to become a charity officially.

Except. Except we had a rare orphan coincidence and a miraculous, collaborative opportunity to join forces with Dr. Katja Van Herle, who had recently established a foundation of her own that was dedicated to public health and education. (Well, of course she did. What else was a gal to do with all that extra time?) A month after we returned from the Mayo the All Greater Good Foundation had jumped its final bureaucratic hurdle and was ready to roll. The timing was perfect. Katja and I agreed to merge heads, hearts, and minds, and wrap the whole package in lovely leftover red tape. By midsummer it made a pretty bow, and we could go to work.

When does this happen so seamlessly? Rarely. Maybe 2% of the time. (The gifts do keep on giving.)

And so the Guthy-Jackson Charitable Foundation, conceived at the Mayo, was born that July—kind of a preemie, like me. A little wobbly but standing on its own four feet, like a newborn giraffe we'd seen on the Discovery channel—stunned and still wet but with high ambitions, already nibbling at the treetops.

My newly inspired logo was a branch with two big leaves on one side and three smaller leaves on the other, each leaf representing the members of our family.

Because we were trying to raise awareness as well as mobilize the leading players, a battle cry also seemed fitting, something like "Stand up for cancer!" But being that we had to overcompensate as the rare orphan disease, I went with "Jump up really high for NMO!"

It wasn't much as a slogan, but the foundation did seem to present more possibilities than one-humped-camel-milk cures.

July 16, 2008

At the UCLA medical complex where Ali will be receiving her first "R" drug IV infusion, Katja and I, the advance team, stop by the imaging division to pick up recent MRIs before heading over to the clinic where Ali waits with Bill and Nanny.

With Ali's first spinal attack a month behind us and the follow-up blasts of IV steroid infusions and an oral regimen of lower doses of steroids after that, she ostensibly shows no remaining deficits, leaving our team to feel incredibly lucky. At the same time we are now officially in mourning. The theory of the NMO one-off has now been killed. With no turning back, no ejector seat for Ali to leave this ride, I accept a familiar fearful warrior truth: action is the only remedy.

Action in this case rests on the hope that B-cell inhibition via the "R" drug may prevent attacks from happening again. The operative word being "may."

In reviewing the literature—a confidence-building manner of saying that the only way for a high school dropout like me to begin to converse with world-renowned medical specialists about why I should fund their research and how it's going to save my child is by devouring everything and anything remotely connected to autoimmune diseases—I have found little to get me past "may prevent."

Although the "R" drug won FDA approval for B-cell inhibition, it's too early for studies of long-term effects. But then again, in medical studies overall, NMO is still a newborn, so there really isn't a "long-term" anything. Anecdotally, however, tidings of positive possibilities do exist. One story, told to me by an eminent doctor, was a testimonial about a woman stricken with NMO. After full paralysis caused her to be on a ventilator, close to death, the "R" drug miraculously brought her back, and within weeks she was able to walk into her doctor's office on her own strength.

I want to believe. I need to believe. But why does that sound like the same woo-woo stories told by the energy-clearing lady while burning sage, throwing salt and rice in our house?

Because, I tell myself, I don't know the science. And if I can learn it or, better yet, make sure that the people who can figure it out are focused on finding treatments that promise more than "may prevent," then I will have a reason to believe.

Ali's doctors who are in the arena of research explain that before approaching the issue of better treatment—let alone a cure—their quest is to find the NMO trigger, the inciting incident that causes the immune system to attack itself. Ali's doctors say that if they can find the trigger, they'll wipe NMO off the face of the earth. They say that finding the trigger will be like finding the Grail.

Yes, God, yes. We can do that, right? We can take the action needed to do that and get started now. This is how we change the orphan disease story.

Except, Ali's doctors say, in the real world and in the real time of medical research, even if they found the trigger today, it wouldn't help my baby. That's what the specialists say.

These are my thoughts in the hours before the "R" drug infusion that may prevent further attacks as I confer with the radiologist who has handed me Ali's most recent spinal cord MRI. Instead of the perfect portrait of a spinal cord that we saw before the New York attack, this MRI shows something very different. A long chain-like lesion, or series of lesions, appears all the way down the thoracic spine, as if a fire-breathing dragon attack has caused inflammation in one fell swoop.

Looking at it with me, the radiologist exhales sadly, saying, "Well, I assume this patient must be in a wheelchair." Translation? With that kind of damage, it would be surprising for anyone to be up and around walking.

Later, when I ask Katja why my daughter isn't in a wheelchair or having problems walking with that intensity of damage, she isn't sure, except to suggest that early diagnosis and treatment are making a difference. "And, of course," Katja adds, "Ali is a miracle."

~

***Without knowing the specifics yet**, the reality of my autoimmune condition hit home. Three spinal attacks came on in a random pattern over the rest of the summer and into the fall of my sophomore year. No let-up either when tennis season started. At the time I wasn't aware how many matches my health caused me to miss, but I do remember at the beginning of the season that we had to go talk to Sherm and make special arrangements for me to avoid getting overheated and fatigued. The decision was for me to play mainly the important league matches.*

I hated asking for special treatment, but if we didn't, the doctors would have asked me to stop playing altogether. They weren't saying that tennis was causing attacks. Though I wasn't asking, I got the impression they didn't know what brought on the attacks exactly.

One bout of attacking inflammation did occur in the middle of a tennis match, in early October as it happened. We had traveled a good distance to play a school in Temple City, out in the vicinity of the Santa Anita racetrack. I was through my first match when all of a sudden I felt that nuance of a back pain. The school we were playing was not very strong. Knowing we would win no matter what, I decided to call it quits and go home. Traffic was surprisingly light, and I was able to get medication within an hour. That helped make the pain go away.

The next morning I was fine—I mean pain-free—and later that night I went to a Dodgers playoff game. It was a ton of fun. Over the weekend I didn't push it and, by Monday, felt perfect, so I decided to play in tennis practice, although not at an intense level.

After practice I came home—still feeling great—did some homework, then ate some dinner. Later that night, however, I began to get the back pain, and before you know it, Dr. Katja Van Herle was over next to my bed giving me an assortment of medications.

Usually, I'm able to sleep after pain meds. But that night, for some reason, I was too agitated and eventually forced myself to buckle down and do more homework if I was going to be awake. Finally, at 4:45 a.m. I completely passed out from exhaustion.

The real bummer was having to be awakened early and dragged off to get an MRI, confirm inflammation, and then hear the news that another five nights of IV-steroid treatment was in order.

My coping skills thankfully were there for me. After all, it wasn't that bad, and a lot of people have much worse things to worry about. No surprise: I came home and ran into my room and literally the first thing I did was turn on my WICKED *CD. Of course, I still cried for a good ten minutes, but then by listening to the music, I was reminded of those people in the world who have it far worse than I do. Some can't even afford to see a great doctor, let alone get treated.*

And that's where I am now. So it's unfortunate I'm dealing with what I'm going through, but I'm lucky in the sense that I can take care of it.

~

Even though Ali doesn't yet know the name of her incurable disease, by the eve of the first Annual Symposium in fall 2008, sponsored by the Guthy-Jackson Charitable Foundation, she knows by the flurry of activity that's overtaken the house in preparation that big things are in the works. She knows that the storm of research that's overtaken my desk and in-box has to do with the intensified search for a cure. In fact, knowing generally about the autoimmune science that I'm trying to teach myself, she has suggested that when the antibody is identified that will fight off inflammation, we should call it the "Alibody."

These are earthquake days. Still, uncertain, terrifying. We now have seen three major attacks, and it feels as if they're coming with increased regularity. By this point in time, in addition to our friends at the Mayo, Ali has a new main doctor who we love and adore—the young, kind, handsome big teddy bear of a brilliant doc, Ben Greenberg, who is based in Texas but works closely with our local team. After seeing no encouraging results from the "R" drug, we are investigating the possibility of using cancer drugs to suppress her immune system.

In the midst of gearing up for this first symposium and the gathering of the little band of NMO experts, I am in my bedroom going over reports and grant requests for research to be conducted, remembering how Dr. Greenberg had stated that with NMO, it's 5 percent science and 95 percent art. (Well, maybe not his exact words, but my interpretation of them.)

I'm remembering again that the start of my other career was a foundation—a base for the face. I'm thinking of other mothers, other fathers, wondering if their children have also asked not to know, whatever their diagnosis, whatever their fear for their children. Have other parents made it their mission not to pass on the fears, both unreasonable and justified, to their kids? Do other moms and dads greet the night by pretending, as we do?

Sometimes it helps to pretend that all is well, even when it's not. Sometimes by not naming or claiming the pain, it passes. On good nights. On bad nights—well, I know Ali waits to the point of unbearable before she'll say anything anyway. She doesn't want to bother us. She's embarrassed. She cries, but not loudly—she doesn't want to wake Jackson.

Alexandra Rose Guthy has one of the highest pain thresholds that any of us have ever seen. She waits to complain until it gets so bad and she's so scared that she's forced to say something.

Ali leaves her room, hesitating. However long it takes her to get down the dark road of the hallway, I don't know, except that I'm sure she dislikes dark roads more than ever. I think she understands that we are as powerless to banish the pain as she is. We have no magic powers for our precious daughter. We're trying to be wizards, trying to use resources, not willing to give up, but for now. . . .God, we feel so helpless.

By the time Ali makes it to our room, she's in agony, she's in tears, she can't calm herself. She can't lie down, she can only sit. We have a protocol now, a checklist of action steps to address the pain, but the fear towers over the situation—because we don't know what deficits will exist after the attack. We don't know if what we're giving her will cause other deficits.

On the eve of our very first conference I'm riding a wave with my little girl. There's no place else I'd rather be. At least she knows: she is absolutely certain I'm going to be here, come what may, I'm gonna be right here, right now, and never leave her. We're the same heart, the same mind, the same body. This long, beautiful, wobbly girl came out of me. I breathe with her, laugh with her, dream with her.

But I refuse to let her share my fear. When the pain subsides, I know she'll feel a different kind of pain—"worry pain"—watching me while I watch her. She knows how excruciating it is for me to see her suffer, but I'll never let on, no matter what she's suspicious of, no matter what she secretly knows or what she pretends not to, I will never let her feel that burden. I'm her mother, I will ride the wave, any wave, I can ride with her, but, man, I am telling you I need to harden myself every time I see that look in her eyes—the feeling-bad-for-Mom look—because if I don't harden myself . . .

I'll go down.

A few months earlier my gynecologist's office found a lump in my breast. The radiologist showed me this potential thing on the ultrasound. I lost it. I said, "No! I am not leaving this room until you tell me there is nothing there."

"But there is something there."

I said, "You don't know me. I cannot have anything be wrong right now, and you need to understand that I am not leaving this office until you tell me there is nothing there."

When I repeated this at an even louder volume, the radiologist must have thought I was dangerous. Which I was. He took his marker and scrawled *THIS IS PROBABLY NOTHING/BENIGN* on the report.

I went to the front desk. The surgeon happened to be standing there. I gave him the report.

"Oh look," he said. "'Benign.' Well, that's great. 'Probably nothing.'" He looked pleased but perplexed. Clearly this wasn't the standard notation for his radiologist. Well, there you have it. The power of positive writing!

Ultimately, everything ended up being okay with me, but I have to say, even at the mere mention that something like this could happen at a time like this, that I could get sick and lose my focus on what I was trying to fix . . . to be blunt: it made me fucking nuts.

I think it's true what they say: that knowledge is power, but sometimes a little knowledge isn't such a good thing. All I hear is that Ali could be watching *So You Think You Can Dance* with friends—laughing and eating popcorn and doing whatever teenage girls do at slumber parties during commercials—and be blind and half-paralyzed in time for the 11 o'clock news.

So now I am going to find rescue in a lot of knowledge, in going into every laboratory or garage in America—no, in the world—and finding the genius formulator for the cure.

Even if it kills me.

~

***What's so interesting at this stage** of the journey—as the midpoint of my sophomore year approaches—is that just as I'm still in the dark about my actual diagnosis and prognosis, I would have to say that Mom is still in the dark about how fearless she really is! I may not know the name yet or the true nature of the autoimmune disorder that has started to bring on a few dark days for me, but one thing I have already learned from this experience is that my mother is a pretty spectacular human being.*

Now I know she says the same about me, but I just need to point out that while she's allowing me to tentatively sip from the fountain of knowledge about what's really going on with me, she's up all night gulping down buckets of science, relentlessly and endlessly, in full-on warrior mode to get to the bottom of the cause and possible cure for the condition that has attached itself to me.

I'm fine with taking the sips because (deep down I think we all know) slowly but surely I'll get there.

I have the luxury of doing that (a) because I'm fifteen and a half and (b) because it's part of how I cope. But Mom doesn't have the luxury, so she has to go Kamikaze on the attacking inflammation—and that's what she's doing. Oh, in case it isn't glaringly apparent yet: my mother doesn't do anything halfway.

The irony is that even though this is happening to me, it's my mom's burden to stop the war, to figure out what sparked the inflammation in the first place.

That requires a recognition of some patterns, something I understand too, especially as they keep messing with my tennis season and have no apparent cause and effect. Bad attacks came in July and August, exactly a month apart, no attacks in September, then a very bad attack in October, another a month later, followed by something I'm feeling possibly coming on now.

Probably the third-worst ordeal so far—after earlier ordeals of having to go to the Mayo and the attack in the night in New York, each tied for THE *worst—happened in an important tennis game. The previous year, my freshman season, for the first time ever in the history of girls' tennis at Buckley, we had made it to the quarter-finals. We lost, but it was still a huge deal to have come that far. It was a monumental feat, and I was absolutely determined this sophomore year not to let the inflammation issues interfere with my goals for surpassing our previous record—for myself and the rest of our team.*

And there I was on the eve of a game with our archrival, Viewpoint. In matches Buckley always lost to Viewpoint. To claim League Champion, teams had to win twice over their nearest competitor, and this was our first of two opportunities for the season to rewrite our losing history. But because our ranking had improved this year, it was either us or them, and the victor would win our league, which meant, in short, there was no way that I could accept having an attack.

But I started to have that sixth sense—sort of a junior version of what my mom has—that soon I was going to begin to feel prickles of pain and tingling of numbness. There was this other superstitious part of me that wondered if maybe my worrying about getting an attack was actually going to cause it. Or just trying to psyche me out. Refusing to give in, I put the worries out of my mind. But of course within a couple hours, by eight o' clock that night, the machete attack was in full swing, bringing waves of nausea with it, and I was overwhelmed, sobbing all night, not sleeping, and knowing I was going to miss my game the next day. And that's what happened. Oh, and Buckley lost to Viewpoint.

But once the five-day treatment was over, or even before that, I was back into the mode of how to find a silver lining. There is nothing heroic about that, I should add. I think it's just human nature that when you are in a tough spot, the last thing you want to do is to focus on the situation.

The simple truth is that the less time you spend on saying that you're having a bad day, the more you can remember, in the words of my favorite orphan, "The sun will come out tomorrow." It will, hard-knock life and all—it really will.

Don't let me fool you. This autoimmune smackdown that I'm watching from in the shadows as my mother does battle for me, like dodging machete blows while wearing a blindfold, is not going to be solved or cured during an episode of HOUSE. Maybe that's why I stopped watching those shows.

~

With Christmas approaching, Bill and I start to ask ourselves whether we should rethink our approach and tell Ali the name of the rare autoimmune disease she's been battling.

We decide to wait and honor her wishes for as long as that's what they are. We continue to be vigilant whenever she sees doctors or has MRIs—or when it's necessary for a nurse to be at the house for a steroid infusion during an attack—and everyone is super careful to speak about the onset of symptoms as "the inflammation."

Bill carefully brings up the subject to Ali, saying, "If you change your mind, let us know."

I add, "Come talk to us anytime, honey." Especially, I offer, "Come ask us whatever you want to know, whatever questions you have, and we'll tell you. But don't use the Internet or Google something you might overhear, okay?"

Ali shrugs, as if to use my least favorite phrase: "Don't worry."

Then I make her promise, as crazy as that sounds.

She promises and I believe her.

Yes, I know that (a) I suffer from Smother Mother tendencies and that (b) I can't control the universe to protect my babies from everything that's lurking in the shadows to hurt them. But during this period I've already learned about two people who came home after being diagnosed with NMO and then went straight to their computers. There, they found the information (I almost just typed "the inflammation") that was sensational, scant, and stark, with that doomsday spin the Internet often thrives on.

Within a short period of time their symptoms became so debilitating, their spirits so destroyed, that both of those NMO patients chose to take their own lives.

Does making her promise still sound nuts?

Ali's continued stance of "I don't want to know" still seems to be the sanest approach.

By Christmas 2008, having lived lifetimes in the less than ten months since the inflammation entered our world, I have definitely come to understand Dr. Ben Greenberg's assessment of Devic's disease/Neuromyelitis Optica (or how I interpreted it) treatment as being "5 percent science and 95 percent voodoo." The first time I heard him say something to that effect was back in May at a medical symposium on MS that was sponsored by a foundation created by a good friend of mine, Nancy Davis. After Nancy was diagnosed with multiple sclerosis, she had established her charity, the Race to Erase MS, which hosts an annual star-studded extravaganza as a fundraiser for research into effective treatments for MS sufferers. Some of the MS research, of course, was already ongoing and had been for years, and there were also other well-established national and international organizations that had done a lot to raise MS awareness. So naturally, in the early years of her work other groups might have felt proprietary of their research or threatened by having a new charity in the mix. Nancy Davis had navigated that challenge well, and I had much to learn from her experiences.

And yet instead of wanting to stake out NMO as my foundation's exclusive turf, Bill and I really only wanted to march out there and raise our hands, hoping that the groups already in existence would pick us for their team. But when I started asking around for names of potential collaborators, we found a situation very different from that of the playing field usually faced by new organizations championing research for other, better-known diseases. Besides there being little ongoing research, the number of philanthropic groups actively devoted to raising NMO awareness and specifically funding the research came to a grand total of zero. Actually, when I double-checked with one of the doctors on our team at the Mayo, to see if they had tracked down any organizations focused on NMO, the answer came back that there was *one* group—us.

By Christmas time, however, I'm starting to see the tiniest of silver linings in the fact that because we're the only game going, we not only set the ground rules for encouraging greater cooperation and collaboration but we could also mobilize our troops to move faster—in part because we are self-contained.

With my formation of the GJCF, we've been able to come up with a "Knights of the Round Table" paradigm that is as rare as the disease we hope to understand. The basic concept is that in order to bring leading researchers and medical centers together at this unprecedented level of noncompetitive cooperation, we only fund research whose results are mutually shared, nationwide and worldwide. And most importantly, we can focus on accelerating ways of going from bench to bedside—the critical path to a cure.

Even though the results of this approach over our less than six months of existence have been extremely impressive (proof of the silver lining), I recognize that none of the research is guaranteed to open the locked door. That thought alone *terrifies* me beyond sleep, beyond words. What if this is all for naught? What if all this sharing of findings is only enough to confirm that nobody's research is taking us on the right track?

So I start to ask more questions. All kinds of questions. And I'm not afraid to ask them. The most random, nonlinear, dumb questions that I can ask, believing that I'll be forgiven for my layperson's ignorance and hoping that somehow, maybe accidentally, one crazy question or another asked from my own observations of Ali's symptoms could maybe spark an insight that might lead to new answers.

That alone takes a lot of nerve on my part, but nothing puts me out of my comfort zone more than the need to look back into the past. But some hunch tells me doing so is important, like the question that I've brought up to the doctors and researchers who are funded by the foundation—a question that has to do with a possible trigger for the onset of the first attack.

None of them have completely dismissed its potential as maybe one stressor among others. But I can tell, in those moments when I raise the question and bring up the name of the vaccine that Ali was given in the year that preceded her Eyeball Headache—and when I mention the skin rashes that occurred partly in conjunction with the three shots—the physician/scientists always react cautiously.

Why? Well, any search for causation can become a slippery slope. The classic response is, no, we can't discount rain as a cause (if rain preceded the first appearance of symptoms); but because it was raining on the day before NMO symptoms came on, we can't really conclude that rain caused the disease—since all the other rainy days didn't trigger the first attack. Unless your hypothesis can be tested in the lab, either in some sort of assay that can pinpoint the immunological chain reaction set off by your supposed triggering agent or in lab animals with results that may or may not apply to humans, all you've got in the end is circumstantial evidence.

There is another issue. Nobody has to spell it out for me, but I understand that any effort that appears to question the safety of a vaccine that is both distributed by a top pharmaceutical company (usually after spending millions of dollars to develop the vaccine) and that has also been FDA approved, is just asking for trouble. From a practical standpoint, when the hope is that you can push research to develop therapies and get them fast tracked for approval even for experimental trials, you would generally want those top pharmaceutical companies and the government approval agencies on your side. Especially when money for research is scarce and everybody wants to limit legal liabilities. Oh, and especially when we're talking about an uber-rare orphan disease that may afflict only twenty thousand people in the world, factoring in estimates of the undiagnosed and the misdiagnosed still being a very unscientific effort. So why go asking questions that might annoy potential allies? Why jeopardize the work of researchers, doctors, and scientists being funded by pharmaceutical companies?

Why open up a Pandora's box?

In fact, a prominent public relations firm that I wanted to hire to help raise public awareness about NMO—vital to finding more patients—declined to represent me because, and I'm not quoting, they were afraid that I was going to go all Erin Brockovich and wind up suing the corporate drug-making overlords.

Who, me?

I had to laugh. Who was I to threaten the status quo? A makeup artist turned entrepreneur who markets mascara and lip gloss.

Then again, I knew from more than a few rare stories that there have been other laypeople in the form of desperate parents refusing to accept the possibility of losing their kids who dared to question science and pushed it toward life-saving discoveries.

And that's all I was going to do, mascara wand and blush brush in hand.

~

Anyone who lives and plays high school sports *in the Los Angeles area is well versed on the powerhouse athleticism of Oaks Christian. Toward the end of our season Buckley has a most memorable match in facing this powerhouse. Because Buckley is known as the brainy school and has been unsung in some sports, especially girls' tennis, facing Oaks Christian and winning is a big deal.*

So we're in the semifinal round and we're just barely up 9–8 at the end of the third round. My partner and I are the last team playing. If we lose our match, our team will lose by what's called "counting games," in which the margin is so close that the count of the games in the match determines the winner. If we win, our team will advance to the CIF finals for the first time in school history. I'm a wreck! My mental calm is failing me, and I begin to resort to wimpy, beginner's shots just to keep the ball in play. My partner is understandably getting frustrated, but she keeps her cool, talks me through it, and helps bring us to victory!

Seeing how she handled that situation, I've since been thinking about ways to grow as a leader and a player. In the matches that follow, when I'm faced with similar challenges, I find a new level of confidence and poise that carries us to the finals.

That marked the end of the tennis this particular year when we lost to a team called Arlington in a very close heart breaker.

But this story was not over. We were coming back the next year stronger than ever.

~

The truth has a way of revealing itself. Give it time, and the truth eventually comes to the fore.

I know that now. I trust that.

But the problem with getting to the truth of NMO is that we don't have the time. So I need to find the trigger, the thing that lit up this whole immunological inferno and meltdown in the beginning, so I can know. Because there is power in knowledge, as much as we fear it. Because then we can take action, we can do something about it. Not only for Ali but also for fellow current NMO patients and for the next wave of them who, science tells us, are going to be increasing in numbers the more we learn about the many undiagnosed patients and possibly thousands of misdiagnosed.

Was I, unknowingly or not, to blame for triggering Ali's NMO?

In my brain I've gone over this question from every angle, every timeline imaginable, returning again and again to early 2007, a year before her Eyeball Headache, asking myself if we had known more about Ali already having the classic autoimmune profile, would I have made the decision to go ahead with the series of three shots that were part of the Gardisil protocol, a vaccination against the devastating cancers of the uterus and ovaries?

Awake during another sleepless night, I don't know if Ali is having an attack or not. I tiptoe down the hall, see the light on under the door, hope and pray she's not suffering in silence. Again, this is our routine. When we do address it, Ali says she does that because, she says, I need my sleep to cure her inflammation once and for all. She's promised now that if she feels an attack coming on, she'll call Katja any time of the night. And Dr. Ben Greenberg is her next phone call.

I also have to mention that we are so grateful and lucky that we can even do this and have the support system in place, knowing especially that most patients certainly can't.

Because Ali still doesn't know that her next attack can be the one that leaves her blind or that puts her in a wheelchair or worse, we continue to have a stealth war going on in our midst, part of which involves finding back-up nurses if the one Ali likes isn't available. Sometimes finding a vein isn't easy and also some of her stress is waiting for the nurse to come when an attack is underway.

Once it is, our weapon of choice is an IV infusion of solumedrol/steroids, a highly effective treatment. And usually, within a matter of hours, she starts to respond.

This approach seems to be working, so far so good, but with NMO we're all so powerless, never knowing what's lurking around the next corner. Somehow this staging that puts me at Def-Com special-ops level feels like the middle ground between no control at all and going full on nuclear with a treatment, say, like plasmapheresis. It's a procedure that separates blood cells from plasma, allowing doctors to replace plasma and reduce toxicity, theoretically halting attacks. It sounds scary, yes, and is usually more of a last resort. So I hold out on that and remain engaged with the enemy, cloak and dagger, stalking it before it can stalk my daughter.

We don't know enough. We know more about the antibodies and molecules being targeted with NMO, but we don't know what the trigger events are that rouse the targeters to go on attacks. I can't connect the dots, no matter how much I read or, as I once put it when pitching my makeup line to the infomercial investors, no matter how much I try to "think outside the compact."

All of this is so above my pay grade. I'll sit up in the middle of the night and suddenly remember my pregnancy with Ali, recalling that I had shingles when she was born. But what do I do with that?

Is there a herpetic link?

Am I going crazy?

Are the attacks linked to her menstrual cycle? Or flying?

Or is it because some of her vaccines didn't take when she was little? Why didn't they?

Am I going crazy?

What if I have to make the decisions on her treatment? One that's going to cause her to become infertile? Or that's not going to work and her systems start to shut down as can happen to kids with NMO who die at seventeen, fifteen, twelve.

Am I going crazy?

One weekend up at Carpinteria we're walking together along the sand, the two of us, mother and daughter, and she is saying that she wants to get married there and can see having a husband—she can see finding that right man. And that she wants to have children. She sees that future. My heart races. Could I have taken it away from her?

What if I made the wrong decision and now she can't have children? Or she goes blind? The three injections of Gardisil—which I later learn that Erin Brockovich is, in fact, investigating—began in March 2007. And Ali had a really bad reaction to the first shot, a horrible, horrible rash. She had skin eruptions, ongoing eczema. I took her to the dermatologist and he said "nonspecific."

Nonspecific! I got nonspecific'ed to death. They thought she had ringworm.

And I let them give her the second of three shots. The rash returned. I didn't listen to the Voice saying that something was wrong. I did my research and I thought, *Amazing. We can actually prevent uterine cancer! Like a polio vaccine.*

Then we had the third shot in September 2007. Same rash. Could that have done us in?

But none of Ali's doctors believe there is a connection. They don't say there is not a connection either. Well, what if all vaccinations have the capacity to trigger the person with the classic autoimmune profile who might be at risk for a disease like NMO or Lupus or MS? Isn't that worth a closer look? Doesn't Erin Brockovich have a point?

These are the questions I have to have the courage to ask.

Even if I am to blame.

~

I understand why my mother *needs to ask the tough questions, but the issue of the shots and rashes is what you might call in mystery books a red herring. What, you say? How do I know? Because there were other clues—like the vomiting and nausea that everyone thought might be some kind of anorexia—all of that came before the shots that really began the saga of too much inflammation.*

In hindsight I can't blame my family at all, but I remember this as an extremely frustrating time—especially because no one could find anything wrong with me.

When I was diagnosed with an autoimmune inflammation problem, we still didn't make a connection. Then finally here in the middle of sophomore year, now about two years after the vomiting episodes, it comes out that prolonged nausea is a symptom of whatever it is that I have!

And of course, I am like, HA, SUCKERS. PROOF! NO, NOT ANOREXIA. NOT BODY IMAGE ISSUES. NOT AN EATING DISORDER.

For a few days or so I'm on my mom's case, and she feels so bad, telling me, "Well we didn't know."

Meanwhile, I am so relieved that I can claim once and for all that I am not anorexic! It's the only moment in which having this enemy in my central nervous system makes me feel happy. At least a little bit.

I don't think that the self-blame approach ever works, not with mystery diseases. I know this because there was a time when I thought that my ninth-grade biology class had, through the power of suggestion, caused me to develop an autoimmune dysfunction! That's a confession.

Seriously. The same year that I was taking biology and we were learning about autoimmune diseases and we were learning about T and B cells, I came down with apparently something so obscure that a foundation has to be started to look into it. Everything that I read about and studied and had imagined as far as worst-case scenarios was happening to me. Maybe that helps to explain why I was not ready even in the tenth grade to get the specific lowdown on how bad this thing was going to be for me.

I don't know if it does or doesn't explain my logic a bit more. But I do blame that biology class for scaring me to death about just how bad my inflammation problem, whatever its name, could possibly be. And people wonder why I hate biology. Clearly, I was cursed in the ninth grade never to like science.

The truth will set you free,
but first it will piss you off.

—GLORIA STEINEM

~

Carpinteria, at the Ranch

I awaken at two a.m. The bewitching hour. My usual waking hour as of these last eleven months, give or take. It's when all the ghosts—past, present, and future—arrive to cause havoc. Mean old antibodies.

Then again, there are some who call these awakenings, at two, three, four in the morning, the darkest, most lonely times, as visitations that come during the "poet's hour"—maybe because the only way to grope successfully for the light is to be awake without it.

I fell asleep at eleven or twelve, at around page forty-two of a fifty-page medical grant proposal, and was up again around twelve or one before dozing off. I consider three to four hours of sleep not bad at all. Well, not bad compared to other epic nights when I've stared sleeplessly at the dawn.

The sleep thing, I have heard, has gotten worse for many of us in the information-overload digital age, not to mention the whole hormonal cascade of menopausal symptoms for women of a certain age—that being me, fifty-three years old now on the cusp of the New Year. Just add that to my Cure-NMO-or-Bust brain squeeze, and my insomnia becomes the one mystery I don't need to unravel.

My friends, bless them, have continued to offer me their secret, alternative, and other remedies to cure my inability to sleep or at least to still my mind. These potions and tinctures and relaxation CDs and reading materials promising sweet serenity are at my bedside both at home and when I travel.

I've got your Goodnight Moon tea (actually), your industrial-strength Tryptophan (I'm exaggerating), various drops, sprays, and lozenges from Rescue Remedy, herbs, homeopathic sleep aids, aromatherapy mixes, calming prayers to recite from every denomination (gotta cover all the spiritual bases), and then the nighttime reading, all lined up like soldiers ready for duty, offering me help to quiet the mental cacophony, whether I should decide to harness *The Power of Now* or follow the guidance of *When Your Life Changes Change Everything* or listen to Pema Chodron in

Start Where You Are and begin with the preliminaries—"I prostrate to the Great Compassionate One."

These are usually the nights this past year when, at two or three in the morning, at home or away, that I'll go outside into the cold night air and walk, crying or not, trying just to breathe. But something is different when I wake up this time. What is it?

A new clarity? Maybe.

I'm not yet clear on that.

But you know what? I'm sensing a stillness on this night, a clearing in the emotional woods in which I have been lost for so long—at least since Ali's diagnosis, but maybe even longer, maybe since girlhood. Something is missing. A weight perhaps?

Then it hits me. From the moment of that terrible Phone Call that we took in Bill's study just after last Valentine's Day, I haven't had one anxiety attack.

Fear, obviously, hasn't fled. I've had nothing but fear since Ali's diagnosis. On the other hand, the anxiety disorder that I self-diagnosed when I was in my twenties (and that has been with me most of my life) has been curiously in remission.

Back in the day I attributed the major anxiety attacks that prevented me from flying, with overlapping aspects of claustrophobia and agoraphobia, to post-traumatic stress disorder caused by being attacked. Then there was the survival struggle of being a preemie and stuck in an incubator fighting for life as well as the abandonment issues that arose when Dad summarily dismissed my sister and me from his life. A trip to visit him as an adolescent had been a nightmare, and on the turbulent flight home, alone, I was so terrified that, when we touched down, that was it. I swore that I'd never fly again. And I didn't for thirty-four years.

When Bill and I started dating, I wanted so badly not to let my fears and old anxiety issues be brought along into our new life together that I attempted to Act-as-if I was in the process of getting them behind me. I was upfront about the fact that flying was out of the question—which bothered Bill because he loved to travel—but he was unaware of perhaps how difficult it was for me to ever be out of my comfort zone.

The first time he caught a glimpse of the ugly truth we were driving up to Big Sur for a romantic weekend getaway. For reasons neither one of us could recall, we had set off without reservations.

For Bill, that meant adventure and spontaneity. Cool. For me, that meant uncertainty, lack of control, a blowout on the side of a darkened road. A horror movie.

After stopping at a couple hotels and hearing that everything was sold out, I could feel anxiety setting in. Bill didn't seem to have a care in the world as he cruised up the coast, suggesting we just enjoy the journey, that we could try to find a camping area and sleep in the car.

He made it sound so perfect, and I wanted to enjoy the journey. But I could barely breathe; I had to hold onto the door to keep myself from fainting. Up until this trip I had probably shielded Bill from how close to home and familiarity I needed to stay. But now he would know. Now he would see. Finally we did find a hotel and checked in. Instead of being able to relax and feel relieved, my entire body started to tremble, and I gasped for air like a fish out of water. Unable to form coherent sentences, I heard strange stuttering sounds coming out of my mouth that mortified me even more.

"C'mon," Bill said, and got me to lay down in the bed with him. Without saying anything, he let me know that things would be better in the morning. He held me and got me through the night.

By the next day I was better. But would Bill change his mind about us, especially after this major preview of the unpredictable affliction known as anxiety disorder?

No, he didn't.

We dealt with it, as we often would, with humor.

That first episode provided the inspiration for "the Ditch Lady," a nickname Bill affectionately gave me, meaning that whenever an extreme propelled me to the side of the road into one ditch, I could get myself out but in the process would careen to the ditch on the other side of the road.

On the flip side, though, nothing really would throw him. "You're just dysfunctionally healthy," I observed early on, thinking that would change as time went on, once I'd gotten below the surface more. Wrong. That's who he was. No pathos, no dark.

So whereas I, the Ditch Lady, was able to go from extreme to extreme in no time, Bill stayed out of all ditches by being Mr. In Between, usually aloof and above the fray. Dysfunctionally healthy. There were two ways of looking at the differences. On the one hand, we were from such different planets we would never speak the same language. On the other hand, we would let our differences balance each other out, like Yin and Yang.

Or so I wanted to believe when, after being together for about six months, I found out that I was pregnant. We were in love, but we hadn't been together that long. Bill insisted that he was planning on proposing on the very night we conceived, and we set a date to get married—when I would be four months pregnant—and found a house in Encino.

Right before one of the first business trips that Bill was scheduled to take after we'd moved into the house, I became convinced that his plane was going to go down and I had to prevent him from leaving the property. How? By throwing myself on the hood of his car.

I spread-eagled myself on the hood and wouldn't get off.

Don't go, don't leave!

Bill quietly got out of the car and lifted me off the hood and then left.

Years later, I asked him what he had thought that day.

"Well, I thought, okay, this is going to be interesting."

Interesting. As in challenging?

"No, I knew there were going to be some adjustments ahead. And we were going to have to figure it out."

That was more or less his reaction after an incident that took place at our wedding. We couldn't think of anywhere we'd rather be than in our rented vacation beach house in Carpinteria. We also planned a storybook honeymoon with a drive up the coast and stops at wonderful hotels—where we had reservations.

Evan, now six and a half, was excited about becoming a brother and proud to take part in the ceremony. Dressed in his tux, he stood next to Bill and me throughout the service. I had made it a point to present him with his own little ring before Bill and I exchanged our vows. This way, Evan would know he was as much a part of my new life as I was.

Once the service was over, I knew that Mom wanted to get Evan home and not keep him up late at the party. Prickling tingles of separation anxiety started to set in. Leaving my guests, I walked the two of them out to the car, telling my little boy, "I'll miss you on my honeymoon, but I'll call you every day, all right?"

He nodded bravely, gave me a huge hug, and then started off to the car with Mom. I waved back, "Love you! I'll miss you. You were the star of the wedding!"

Evan started to answer, and then he dashed back to me for another good-bye hug. He wasn't upset, just enjoying the moment. But I was starting to lose it. Why was I going on this long trip when I was four months pregnant, exhausted, and really wanted nothing more than to hang out with my little boy and put my feet up?

I think Evan knew me so well at that moment that he could have read my mind. "I'll be fine," he said, and gave me one last hug.

Suddenly, something came over me. Probably a surge of pregnancy hormones.

"Wait a few minutes," I told my mother. "I'm coming with you guys."

So I ended up leaving my own wedding, missing most of the festivities and the lavish honeymoon we had planned specifically so as not to require me to get on any airplanes. Before departing the scene, I found Bill, who heard me out and accepted my decision, promising to meet up with me at home later.

I wish that those were the only instances when my anxiety issues interrupted important plans. Sadly, those were only the tip of the iceberg.

And yet, as I'm just noticing these many years later, none of the typical anxiety landmines have exploded in recent months. Nothing like a rare, potentially fatal autoimmune disease threatening your child to cure your own anxiety disorder! Not that I take much comfort in the trade-off. I would gladly, eagerly, desperately have kept my own afflictions to protect my daughter.

But that's just it: there is no negotiating with NMO. Except, that is, for this new awareness that has now shown up to remind me that maybe there is some sort of fearlessness starting to inhabit my psyche.

The Voice is trying to tell me to give myself a bit of credit. After all, I have no trouble volunteering to take the blame, so why not let myself be empowered? And in fact, when I think about it, that has been the story and message of my Act-as-if life to date—that if someone with self-esteem as low as mine can do it, so can anyone. More importantly, nobody else can attain what you want for you other than you.

I'm remembering, here in the poet's hour, why it's important not to put anyone else's expertise so high on a pedestal that you'll always feel intimidated, which so happened to be one of my teaching mantras that I used to try to reinforce in the beauty field when my students lacked confidence in their own abilities; when I would ask if they really believed that José Eber was the only person who truly knew hair. Of course not. No one has a lock on knowledge; no one has a trademark on success.

Act-as-if had always worked for me in those times when I was entering unfamiliar straits, in part because I refused to be intimidated, in part because I was willing to pretend to be someone I wasn't yet, and in part because I allowed myself to use imagery and different forms of visualization in order to know what success looked like even before I knew for certain that success was going to happen.

After creating my no-makeup makeup foundation and color cosmetic line, how did I go from struggling business entrepreneur to successful CEO of my own company? By asking myself first: what does a CEO look like, sound like, and dress like? And then by becoming that—by looking, sounding, dressing and acting like that.

Coming from my low self-esteem perspective let me be a chameleon in terms of attitude, in terms of how to sit, how to stand, how to speak, how to dress, how to behave. The key was always observing and being willing to learn, always visualizing possibilities that I used to call "reading my own success story."

All that was needed was a vivid example to emulate, and what began as pretending and emulating turned into actually being. I had morphed into my own version of me as a CEO.

Now, in this hour of the early morning, the Voice is here to tell me that the same skills that have served me in the past can be effective now.

Really? I ask the Voice. (Yes, I talk that way to my own sixth sense.) This is my daughter's life. What about medical school? What about college? I didn't graduate high school, remember? I mean, searching for clues to solve a medical mystery is not challenging the status quo of the cosmetic business or the infomercial industry. What the hell do I know?

I don't know much at all except that with the sun coming up, I'm looking down the hillside toward the ocean, beyond the horses grazing in the field and beyond the lush avocado and citrus groves, and I'm thinking that if only I could get all the doctors to come here to the ranch, all together, up to this very summit point, something dramatic could happen. If I could get them away from the noise and the daily grind and the life-and-death challenges of their work, they would have some kind of magical mind meld and come up with a cure.

I had to laugh when the idea first came to me. Was this my way of bringing Mohammed to the mountain? Hell, yeah. Forget trying to bring the clarity of the mountaintop to Mohammed. Wasn't this what having a ranch retreat was intended for? Yes, it was, as I reminded Bill when I proposed my concept to him.

Well, okay, I didn't know this was exactly what we would do when the three hundred–acre horse ranch and working farm first went on the market. But now its purpose in our lives had been revealed. No one could argue with that.

Thus, the annual Guthy-Jackson NMO Research Summit had been born, along with the theoretical framework for a clinical consortium that, again, was a classic example of our Acting-as-if, following the few models out there for galvanizing the speed at which bench-to-bedside discoveries could be made. Call it the birth of our own little guacamole Gordon Conference.

Do I dare to be hopeful?

No longer am I in denial that we have seen the worst of Ali's attacks. I know better now. The Voice has promised that we have only been given a preview.

So why am I flirting with hope?

Because it seems we may now have better weapons, or so I'm being told. And because we were going to have a new warrior leading us in the fight: Ali.

~

FEBRUARY 2009, AFTER VALENTINE'S DAY

The truth—and yes, Gloria Steinem is right, *it does set you free but it does piss you off in the beginning (A LOT!)—is that I never intentionally decided to find out the name of my rare orphan disease.*

If it were up to me, I would have waited until at least my eighteenth birthday. Or longer. Maybe I would have decided never to know. In all honesty, back in the fall, with tennis season in full swing—no pun intended, for real—it was easier to keep the whole thing under wraps, without knowing the gritty details. Even here at the one-year mark since first being struck by "too much inflammation," I'm still resistant to telling people, even close friends and members of the tennis team, who clearly knew something was up when I had attacks that were bad enough to keep me from playing.

The timing for the big revelation kinda sucked. My parents had done their best to let me call the shots—oops, not again, pun still not intended—about being ready to hear any more information. When it happened, it was accidental.

Back in December, after a pretty bad attack, I had successfully put everything out of my mind when, in the cheeriest of moods, I came home and saw some mail on the counter in the kitchen. A letter, opened, was addressed to Mom, care of the foundation, and I saw NMO as the subject heading.

There was no turning back now. No Jedi mind trick to forget what I'd just read. In the body of the paragraph I saw what NMO stood for: Neuromyelitis Optica Spectrum Disease. And then as I scanned down below that, I saw that NMO was also known as Devic's Disease.

Later that afternoon Mom was reading the same letter at her desk and I came to the door, leaned in, and asked, "So I guess that's what I have?"

On her face was a mix of relief and sadness—relief that she didn't have to hide the facts anymore, and sadness that I had found out that way. Did I want to talk about it? Nah. Did I want more information? Not right then.

At first—okay, for a while—I was angry. This was not the way I'd planned spending my formative years, after all. But then I began to contemplate making peace with my enemy, strange as that sounds. Not that I had any intention of being lifelong friends, knowing as I do that Mom is in the trenches working on making NMO obsolete. Still, I had to find a way to mentally overpower my opponent and win this game, even if it meant accepting that we both had to share my body for the time being. Anger and all.

I'm not ready to take those big gulps of information yet. But it is empowering to see how the pieces of the puzzle are starting to be put together and how the incentives for scientists to share their findings has already sped up the research dramatically.

Whenever Mom's onto a new idea, instead of protecting me, as she used to do, she can announce, "I think this is what we're doing next—what do you think?"

A Summit with medical geniuses from around the world at our ranch? Maybe a little over the top. But as I've said, she doesn't do anything halfway. She goes all out.

And that's the lowdown on Valentine's Day 2009 as I celebrate another month without an attack. Knowing the little of what I've read now about NMO, I understand that this is a calm that may not last. But for the time being my focus is on anything but NMO.

~

March 1, 2009

After two and a half months without an attack, just when I make the mistake of feeling like we're making progress and that we've cast a no-mo' NMO spell, the enemy returns in force in one of the most debilitating attacks to date.

And it's the first attack since she found out the name of her spectrum disease, spectrum being the foreign-language word that really translates as "no rhyme or reason, no predictable pattern, just immunological chaos brought to you through the channels of your very own central nervous system."

Knowing doesn't make it make any more sense. Knowing doesn't make it go away. Knowing doesn't stop the pain or the look in her eyes that I've seen before, the one asking *Why?*, asking *How did I get here?*, asking *What is this weird NMO land and how do I get home again, Mom?*

This is the rub, of course. The reality that I never wanted my babies to have to ask that question. That I did everything so that our home would be the last place they'd ever want to leave. Ali's so good, so gutsy, even if she's as angry and hurt and scared as she ought to be. This isn't how any child should spend their high school years. Almost sixteen, she's tall and beautiful and brilliant—an innocent. The world should be hers to embrace, her treasure box to open and explore.

Watching Ali battle through this one, I pretend this is just my nightmare and if I can figure out a way to wake up, she'll be saved. Illogical, yes, but there is a logical basis for supposing that somehow my courageous daughter took a wrong turn and landed in my mixed-up bad dreams of a country no one's ever heard of and earned dual citizenship in a place that practices genocide of its own people. But in this mixed-up nightmare logic, before she can leave, she has to see what that country is like—because it's literally in her blood—to meet others like her and know that she's not alone and that she can be their hope.

No wonder she's angry. She did not sign up to be a poster child for a rare orphan disease.

The March attack feels like an assault on the family. Jackson's hurting for his sister but doesn't know what to do or say, so sometimes he pours his fears into his music and sometimes acts out instead—getting on all of our last nerves—and causing Ali to lash out at him in resentment. Bill is shutting down even more, still maintaining his always even keel but detaching emotionally in order to handle the rapids, this descent into the roughest waters yet.

What's happening to us?

After dinner, in my office as I review plans for the first Summit up at the ranch, I turn to see Jackson, my sweet, talented thirteen-year-old, his feelings still bruised from something Ali said to him. He stands there in the doorway and then comes over, pulling up a chair.

"You shouldn't be alone, Mom," he says, as if to say he doesn't want to be alone either. And then he adds, "You're going through a hard time."

I don't need to say that we all are. Jackson William Guthy already knows it.

April 2009

A psychic I've seen periodically over the years does the Tarot for me, then turns the subject to Ali and explains where she is in her journey. She asks first if Ali has seemed angry lately.

Of course, she knows the answer, she's psychic, right? But then she goes on to assure me not only is the anger understandable but it's temporary.

THE PSYCHIC: "Your daughter—does she know why she got this—disease?"

ME: "No. Why?"

THE PSYCHIC: "She needs to understand. I'd love to sit with her. Whenever she's ready, bring her and I'll make her understand."

ME (thinking that's not going to be easy to pull off): "Understand what?"

THE PSYCHIC: "That she's the lucky one. Of all the people in her family, she is the lucky one. Because she is chosen. And she's going to go for something nobody on this earth could volunteer for. She doesn't know that she got that because she wanted to find a cure. She will find a cure and be saved. The reason Ali got this challenge in her health is she chose that."

Is this true? I'm not sure. Do we choose all of our experiences? I don't think so. But sometimes we must act as if we do.

> **The method by which one develops FAITH, where it does not already exist, is extremely difficult to describe, almost as difficult, in fact, as it would be to describe the color of red to a blind man who has never seen color, and has nothing with which to compare what you describe to him.**
>
> —NAPOLEON HILL, *THINK AND GROW RICH*

April 8, 2009

A year after spending Ali's spring vacation traveling to the Mayo for the first official diagnosis of NMO, we make another family pilgrimage over Spring Break. This time we're going to Dallas, to the University of Texas Southwestern medical center, to see Dr. Ben Greenberg.

When we announced to Ali a few weeks earlier that she would once again spend vacation time at an out-of-town medical center mainly devoted to MS and other autoimmune disease–afflicted patients, she was openly pissed about it.

That, in my opinion, was probably a good thing—no more suffering in silence, no more chalking up Brownie points for sainthood. Ali had some rebel in her and decidedly didn't want to be a poster girl for a rare orphan disease.

To make matters more loaded, after a few months of reprieve 2009 has been bringing attacks at the rate of once a month, even once every two to three weeks. In fact, days before traveling to Dallas, without warning, the stabbing pain in her back began and the numbness in her legs and torso knocked her for a loop. She had only wrapped up her last of a five-day infusion of steroids on the night before we left to go see Dr. Greenberg.

That's the thing: we have a protocol now for addressing the pain to stop the attack from doing lasting damage—we think—but still don't have the tools to keep the attacks from triggering in the first place.

Thus, we are ruining our child's vacation and putting her through yet another series of tests, blood work, and MRIs.

Ali accepts this as a valid reason for going. But that doesn't mean she's happy about it. How's that for mature and healthy?

~

APRIL 9, 2009

My mother has this very magical way of creating ambience in the darkest of settings.

In the waiting room at UTSW she makes sure everyone has what we need—a good book, a magazine, the extra deck of cards for me and Nanny to play, just in case. If Mom could have gotten away with catering the event, she would have.

Instead, we all settle into our regular routine, which includes Dr. Katja Van Herle catching up on her work, and Dad, don't ask me why, catching up on his sleep, which he likes to do in waiting rooms. Some kind of coping mechanism, I guess.

The first exam is an eye test that requires me to put a patch over my good eye and wait for drops to take effect. So what does Mom do? When I'm done with the eye patch, she puts it on herself and asks how she looks. Then I put it on Dad and I take pictures of my sleeping father, the pirate.

We leave him there when I'm called in to do blood work and am routed to another waiting area. Mom, Katja, and Nanny follow. Knowing my competitive side, my grandmother just lays out the cards as they were before and engages me in the game again. There's no secret about the fact that though I've gotten used to needles, I still don't love them.

And so, after having the blood taken, I go back to the little waiting area, sort of cradling my arm. Nobody seems to notice. Nobody, that is, except for this old lady who had already been muttering about the card game that Nanny and I have just resumed.

Like someone from a movie, or a real-life character on a cruise ship to Florida—playing shuffle board on the deck—she is overtanned, wrinkled, cranky, and with cheesy old-lady orange hair. And she's obviously not happy with the current state of affairs, in particular that she is attached to an IV pole, a ball and chain that is keeping her from playing her shuffle board or what have you.

As she's sitting there staring at me, at length, finally she turns to Mom and asks, "What's wrong with your daughter?"

This is when everything finally all comes to a head and I have a major meltdown. "What's wrong with me?" I blurt out. "There's nothing wrong with me! What's wrong with you?"

Oh my God. Those words will haunt me the rest of my life. I actually say, "What's wrong with you?" to the creepy old lady and then, fighting off my tears, stick around to be polite and listen to her tell her tale of woe. And then, when she's done, I nod, striving for compassion, and announce, "I'm going to the bathroom," and run out of there at top speed—which, as I believe has been mentioned before, is fast.

Really freaked out, I race to the ladies room, fly inside, and enter the handicapped stall, where I start to sob. I lock myself in, slam down the lid of the toilet, and sit cross-legged on top of it. Just crying my eyes out.

Not many moments later Mom comes in, saying, "Ali, honey, it's gonna be okay. Let's take a break."

I say nothing.

"Ali?"

I'm not mad at her, but right about now I've had it. My tears fall faster, my sobs get louder.

Mom knocks on the door. She says something about the old lady not meaning to hurt me. Of course I know that. I don't answer. "Ali," Mom says now, "would you open the door and come out? Please?"

"No. I'm not coming out."

"They're going to call you for your MRI, and if we miss the window, we'll have to come back tomorrow. You don't want that, do you?" When I don't answer, she repeats, "Honey, come on out."

"Just leave me alone."

"Ali, are you going to open the door?"

"No!"

I hear her take a breath and then she shifts tactics and gets this goofy sound to her voice as she warns me, "Well, if you don't open the door, I'm going to have to come in and get ya!"

Not sure that I believe she will really try to come in by sliding on the floor and squeezing through the one-foot opening, I am slightly amused by the idea that she is threatening to do this in her white Prada blouse.

Who will win? Me, the blouse, or Mom's boobs? Judging from where I'm sitting, there's no way my mother's ample bosom is going to allow her to get under the stall door.

"I'm coming in after you!"

"Leave me alone!"

That does it for my mother, who lays down on the bathroom floor and starts to shimmy her way into the stall, feet first.

"Mom, what about your boobs?

"I had a reduction," she reminds me.

Oh yeah, the reduction, the one that she has always said must have been done by a cosmetic surgeon who didn't want to miss his golf game and barely took anything at all. "I'm telling you," I can't help warning her, "your boobs will not fit."

She curses her former surgeon and vows to have another reduction the minute she gets me out of here.

Meanwhile, she has now slid halfway into my stall, legs and hips and waist, but is completely stuck, as predicted, by this insane maneuver that involves trying to shmush her bosom down with one hand and push herself along the floor with another. Mom has wedged herself in so tightly that she seems to be having trouble breathing.

A tornado of emotions assaults me. I want to laugh, I can barely keep from laughing. I have let the faucet of my tears open and can't stop crying. Oh, and then, as if that's not enough, I'm mortified that someone is going to walk into the bathroom and spot my mother on the floor, half in the handicapped stall and half out.

But if someone doesn't discover us, we'll be doomed to all eternity in here.

Then I hear my mother doing some kind of panting, maybe a leftover Lamaze technique or two, or a yoga tantric trick. Next thing I know

I'm laughing, and my mother, Supermom on a mission, lets out a primal scream and exhales all the air from her lungs. She gives herself one last push and pops through into the stall with me.

"Fuck," she says. "I ruined my Prada blouse."

We laugh hysterically, hugging, crying, cursing, and sitting there until we both just look at each other and shrug, exhausted.

If that's not love, I don't know what is. That's Mom—my hero, my best friend.

When we finally get to see Dr. Ben Greenberg, he says, "You two seem to be in a great mood."

And we both nod and say that we are.

MAY 15, 2009

Mom knows how to throw a party. *And it's not about extravagance but about details nobody has ever considered. Like the annual "guac-off" she and Dad host every summer, where guests come with their best guacamole recipes, which are then sampled by the other guests. Winners are selected by top chefs. Oh yeah, and I plan on winning with my guacamole one day.*

The only time Mom goes overboard with her entertaining ideas, in my opinion, is when it comes to my birthday parties.

Don't know why, but I never liked celebrating my birthday. I can understand other people who love the big extravaganzas—Jackson being one—but my preference is just to have dinner with the family and be done with it. When Mom threw me a surprise party for my fifteenth birthday, around the same time that I was first being diagnosed with NMO, I knew she had only the best of intentions. How could I be mad? Except I hate surprises. So what was I going to do? None of my friends knew what was going on with me (not to mention that back then I really didn't know what was going on with me). By the way, most of them still don't.

I did, however, tell Mom, as directly as possible, "Next year for my Sweet Sixteen, I don't want a big fuss, okay?"

"Okay, honey. You don't get depressed on your birthday, do you? If you do, that's not unusual."

"I'm not depressed! But if it's my day, I shouldn't have to do something I don't like."

Mom agreed. So we came up with a solution that would give me more control over the planning for my celebration. First, for the night before my birthday I could invite a few really close friends to go out to a movie, no big deal. And then Mom could plan something low key at the ranch. And for the guest list—only the extended family. I also didn't want people to make a fuss with presents.

Dr. Katja Van Herle, who is always so amazing and so involved with everything that's relevant to my well-being, kept asking me before the party, "Ali, is there anything on your birthday list you really want?" She must have asked some form of the question sixteen times.

"I just want a card, a nice big card is fine. Really, you don't have to get me anything else," I kept telling her. Not budging, whenever the topic came up, I would tell Katja, "I only want a card, no gifts."

At the party, as I was greeting everyone, Katja announced, "I have something for you."

"But . . . " and just as I was about to say that she shouldn't have gotten me anything, she led me away from the rest of the guests and around a small wall and there in front of me was a birthday card that was six feet tall—just a little taller than me—and wider than the expanse of my arms. The card was of a bouquet of balloons of every color and had been specially made out of superstrength cardboard. Katja had gotten everyone to sign it—making it that much more perfect. Somehow she also snuck in a gift: a collection of little, rare seashells.

Well, as for the party, I must say that Mom outdid herself—which is saying a lot! And I loved sharing it with the extended family, especially because we were at the ranch, my favorite place to be in the universe. It has everything. The horses and the flowers—and now there's a pub! With the writers' retreats and the medical summits and various events happening, Mom decided we had to put in a pub—a totally real pub!

I know why Mom is holding the Summit there. Your vision changes up there. Maybe it's the view.

I want to live there one day. I WILL *live there one day. Why would I ever leave? Someone not long ago nailed up a sign where you exit out the gate. It reads, "Leaving Paradise."*

If you look at the mountain behind the house, you can see a little brown line snaking up through the trees. A woman who is one of the foremost hiking experts in the world helped design these trails, which you can take all the way to the top. The best way is by horse. You can take a 'gator, but that route only goes about halfway up then just sort of stops. You have to walk the rest.

We had my Sweet Sixteen in the pasture with a tent in the middle of it. Everything about the celebration was beyond magical—very ARABIAN NIGHTS. *The day of my party was sunny and beautiful, but as soon as sunset came, this thick, thick fog rolled in, and you couldn't see your hand out in front of you. Candles were lit on the path to the pasture, and that's how you found the tent. And when we finally arrived inside, we entered another world. Pure enchantment.*

Dad made a movie/montage of my life, with all my favorite songs and photos and videos that took me back. There were all kinds of shots of Evan looking after me and then of Jackson trying to catch up to his big sis. The love that has filled my life for all these sixteen years soared along with the music, making this very happy girl the very happiest.

I have to admit that after this party I may be cured of my dislike of celebrating my birthday!

Mom left the tent up as a reminder of the magic. I don't think she ever wants to take it down.

PART II

By the time we are women, fear is as familiar to us as air. It is our element. We live in it, we inhale it, we exhale it, and most of the time we do not even notice it. Instead of "I am afraid," we say, "I don't want to," or "I don't know how," or "I can't."

—Andrea Dworkin,
author of *The Sexual Politics of Fear and Courage*

4

From Mascara to Medicine

Normally, the immune system is able to distinguish friend from foe, ignoring the body's own components and attacking foreign invaders. Unfortunately, the immunological weapons can, like friendly fire, sometimes turn against the self, causing severe illness and even death.

—Dr. Lawrence Steinman, Stanford University, from "Autoimmune Disease," *Scientific American*, September 1993

August 2009

By the middle of the year, with Ali's attacks coming on an almost weekly basis, I am starting to feel nostalgic for the days when we had to tiptoe around and protect her from knowing the name of her affliction. Now I get to worry not just about what's happening to her physically but also what's happening inside her brain and to her spirit—about where she is filing away the tragic stories of fellow NMO patients that are beginning to accumulate in our data base.

Lately, Ali admits, she's had a scary dream or two at night. Like she'll find herself trying to run but can't feel her legs and then realizes that she's in a wheelchair.

In the dream, in the bad dream.

What power of white light or dark magic can prevent her from seeing those images, even if only in her dreams? What tonic, amulet, wooden stake, or garlic on steroids can ward off the forces that enable us to turn visualization into reality? The same power that changes straw to gold and rags to riches but that can go awry and work in reverse?

Why would you do that? Because, as I've learned, the first step to making something happen is embracing the belief that it can happen. And the step before believing is the seeing of it, so that belief can bind to the image and make it real.

My dreams are much worse. They are so tortured, so fear infected, that I compensate and careen crazily over to the ditch on the other side of the road, grasping at and trumpeting any shred of good news from the foundation and the research front that I can dig up for the day.

Every time a patient is located and identified for tracking on our database, I dash up the stairs and down the hall to Ali's bedroom and burst in with an announcement.

"Guess what? Someone in Ethiopia has NMO!"

We hug. We high five.

"Wow, Ethiopia? That's so cool, Mom!"

I show her the "Connect the Docs" map. The foundation has developed it as a global resource for identifying doctors whose patients have tested positive for the NMO-IgG antibody as well as a communication network for physicians anywhere in the world who may be onto valuable research in their own labs, kitchens, and garages—or who simply want to tap the latest findings of others.

And Ali, being Ali, will look at the map and see all the good that is being accomplished. Or even if she can't see that, she will find the silver lining, the thread of positivity that has eluded me, and she'll say something sparkling like, "Who knew that NMO would help my knowledge of world geography?"

So in this way, together, we surf the tidal waves, clinging to hope's slippery wet backside, like trying to ride a whale as it surfaces from churning waters. Holding our breath when it submerges again. Into the deep.

Not every day is dark. But there is an undertow we're always watching out for, all part of living with the disease's unpredictability. Dr. Larry Steinman, one of our chief investigators and the head of the neurology department at Stanford as well as a professor of immunology, wrote about how anxiety can feed the manifestation of an attack during lulls that fool patients into thinking they're in remission:

> If fear can produce relapses, then even the fear of a relapse may become a self-fulfilling prophecy. Indeed, uncertainty about the future is perhaps the most bitter aspect of autoimmune disease. Remissions may last for months or for years, disease may progress slowly or rapidly, complaints beyond the primary autoimmune process may or may not ensue. Moreover, the chances of developing another autoimmune condition are much enhanced in those who already have one.

This isn't excerpted here to add to the woe. Just to keep it real, folks.

That said, woe or not, 2009 is my time for reclaiming the edge that I'd first developed as a businesswoman, back in the day when it was very helpful to have that don't-fuck-with-me attitude. This was especially true in that era when I was a wide-eyed makeup artist with a great product line but little marketing experience and was preparing for my big meeting with the infomercial investors that my student at UCLA had set up.

Well, then again, I wasn't completely green. My first line, Victoria Jackson Beauty Basics, created around no-makeup makeup foundation and expanded to include a full color product collection for eyes and lips too, had been in the beauty supply stores for a while. I designed a plexiglass display case and my own poster, featuring actresses like Kathleen Beller (the gorgeous star of *Dynasty* and one of my best friends). That was an attention grabber. Plus, I started doing makeovers at little cookie gatherings that were hosted by friends and clients, where I took orders and began selling by fast-moving word-of-mouth.

My first employee was my mother. Divorced from my stepfather, Mort, by that point, Mom had been supporting herself as a bookkeeper. In her off-hours she would show up at my garage and help me pack orders for delivery. To save on postage when the shipment was going to a local address, Mom would often deliver the packages for me on her lunch hour.

Everyone who tried my makeup even once became almost a lifelong devotee. But getting investors on board had been tough. When I landed meetings with Beverly Sassoon and a few other entrepreneurial women who were pioneers in the cosmetics field, I really got my hopes up that these new associations would help raise my profile in some way. But even with some interesting ideas that were discussed, nothing really came from the encounters.

After those disappointments, I was excited and hopeful when the meeting was arranged in late 1989 for me to meet my student's contacts who were involved with a new East Coast marketing company just getting into infomercials.

Ironically, I was close to clueless as to just what infomercials were all about. Not quite in its infancy but probably more like its toddlerhood, the field of televised direct marketing was nearly uncharted territory. With the advent of cable and a growing number of channels, it was like the Wild Wild West—lots of opportunity, but also lots of risk.

The big expense, I understood, was purchasing the air time. The product had to beckon so powerfully that consumers would respond in masses. In other words, I had to go to the meeting—the power lunch, to be more specific (this was the 1980s after all)—and seriously wow the two women who were screening candidates for the investors to subsequently meet.

Lynn and Patti stated from the outset that I wasn't the typical infomercial product marketer. Right, I agreed, but wouldn't that be refreshing and different? In answer to how I was going to overcome the objection that color cosmetics had never been sold successfully via direct marketing, I again went with how my product line, now simply called Victoria Jackson Cosmetics, was different and was based on the natural beauty of all women. They liked that point as well and suggested a phrase that stuck: "The Victoria Jackson difference."

With that, I was waved on to the next meeting with executives from the marketing company, the two women also in tow, and after looking at photographs of my Before's and After's, in under five minutes the men were quick to tell me that previous efforts to market color cosmetics via infomercials had bombed.

"Yes," I nodded and smiled. "But I have a way to present my line that will be so inviting, women won't feel the need to see, touch, and test the products." Silence. They all sat there and waited. "Kits," I declared, after several beats. "Color-coordinated kits. Everything you need to go from Before to After." I pointed to the photos showing dramatic changes, describing the instruction cards and videos that could accompany the products, the components of the kits, and why there would be an appeal to all women. Who wouldn't want to buy movie-star natural beauty that you could do yourself *and* achieve the same look as having your own makeup artist at home?

Everyone stared back at me, showing nothing, except for one of the men, who asked, "You really think kits would sell?"

"I know they will," I predicted. "And if you put your money where my mouth is, I'll prove it."

No, I wasn't quite "don't-fuck-with-me" yet, but when they eventually came back to me and asked for a full-on presentation, like immediately, I swung into gear.

During the presentation I did one of my "half-face" demonstrations. The simple concept was to hold a card over the made-up side of my face, showing what no makeup at all looked like, and then to move the card to show the half-face with makeup. Then I raised my sponge and put only a tiny amount of no-makeup makeup on it and showed how little was required for the non-made-up side to match the other. The half-face demo clinched it. My first infomercial was a go.

The best news was that the beautiful Ali McGraw and lovely Lisa Hartman had been signed as the celebrity spokeswomen for Victoria Jackson Cosmetics. Then the UCLA professor in me came out, and I persuaded them to hire a cinematographer for the special features that could be inserted with the video that gave a live and unscripted feeling. A great blend, I thought!

Once I approved of the set-up, I went to check my makeup before we started shooting. Nervous but excited, I felt like my moment in the sun had arrived. Looking in the mirror, I was pleased to see a little Estée Lauder attitude that I was projecting. Me, a cosmetics entrepreneur? Who knew? An expert in beauty with my own sense of style and grace? Seemed like that's who I was growing up to be after all.

Just then, there was a knock at the door.

The French cinematographer had arrived and came to introduce himself. His accent was so thick, it sounded put on.

He peered closely at me after we said hello and then took my face in his hands, tilting it to various subtle degrees. He smiled. Probably he saw the new confidence, the woman on the edge of success.

"You know," he said, smiling, studying me, "I have photographed the most gorgeous women in the world."

I smiled back, modestly, graciously, as Estée Lauder might have, ready for a compliment.

"In my experiences photographing the most gorgeous women in the world, I have found there to be two kinds. There are women of great beauty, and women of great brains. You . . . are a woman of great brains."

Wait. Did he just insult me in his excessive French accent? Screw him.

But then it didn't matter. I surrendered. I went from fearless beauty to panic-stricken mutt and back again, all in a nanosecond. Total makeover! With a laugh, I tossed my hair, leaned back, pointed at him, and said, "Well, then I know *you* are going to make me look beautiful."

And he did.

Something magical happened over the course of the first week when the infomercial ran. The conventional wisdom that women wouldn't buy color cosmetics without being able to touch, feel, and test products in person was disproved. Beyond a shadow of a doubt.

True to my word, I had set the investors on a fast track to grossing a hundred million dollars a year from Victoria Jackson Cosmetics. Before the term "going viral" existed, that's what infomercials did for no-makeup makeup.

So where did the need for an edge come from? Because, as it turned out, the infomercials were making money—to the tune of nearly a million dollars in the first week. Before long we were adding ten thousand new customers a week, but I was the last and the least to get paid, other than the small monthly advance against future royalties that allowed me to cover living expenses.

I was becoming a household name, but unless I found a serious edge, I was going to be left with nothing to show for my own success.

That was what I did, ultimately, by improving my terms over time and eventually parting ways with that marketing company. And that's when "don't-fuck-with-me" became a business survival necessity.

So here in August of the second year in the land of NMO, I summon my inner Hell on Wheels that you wouldn't normally associate with the people pleaser I usually am. With no particular target, I'm on everyone's case—at work and at home.

I'm angry, yes. I'm angry that I didn't get this disease and Ali did. There I said it. There is nothing I wouldn't give or do if we could go back and rewrite the narrative and have the universe realize it sent the overvigilant immune system to the wrong person. It should have been me.

Scientifically, now that I'm making the switch-over from mascara to medicine, I know that given genetics as a factor, the likelihood of my having an autoimmune disease is increased. In fact, our doctors at the Mayo—where the NMO IgG test was developed—keep asking whether I want us all to be tested, and I keep saying, "No!"

At this stage, if anybody else's test came back positive, I'd lose it entirely. I'd seriously freak out beyond anything that's happened so far. I just don't want to know.

I do, however, accept that Ali's specific genetic profile may have allowed for a predisposition for autoimmune diseases. In chasing a mystery disease, the question is at least worth asking. Our researchers agree that in our case it's another clue to the mechanism that fires up the inflammatory cascade. It's another piece of the puzzle.

One of millions.

Dr. Michael Yeaman is Professor of Medicine at UCLA and Chief of Molecular Medicine at Harbor-UCLA Medical Center as well as our investigative team's lead advisor. He has pointed out that not only are there many clues that can be relevant in understanding the mysterious behavior of the immune system but also that they happen at very specific times and places in the body—a sort of biological 3-D. "Kind of like a game of 3-D chess moving at one hundred miles an hour." So the challenge of identifying the key pieces involved in NMO becomes that much harder.

Like a needle in a haystack?

"More like a needle in a sea of needles."

Suddenly I have to agree with Ali that I too hate needles.

The odds of finding the right needle can keep the most desperate parents and the most dedicated researchers up at night. But that won't stop us from trying.

And as I'm reminded by many of our Knights of the Round Table, as I call our growing medical team, we actually know something with NMO that we don't have with most other autoimmune diseases. Thanks to the work of the team at the Mayo in identifying the biomarker that redefined NMO, there is proof that needles critical to the cure can be found—the equivalent of having a major edge, I have to admit.

This had come about because of the vision of the Wizard of the Mayo, Dr. Brian Weinshenker, who in 1999 had joined forces with another brilliant Mayo neurologist, Dr. Dean M. Wingerchuk, in publishing research from sixty different cases that distinguished Devic's Disease as a separate entity from MS, as it had been understood for about a century.

In paying attention to their work, a leading Mayo research immunologist, Dr. Vanda Lennon, had a lightbulb go off that sent her in search of the first needle in the stack of needles. Dr. Lennon wanted to understand what was happening to NMO patients who frequently had accompanying autoimmune disorders that weren't part of the MS profile. To do that, she acquired blood samples from NMO patients and, lo and behold, discovered a previously unnamed antibody that showed up consistently in tests used to rule out another disease. Vanda and Brian then went back to check patient histories, twelve of them that they could track, and found—guess what?—they all had both optic neuritis and transverse myelitis. Realizing that they had found the antibody for Devic's, they called it NMO-immunoglobulin G (NMO-IgG).

While that was happening, another gifted Mayo neurologist and MS investigator, Dr. Claudia Luccinetti, had been studying the mechanisms of tissue damage in demyelinating diseases of the central nervous system and also discovered unique traits of the damage being done to myelin in NMO.

All of these findings thus far from the Mayo team had been published by 2004. Then, two years later Vanda Lennon had another research breakthrough when she identified the actual target of the NMO-IgG antibody: a water channel protein called aquaporin-4, or, as those of us in the know refer to the protein molecule, AQP-4, a fairly common, hard-working protein that serves as a channel for water to enter and leave the central nervous system, commonly found in the areas affected by NMO.

So in the grand scheme of things, that would be two needles: (1) the antibody that unfairly and irrationally attacks a target *and* (2) the target itself, the unwitting AQP-4. The completion of this work then led to the development of the NMO-IgG blood test by Dr. Lennon's lab. At the time of Ali's diagnosis the test had only been available for a little more than a year.

Here we were now, about eighteen months since she tested positive, and we're looking for more needles. One of those will allow us to understand why the immune system is making the antibodies that are causing the attacks. The other, all-important needle will be the one that gives us the means to stop attacks for good.

The question that's causing me to lose the most sleep these nights is whether I dare believe we're closer than we were before.

The raw-edged answer is that I still don't know.

Carpe diem. Seize the day, boys.
Make your lives extraordinary.

—Robin Williams,
Dead Poets Society, 1989

~

AUGUST 14, 2009, AT THE BEACH IN CARPINTERIA

***As you may have noticed already**, Mom has a few control issues and a couple trust issues, which I guess is kind of a double whammy, because they're different but connected. Apparently I have inherited some of the need for control that comes along with being Type A (for Ali), so I understand and share that with her.*

The metaphor for control, of course, is Mom and cars. She doesn't like other people driving. (After three months with my driver's license, neither do I.) She has always loved fast cars and vintage cars. I guess there's something about getting behind the wheel that lets her feel in charge. Mom and I are the worst backseat drivers—including with each other.

Obviously, in business and in running the foundation and overseeing the research, having that control is necessary to make sure that everything is done right. Not just done "right" but done at a level that pushes the science beyond the limits of where it has been before. But in that need to get it right, Mom accepts that she has to give up a lot of control and trust others who have the knowledge to achieve what everyone else has failed to do. And the responsibility when she does let go and trust others has to be overwhelming. Because, I mean, it is my life and the lives of a lot other parents' kids.

Out of this need to control what she doesn't even understand, my mother has come up with some amazing innovations. Take, for example, the blood bank she started for the research. That all came about because of a mix-up in a lab with vials of my blood that were lost back when I was trying the "R" drug. As luck would have it, the Mayo still had two extra vials of blood from when we first visited.

Sharing blood was not exactly the policy among the different medical institutions, but Mom managed to get the vials sent to the team monitoring the "R" drug trials.

The story wasn't over, though.

Later in the year, after I stopped the "R" drug trials and went on the Victoria Jackson/Ali Guthy cocktail (that we're still refining), Mom burst into my room one afternoon with a wild look in her eyes. She had just come up with this brainstorm about how one of the biggest hurdles for most researchers is lack of blood specimens for testing. Obviously this was especially true for a rare disease like NMO.

"And do you know what's the most test-worthy blood?" Not waiting for an answer, she continued, "Untreated blood. That's the gold standard."

"Right?" I said, not sure what was next.

Well, Mom had devised an ambitious plan to create a blood repository for samples taken from NMO patients everywhere around the world, under treatment or newly diagnosed. How was she going to encourage patients to donate their blood to research? By giving them a thank you gift of some of her private collection Victoria Jackson Cosmetics. "I'm going to call it 'Blush for Blood.' Do you like the idea?"

Like it? I loved it!

Next thing I knew, the framework was set up for the Guthy-Jackson Repository for NMO. Mom teamed up with the Accelerated Cure Project and the University of Texas Southwestern for the collecting, storing, and sharing of blood specimens and data—necessary blood samples and data in a secure repository. Before long, there were ten blood collection sites that had been identified for adult patients with NMO and five pediatric collection sites. Oh, and then my mother suggested the idea of a traveling nurse sent out by the repository to draw blood from NMO patients who didn't have access to any nearby collection sites.

Blush for Blood? Genius! Who comes up with a traveling nurse who spreads the cheer of blush or mascara or lip gloss wherever she goes? My mom. I think what I'm trying to point out is that the need for control can be a very positive force when properly harnessed.

She doesn't say it in so many words, but she wants to give me the girlhood and the teenage years that she never had. She doesn't say it in so many words, but I know she worries that NMO is robbing me of those options.

But I don't believe it is. The only feeling I have of being robbed, which has come about this summer with the increased frequency of attacks, has to do with not getting to go on the much-anticipated trip to Europe.

When Mom canceled our trip, I was crushed. She didn't say that she was worried about me having an attack overseas, and I didn't say, "So what? There are hospitals in Europe."

All Mom said was, "There's too much going on. Let's stay close to home," as a way of making it be about her and her own anxiety about travel.

But I knew in this instance, canceling Rome was about her fears for me. Otherwise, Dad would have just said, "No problem," and he would have taken the entourage and led us off on the European expedition himself. That's what we used to do before Mom figured out the flying thing, a back story I don't have full knowledge of.

The one real upset for me during this period happened toward the end of the summer—August 15 to be exact. We were up at the beach in Carp for what was probably the worst attack of the summer. To make it that much more annoying, it had only been two days since I finished the IV treatments for the previous attacks. No catching a break, as Mom would say. I was getting ready for a walk on the beach when, all of sudden, my foot went numb.

Normally, the instant the tingling begins we go into triage mode. But because we weren't expecting the attack and were up at the beach without anyone who could administer the IV, I had to wait a couple hours for a nurse to arrive. And it was sort of nerve wracking because I could only hop on one foot, with that awful feeling of sand falling down through my legs and the numbness spreading until I couldn't walk.

Watching me go through the ordeal, Mom almost appeared to be having the same symptoms. Crazy! It was like she was hobbling around after me, trying to assure me that it's all going to be fine—not too convincingly.

Suddenly, her eyes lit up and she bolted from the room, returning moments later with—oh, my God!—marijuana! And a shopping bag of apparently laced baked items.

"Here, honey" she said, extending the jar of weed in my direction. "It's supposed to calm you down and make you feel better. Kind of like Xanax."

"Xanax? Great help that is."

"But it's not a pill. It's natural."

"Mom, get that away from me! I can't believe you're trying to give me pot."

"I've been reading how many people in pain or on meds get relief from smoking just a little bit." My mother paused, then added, with the same desperate expression she wore when we were going the one-humped-camel-milk route. "And besides, think of how popular you'll be with all your friends."

~

Just after Labor Day, 2009

Year two with NMO is life in Limbo-land.

It's a month since my failed attempt to offer Ali medical marijuana. Not really something that I thought through all the way, the idea was to have some sort of emergency remedy that we could keep under glass, only to be broken during a severe attack when relief appeared out of reach.

The effort began with a foray into a very sketchy area of the Valley to apply for a license for myself and my insomnia-induced headaches (true). When the license was approved, I ventured off to the dispensary located in an even sketchier neighborhood.

Number one, I felt funny going into that world, definitely a through-the-looking-glass experience. To my shock, there were medical marijuana vending machines! I watched a mixed clientele peruse and legally purchase items from vending machines! That was weird enough. But I was also surprised at how dated my street smarts were. Once upon a time I did know the lingo, even if I've always been too afraid to put any kind of mind-altering substances into my body.

But so much had changed from the days of the nickel bags and single joints that I used to see at parties my friends held when I was a kid. There were now not only so many different strains and strengths of pot, but you could also choose between the kind that brings you up and the other kind that brings you down. I decided to get both kinds—why do less when you can choose more?—as well as a batch of brownies and an assortment of pot accessories and a "piece."

Ali instantly forgot her numb foot and her stoicism and whatever other emotions were bubbling up inside her and looked at the jar of weed with its medicinal label and screamed, "Oooh, Mom, get that out of here!"

On the phone later, when she was telling Dr. Ben Greenberg about the progression of the numbness from her foot to the rest of her right side, I heard Ali add, "Oh, Mom tried to give me drugs!"

No laughter followed. After a beat she added, "Yeah, uh-huh, she thought I should try medical marijuana." In all seriousness, Ali put her hand over the phone, shook her head, and warned, "Just say 'no,' Mom."

She is so astounding, how she keeps fear at arms' length, as she did a few days after the attack. We took a walk on the beach, and she again described her future, telling me, "Mom, I want my dream man to walk me down the beach in a sunset like this. Just like we are now."

Me too.

"We'll be walking along right here, drinking champagne. I'm not sure why we happen to be so festive, but I'll figure that out. Anyway, right when we turn to go back to the party, he'll drop to one knee and ask me to marry him."

By chance or maybe not, the place where she chose for her future dream man to propose to her happened to be in back of the house where I married Bill.

All I could think was, *Oh God, she's going to have that, right?*

An image stuck in my head. The wedding day. The beautiful gown. Perfect. It's perfect.

But then in the days that followed, fear altered the picture to the point that I imagined I could see Bill as father of the bride, taking a breath in before wheeling her out on the ramp laid over the sand.

I want to talk science and logic with the fear and say, "Look, you're really not helping here." But that doesn't seem to stop the taunts and jeers telling me that all my fears were justified during attacks or that I allowed myself to get too all high and mighty during states of calm.

Plus, the more science I pack into my head, the harder time I have shaking the familiar sense of foreboding. Putting my feelings down on paper helps, my own version of a journal, scratched out in notes on the margins of medical studies. But I've come to feel that fear, like anger or revenge, is a terrible author. What's worse is in the no-writing writing zone, as I've come to think of these dear-diary entries—perhaps as homage to no-makeup makeup—I'm never able to stop myself from trying to write the story before it's written itself.

Those are control issues. Big ones. As though it's all about me. But of course it isn't. It isn't even all about Ali.

It's about living in the moment, hour by hour, day to day. It's about how we choose to write the story as it unfolds.

Such is the next lesson that Ali steps forward to help me learn as I sit at my desk at night reviewing funding requests for studies already begun or waiting for dollars. Something major is starting to take shape with the research our investigators are conducting. I'm so ready for us to spread our wings to fly, but something's blocking the runway.

Could it be the old refrain from the Voice that predicted the story of my angel child would not be easy and would not have a happy ending? What medicine was there to erase that prediction? I need that. God, I need that.

Right then, Light and Reason enter the room, and the incredible happens.

Ali walks in with wings enough for the both of us.

She wants to talk about the homework assignment for her writing class, an essay she's working on about a famous short story by the American writer Willa Cather. Ali says that the story focuses on a boy who was supposed to make a bank deposit for his dad but instead steals the money and runs away to Manhattan. He checks into a hotel and lives it up, but when he learns that his father is coming for him, he kills himself.

"God, Ali, that is so depressing."

"It's really beautiful. She's an amazing writer."

The assignment, she explains, is to rewrite the ending, starting from when the boy arrives in New York.

"Rewrite the ending how?"

"The teacher wants us to change the Narrative."

The Narrative. I love that Ali's teacher used that word. Ali's only a junior, but she knows what it means. I certainly didn't know what it meant when I was in high school.

"The point isn't just to give the story a happy ending but to actually write in the same style of the author. It's not, like, 'Oh, this story is so depressing! We need to put a smiley face on it!' It's more like an exercise to see if you can write it in the style and voice of the author." Ali goes on to explain that they have to use a special symbol because Cather uses symbolism in her work.

I am holding back tears as Ali tells me she is going to use a rose for her symbol. In her ending, when the father comes to get the son, they're both carrying these white roses for each other, without either having known about it. The son uses roses to say he's sorry and the father to say he forgives him. When they hug at the end, the rose petals fall like snow.

I am altered somehow by my daughter's gifts of storytelling and belief and vision. Maybe on purpose or on instinct, she has chosen this moment to remind me of my own narrative-changing powers, taking me back again to the past and then back to the future.

The runway was clear. The wings had been de-iced of all those miserable story endings.

Soon we would be ready for takeoff, and I would be able to go along for the ride.

Mid-September 2009

Summer fades, and a new season, both promising and worrying, begins.

Ali is on alert, warding off threats, intent on making up for any loss of time that hasn't even occurred yet, not letting a moment go by, like someone bear-hugging life and squeezing every ounce of possibility out of it.

During a check-in with Dr. Ben, as we discuss potential changes to Ali's meds and I ask about some of the newer approaches I've been reading about, he agrees that there is nothing wrong with wanting to turn over all stones. But he also cautions me not to give up on the combination of meds we've already taken—just stopping short of "going nuclear," which would entail the equivalent of blood plasma replacement.

As a home-schooled medical researcher in training, I had by now come to the conclusion that just because we discontinued the "R" drug and didn't pursue the "A" drug that wasn't to take away from the excellent results patients were having with both. In fact, the foundation increased funding for work that Dr. R. was doing because of the potential of the ongoing studies.

Interestingly enough, after Dr. R.'s doom and gloom had devastated me so much early on, once he was no longer Ali's primary NMO doctor, he and I arrived at a place of mutual respect. During review sessions by phone or in person, whenever I made a comment or asked a question, he shocked me by saying things like, "That's an excellent point, Victoria. I hadn't thought of that."

After talking further, I had felt at ease enough to finally ask him, "Why do you seem so angry?"

Dr. R. took a breath and then explained that he lived through the recent loss of his wife. Ah, then it made sense. He was part of the same club, the bad-deal-of-the-cards club that none of us ask to join. That's all he revealed really, but after that he became much more human in my eyes. And that was the kind of guy I wanted in the trenches with us—with that sense of life-and-death urgency that is often absent in the laboratory.

In the interim we had tried different combinations of meds. The efficacy was hard to assess, especially through the summer, with attacks coming almost weekly. In close consultation with Ben Greenberg and Katja Van Herle, Ali, Bill, and I finally settled on what we're calling the "cocktail" because it combines potent drugs with natural supplements and items I've added to the mix intuitively. This includes steroids and CellCept, a chemo/immune-suppressing drug that is often given to transplant patients to prevent their immune system from attacking the foreign invasion of the transplanted organ. These aggressive meds combined with certain vitamins and minerals, along with a gluten-free (or lowered gluten) diet and an avoidance of triggers such as excessive heat and stress (not easy to limit with Ali's tennis schedule), are beginning to feel like the right mix. That is, with the exception of the complications of hormones, which tend to exacerbate milder symptoms.

When I mention this to Ben and suggest that maybe putting her on birth control might be helpful, he agrees. And, as we knock on wood, whether or not we can connect the cocktail to a decrease in attacks, September brings a reprieve.

I know better than to count my chickens before they hatch, even though I try never to forget to count my blessings before they hatch too.

~

LATE SEPTEMBER, 2009

***I've always felt that our family** has a charmed life and don't feel that's been changed because of the unfortunate draw of the card that is NMO.*

By the same token, I never thought that having a certain lifestyle made our existence any more charmed than it already was when I was young and my parents were still getting their businesses going. Mom likes to joke about how we were the Beverly Hillbillies when we moved away from the Valley to the 90210. We weren't any different from who we were in the Valley; we just lived in a different zip code. At first, I was unhappy about the move. The Valley was my very first home. It's where I grew up and where we had a very normal family life. The house and the narrow street with shade trees and little traffic—where we could ride our bikes and skateboards—will always have a special place in my heart.

So yeah, the move to Beverly Hills was something I initially opposed—quite vocally, I might add. At first, the house we had moved into didn't feel like much of a home either, although it had a sort of character that captured bygone movie-star eras. That was pretty cool, I have to admit.

After about a year the place started to grow on me, not just the house but also the proximity to different parts of LA, kind of smack dab between its west and east sides. But the idea that good fortune had given us more of a charmed life never figured into the equation.

What I'm trying to emphasize is that it's not like when I got diagnosed the whole world came crashing down. And maybe that's just my view because I didn't know about NMO or its consequences right away. Because I was so oblivious, I had the luxury of being kept in this bubble, believing and really living like nothing had changed. The act of discovery since then has been a slow and steady process, so it's not like the rug has been pulled out from under me.

Other than the obvious increase in medical visits and frequent bouts of illness, I haven't seen anything about our journey as a family to make it feel less charmed. In fact, if anything, the diagnosis has only increased my awareness of our charmed life. After all, my parents' successes are making the foundation possible, along with the research that will result in treatment and a cure for NMO. So essentially, my family's charmed life and the success of the foundation are inherently linked.

The bottom line decreed by me, Alexandra Rose Guthy, in September 2009, early in my junior year of high school, is that I don't think the diagnosis has had any effect on our charmed life other than to increase its impact on a more universal scale.

Life is best understood backward
but must be lived forward.

—Søren Kierkegaard (1813–1855)

~

When Bill and I went out on our first date, back in the early 1990s, I actually was the one who asked him out. The twist in that tale is that he thought I wanted to talk to him about business because his company was a newer competitor to the infomercial group that marketed my line.

The truth? I thought he was one of the most handsome, smartest, and charismatic men I'd ever met and wanted to get to know him better.

Being in the same industry, our paths had crossed earlier, but we were officially introduced at the first-ever infomercial industry award/trade show and convention held in Las Vegas in 1991, where I won the coveted award for Best Female in an Infomercial and was treated as the reigning queen of our industry. The reigning king, motivational guru Tony Robbins, took home the award for Best Male.

Bill's company, Guthy-Renker, had really put itself on the map with Tony's motivational program, *Unlimited Power*. So that's how the stars aligned, all of us in that room in Vegas with Tony Robbins as the unwitting matchmaker who introduced me to Mr. Guthy.

Everyone seemed to be very taken with a speech I had given during the program about how we as infomercial pioneers should improve our image. I'd addressed my concern that much of the public associated what we did with snake-oil salesmen. The idea that we were all hawkers trying to lure buyers into making purchases they didn't need was not who we were. The way to counteract the portrayal, I suggested, was to be as honest and reputable as we could.

I made other comments about broadening our demographics and reaching out to all market groups. Whatever I said that got Bill Guthy's attention, he didn't say. But when Tony introduced us, he complimented me on my remarks. All of that was in my mind almost a year later when I called and asked him to dinner.

A wonderful raconteur, Bill gave me a lively account of some of his ups and downs in the business world. They were mostly ups. His first endeavor had begun in his late teens when he attended Ambassador College (affiliated with the Worldwide Church of God). To pay for tuition, he had tapped his lifelong curiosity in technology and new trends by duplicating cassette tapes for the Blind Department at the college.

With the boom in the recording industry's transition from vinyl to audio tapes, he saw other opportunities, and by the time he was out of college he had his own company, Cassette Productions Unlimited, operating first out of an apartment and then a small office. In time CPU would become one of the premiere audio/video duplication companies in the world, including over two hundred thousand square feet of manufacturing space and employing nearly two hundred employees.

In the early 1980s Bill started spending weekends in Palm Desert, where he met Greg Renker, a budding entrepreneur whose family owned real estate in the area. When Bill and Greg were first batting around business ideas, they discovered they had a shared love for motivational books, in particular a book written in 1937 by Napoleon Hill entitled *Think and Grow Rich*. (Interestingly enough, I had also read the book before its reissue and found it to be life changing.)

Bill and Greg were amazed that the book was so little known to contemporary readers. They weren't sure what to do about that until Bill had a brainstorm after CPU was given an order to duplicate 120,000 audio cassettes for a real estate sales motivational/instructional series being marketed via infomercials, a new medium.

Bill recalled, "It occurred to me one day that if I could get into the infomercial business, I'd have an edge." Because CPU already had cassette-duplicating technology, he could save himself a fortune. As he put it, "With an infomercial company of my own, I could be my own best customer."

The stage was set. Joining forces with Greg Renker, their direct-response television marketing company Guthy-Renker was born. Their first product for promotion was the result of obtaining the rights to *Think and Grow Rich* from the Napoleon Hill estate. Between the book and an audio series that included Hill's lectures, and sports/motivation legend Fran Tarkenton brought in as pitch man, they had hit upon a recipe that led to somewhere around $10 million of revenue.

All that from a discussion about favorite books!

Aware that their success was one of those 2% amazing strokes of great timing and entrepreneurial thinking, Bill and Greg now had to try to make it happen again. But on an even more impressive scale.

The two had met Tony Robbins when they went in search of a young voice to provide a testimonial for the Napoleon Hill book. Bill told me that Tony had been so compelling and empowering in the process, he and Greg decided that instead of looking for a gadget or celebrity to push a new product, they would look no further than their own backyard and launch Tony Robbins and his *Personal Power* program into the infomercial stratosphere.

From the beginning of my relationship with Bill—when I quickly got past the impression that he was a male version of me and found out how different we were in our emotional response to everything—I was clear on how uncomfortable he was claiming glory. For better and for worse, he never wanted to draw too much attention to himself. But it was nonetheless apparent that he knew how to harness talent, to recognize someone else's big, broad idea, and then find a way to build it, first giving the concept real form and then figuring out not just how to launch the product or program but also how to give it legs. He was also *not* a control person and knew how to trust his partner and his team when the company really started to take off.

With the success of Tony's tapes, books, and lecture series, you might say that for Guthy-Renker, the rest was a slow-burn history—leading to everything from Principal Secret (Victoria Principal's skin care products), the Power Trainer exerciser with Bruce and Kris Jenner, a teeth whitening system with Vanna White, and, of course, later on, to the crown jewel: Proactiv™, first launched with Judith Light, subsequently promoted by stars ranging from Vanessa Williams to Justin Bieber.

We are so grateful to every sufferer of pimples on the planet who has helped make Proactiv™ the worldwide number-one nonprescription treatment for adolescent and adult acne. Because of that, we are able to afford to seek accelerated treatment and a cure for NMO.

Who knew that we would be having so much gratitude for skin breakouts?

Aha! A silver lining for acne!

What that tells me, what I am trying to face and act on, is that for most of us who embrace our own journeys—whatever they happen to be—the textbook from the past, complete with all the blessings and the struggles, can serve as a classroom for the challenges of something new, different, and even terrifying.

Or, rather, as boot camp.

If you can't you must, and if you must you can.

—Anthony Robbins

I want to believe that all the early years of struggle have prepared me for the metamorphosis necessary for going from mascara to medicine. True, there are many miles in between when going from the makeup world, which is full of color, to navigating through the dark corridors of medical research. There is a chasm between marketing miracles and actually achieving them in the scientific world.

Medicine has a different energy. It's life and death, black and white, sometimes gray. Overall, the texture of day-to-day work is darker and heavier. Being success driven and having a lot to prove has worked in the past, but I'm coming to terms with the reality that the old rules no longer apply. Unlike earlier endeavors, when I had a clear vision for the destination, I'm not sure what success can realistically look like. Not only that, but I went into makeup with a passion for it—a choice. Just as Napoleon Hill says in *Think and Grow Rich*, the engine of making dreams become real is the burning desire to do something that is organic and true to who you are.

My journey into medicine was not born of a desire. I wasn't raised on dreams of wanting to be a scientist or a researcher or a doctor. But at the same time, I can't imagine a passion more intense for any of us than wanting to give our children their health, safety, and well-being. Somehow that alone makes the science understandable. Not because I'm any different from any parent out there. The only difference is that we have the resources to be "proactive"—as the doctors often like to say.

Sometimes we laugh at the use of the word. Sometimes we want to cry.

Hopefully—yes, I carry hope with me everywhere, tucked in the same bag as the fear, even though I forget to pull it out sometimes—I can apply the power of the makeover to what we're up against.

Obviously, with the amount of self-help titles I read a year, not to mention the fact that I wrote a couple of them, I knew that the power of the makeover isn't something that's been personally discovered just by me. It's old, it's ancient, a predisposition even in our primitive selves, our DNA. And it's the number-one marketing message that's prevailed since time immemorial—the promise that a product, an idea, an experience, a service, a what-have-you can change us and make us better. Like new.

Self-improvement and self-encouragement, I should add, are not the only reasons I gravitate to self-help titles. My biggest motivation for reading them all has been as a mother in search of the secret to not passing on my fear of almost everything to my kids.

Almost a Momtra: *Don't fear as I do.*

Then one evening in September I realize that I've been following the cold trail of how to *not* do something.

Wrong! Never works. The universe only responds to affirmative action—trust me on this—and I have to start thinking about passing on something to my children that I haven't mastered myself: how to be happy.

I know that is insanely counterintuitive to decide to look for joy in the midst of your worst nightmare coming true and an otherwise pretty stressful period in the global history of humankind. But wouldn't that be the ultimate test? Isn't that what the Buddhists and Yogis and the other enlightened ones have been trying to teach throughout the millennia? And I have the best teacher in the world right next to me—my daughter.

Still, I'm starting to suspect that I might not be genetically predisposed for true joy.

Time for cramming as part of my own mascara-into-medicine makeover. I come up with a list of no less than one hundred self-help books that incorporate the teaching of happiness and buy them all. True.

Guess what I learned from perusing every single last one of them? Sorry about not giving you a spoiler alert, but the message—the takeaway as Bill would say—is that happiness is not all it's cracked up to be. Turns out, it's as elusive to a majority of other people as it is to me.

The message is not entirely discouraging, however. The antidote to fear, the experts all seem to agree, is less about the ability to experience happiness and more about the ability to experience purpose. Like

soldiers in a war who win medals of bravery and mothers who fend off overpowering predators to protect their young. They never say they weren't afraid.

Purpose! That is the key for making the transition from makeup to medicine.

There is more to this lesson than meets the eye. It's about being able to inhabit the dark and acknowledge day terrors while still believing there can be a happy ending.

~

FALL 2009

Until this period*, in the weeks leading up to the Symposium, I didn't really get how visionary my mother's thinking with the foundation really is. Blush for Blood and the GJCF Repository is only one example. The Connect the Docs map that identifies where specialists in NMO exist all over the globe is another.*

What's the secret? She goes with her gut. She knows who to trust, who not to. She knows who she needs to have on her team and who needs to go. She's very intuitive, but that intuition is also balanced with a brilliant mind that understands how the world operates. She may not have graduated high school or gone to college, but her intuition is by far one of her most valuable assets that has allowed her to achieve so much.

She wouldn't admit it, but I have to say that my mom is not just out to change how research is done but also to challenge the terrible unfairness that exists when it comes to access to great medical care. In the process, maybe without trying, she has kind of made a reformer out of me. I'm in no way denying many valuable aspects to the current medical system. It's just that I feel so strongly that access to medical treatment shouldn't be so heavily reliant on financial status. And honestly, part of what Mom is doing with the foundation is coming at that problem. She's only one person. She can't change the entire world on her own. But in my view she may just prove that the medical field can be a more accessible place for everyone.

Right now, "everyone" is limited just to those with NMO or other closely related autoimmune conditions. Watch out, however, because I wouldn't put it past Victoria Jackson to have an impact on the way the medical community could potentially have its own makeover.

Why shouldn't everyone have access to doctors who collaborate and share their wisdom with one another? Sounds simple—and it is. Again, that's why I feel so fortunate to have a team conferring with one another on my behalf.

And by the way, I do know that there are doctors and then there are healers. Take Dr. Ben Greenberg. Dr. Ben's a rock star, the coolest guy on the planet who you can't help but just love. He's a teddy bear with this unpretentious can-do demeanor of a Southern gentleman on top of the fact that he has a laugh that can make you feel better in a minute. Plus, he looks so young and talks to me, a teen, on my level.

After a bad attack, Ben flew out—as much for Mom as he did for me. He wanted to remind her of how much promise the work of the foundation now holds.

"If you'd have asked me eight years ago," he said to both of us, "what was worse, MS or NMO, I would have said NMO. Now I'm on the fence." He has treated about one hundred people with NMO in the last eight years. That's how rare and little understood it used to be. But the tide is turning because of the collaboration of the team that the foundation has put together.

During his visit I have to note that their conversation provides the most science I've heard, and it's staggering how Mom just speaks that language already, whereas it's way too abstract to me.

Ben says, "So you understand that you make antibodies that target the spine and the optic nerve. They're trained to defend against invaders but are misfiring against noninvaders. How do you get them to stop doing that?"

Mom nods. She's on board. Dad's there too.

Ben continues, "I have a cat at home."

Ah, he knows me well. I'm an animal person all the way. My closest companion, best beloved friend and confidante, is Scooby Doo, my cat who never leaves my room.

"Go on."

"Well, what I didn't know is, some cats like to chew through wire. Bad cats chew on wires and cause all kinds of problems. So how do we stop that cat from chewing through wire? We can put him in a room where there aren't any wires and lock the door. That won't guarantee that he won't get out and chew wire. Cats are pretty smart. But locking the door will help. There are a number of things we can do."

"But how can you be sure they'll even work?" Mom interjects.

Ben nods, explaining that the only drastic thing to do is to rid the city of all cats who chew on wire. Immune-system suppression, basically.

"Ali is this upsetting you?" my mother asks.

"No, no," I answer. "Scooby has nothing to do with the chewing on my spine."

The inflammation, like a smoldering fire, has been kind of a hotspot in my spine for about a year, Ben reminds me. "I'd like to put that out, get rid of the cats that are causing that."

We can use treatments already on the table to do that, he says, and up some of the dosages as long as I can tolerate them.

"I'm pretty used to the side effects," I say.

We thank him for coming out and then start getting ready to say good-bye when Mom says, "Before you get on the plane, I just want to be sure . . . is there anything else? What else should I worry about?"

Dad leans in. I wait for the answer.

Ben thinks hard and then he says, "Let's see. What else can we put on your plate? World famine?"

5

Flying Blind

It's not the load that breaks you down,
it's how you carry it.

—Lena Horne

October 2009

"Mom?"

Ali's voice echoes down the hallway to our bedroom into my blurry state of almost asleep. It's almost midnight. I've dozed off reading about B cells and T cells, sitting at my desk. Disjointed, distraught, my heart thumping, foreboding wrapped around my throat like a noose, I rouse.

My impulse is to bolt up out of my chair and run toward the Mom Summons.

But, catching my breath, I'm careful not to change the routine. We have a set way of doing this. And when things are going well, as they have been since Dr. Ben Greenberg's visit, without an attack in over three weeks, we are very superstitious about following the unspoken rules.

So I call back, "Yes, Ali, I'm awake."

"Would you come tuck me in?"

"Are you ready?" Wait. One Mississippi, two Mississippi, and then, "Call me when you're ready, Ali."

"No, Mom, come now!"

This is the ritual. I pad down the hallway in my slippers, not too urgently, so I can sit with her as she washes her face and brushes teeth. We chit-chat. Nothing momentous.

There's almost an OCD part to this. It's like, she feels safe if it's the same every night—then she won't have an attack.

"Scooby Doo, where are you?" Ali searches under her bed for the husky, amber-colored Scottish-fold husky who is her constant companion, a cat who has never left her bedroom in the entire time we've lived in our Beverly Hills home. Every night after she finds him—either under the bed or underneath the armchair where Ali does most of her reading when she's not doing homework at her desk—she carries Scooby to her bed and gets him situated on his blanket before she sits down.

My job is then to pull off her socks and touch the bottom of her feet.

"Mom! You didn't touch each foot the same way!" She is teasing but dead serious.

We try again. I poke the bottom of each foot precisely with the exact amount of pressure. "Good?"

Ali detects something not so good in my delivery. "They're cold, aren't they?"

"Yeah, a little cold."

She shrugs, as if to say, *well, we knew that,* and reaches for a needle kept in a drawer of her bedside table. Ali pricks both feet with it, in several spots, testing for numbness. During the day, when no one's watching, she conducts tests for numbness with ice packs, making sure her extremities can feel cold to the touch, although I'm not always privy to those results.

"Did you feel the needle pricks, Ali?"

"No numbness."

"Anything else going on?"

"Well, I've been having some charley horses the past week or so when I first go to bed." She allows a hint of nervousness, a touch of resentment to color her tone. But then she bats it away with a shake of her head.

Charley horses? That sounds bad. But what tennis player doesn't have that symptom now and then, right?

"No big deal." Ali is reassuring me, giving me her own brand of *don't worry*.

God, she is so tough, so fierce, so loving, so good.

I'm thinking of her conversation a year earlier with Ben Greenberg about tennis, when she asked if this was going to keep her from playing—how he would have preferred a sport that didn't set up the potential of overheating. From that point on, even though she wanted to play singles, she has opted to play doubles, sometimes having to miss practice or do what's necessary to keep her core body temperature from getting too warm.

Because both heat and stress can contribute to the onset of attacks, whenever she has a match, I'm in worry mode, having minimeltdowns, especially if it's a hot day. Oh, and it always seems to be broiling.

Ali and Raquel, her "other mother," have come up with a daring, covert approach to remaining cool. Raquel and her cousin Mimi have been part of the family since Ali was born, working as caretakers and helpers in our busy household. Ali has described them as magical fairy godmothers who not only will do anything for her but are also keen on seeing her grow and learn from them by example. They have ridden the NMO roller coaster with us and have helped me through some dark days. After Ali's first few attacks, Raquel decided to take nursing classes that would train her to help administer the IV treatments when emergencies dictated.

With Raquel already the unofficial Team Mom for girls tennis at Buckley, there was never anything unusual about her being on hand during practices or matches. So the way they worked it out with Sherm was that at certain points, when the rest of the team was practicing, Sherm would call Ali over to discuss strategy or send her off on an errand, only for Ali to end up at Raquel's car to get iced down.

At a major match, as the season got underway, I showed up right before Ali's game and couldn't find her. The heat that day was brutal for starters, and on the court everything was just baking. Spectators had even left the stands to grab some shade in between games. Where was she? Where was Raquel, who is never far from her side at every practice and every game?

Finally I spotted Raquel's car and headed toward it. Upon approach, I could see Ali trying to keep herself underneath the opened hatchback door while Raquel helped put cold packs on her stomach, arms, back, and legs. Seconds later, I saw my daughter emerge with her racket and game face—but drenched. Her hair was wet, and I knew that by the time she walked out onto the court, her clothes would still be soaked.

None of her teammates have indicated to Ali that they have any idea what's going on. A friend who is not on the tennis team found out because she was sleeping over. Ali woke up in horrible pain. When the nurse came and the friend saw Ali getting connected to an IV, she was quick to ask, "Hey, what's happening?"

And in a way, that's been a relief that a close friend has found out. But with her tennis team, I understand that Ali's not ready to say anything. There is the concern that no one will want to be her doubles partner, that others would assume her alleged "back trouble" could cause her not to do well. And in some instances they wouldn't want to play with her because their ratings are tied to how she does. At one point, early on, when the coach called to say that she might be matched with a player who was considered to be the weakest link, I saw Ali momentarily shut down.

She knew the drill. Going way deep, way silent, she finally looked up and said, "Oh, is this how it's going to be?"

But of course, she has used the challenges to be stronger, better, and smarter, just pushing herself to win, becoming close to unbeatable. A magic prescription on the court, but tricky, so tricky, because, again, she's got to keep herself from getting overheated.

A couple players on other teams have apparently seen the special treatment and assumed she's a prima donna—you know, pampered by her own personal groomer. Even some of the parents from other schools seemed to have had that misconception.

Sure enough, the day I went to check on her, when Ali returned to the court with Raquel after being iced down, I actually observed a parent rolling her eyes and overheard her say to someone else, "What a diva!"

Jesus, it was like a hiss.

That killed me. It was so cruel, so unfair. I wanted to grab that mom and say, "You listen, bitch. That's my daughter, and she's just trying to stay alive, I mean, if that's fucking okay with you."

Of course, I swallowed my anger. When you're fighting a war, you learn pretty quickly that you can't afford to waste ammunition. And you also learn that your heart can only break so much.

Besides, I don't want Ali to worry about me falling apart, ironic as that may seem. She does her own worrying, much as she may deny it. Lately, I'm also noticing that she's been having trouble sleeping, possibly a side effect of the prednisone. She admits that nighttime can get scary for her. In recent weeks she's traded off—some nights asking Bill to go in and sit at her bedside and sometimes asking me. She's so incredibly thoughtful that she alternates, wanting us to be able to take turns and rest.

Tonight I linger as she falls asleep, not wanting to engage her in any conversation. We're quiet together, and the sounds of the wind stirring in the canyon above us acts like a comforting lullaby, rocking her to sleep—I hope.

The sight of a sleeping child is such a happy touchstone for me, letting me flip through images of the years and summon a joyful past, remembering times when all three were babies and toddlers and preschoolers and preteens, times when their wants and needs seemed so much simpler.

Or maybe that's my romantic view of how it all used to be when we were supposed to be living the charmed life. When were those days, really? Was it back when the alphabet used to have twenty-six letters—back before N, M, and O decided they were going to break off from the Union and start a Civil War? I'm not sure. Maybe our most charmed days are yet to come.

Maybe.

~

I have no clue as to what prompts me to say it. *But the day after Mom came in to sit at my bedside, the words just pop out.*

After arriving home from school and practice, I'm watching my mother with an array of sketches, pamphlets, and floor plans spread out over the kitchen table, as she fine tunes plans for the November Symposium, the second for the foundation. The first one, held the previous year, was back during my days of ignorance. From what I have heard, that first Roundtable was about connecting the few scientists/doctors to each other so the scant knowledge about NMO at the time could be shared. Goals for this next one include the job of the researchers to report back about findings that have been funded so far, building on that information, and then creating a worldwide awareness campaign.

That's when I realize something and finally say what's on my mind: "Mom, you know this isn't just about me and you anymore. This is bigger than the two of us."

Mom looks up at me, and tears come to her eyes, like I've just said something earth shattering. But no thunder claps. No lightning strikes. I mean, I'm just stating the obvious.

Still, when I hurry on up to my bedroom and greet Scooby, it dawns on me that slowly but surely I have officially entered a new phase in my life and in the work of understanding NMO. Up until now, even after getting the lowdown on the diagnosis, I've kept myself at arm's length from the fight, with only a limited understanding of the spectrum the disease inhabits. I'm not sure that this prepares me even yet to know the extent to which NMO can have debilitating effects. Oh, and by the way, I sure as heck am still not ready to become the poster child for a disease I'm barely just beginning to accept myself!

Mom's been battling for me, fighting the elusive, insidious, mean antagonistic disease/disorder/spectrum that hides in the shadows and you never can predict when it's going to spring out at you. The enemy is great at guerilla-style warfare, moving in like a thief in the night or showing up to the battlefield with no regard for the rules of engagement.

Me, I can obviously be a fighter too, ready with my big rifle—my steroids and CellCept—but I'm playing by the rules and here comes the enemy from behind, hitting at my back with a machete, making it hard to see sometimes and other times to even walk.

So what? That doesn't disqualify me from helping to share the burden of the search that the entire team has undertaken to find out what's causing the signals to go haywire and basically go rogue—for lack of a better phrase—in the first place.

Then the question occurs to me: what do I know that might be of help in at least a small way? Well, as a patient, I do offer some first-hand, up-close-and-personal encounters with NMO. That's got to be good for something. And also, from what I can tell, it's the early intervention in my case along with the ability to start treatment fast that nips an attack in the bud, and that's making a huge difference. It seems to me that information would be helpful for the doctors who are starting to think differently about the treatment of NMO and related autoimmune diseases—another reason why awareness is everything.

Hmmm. Maybe I do have a way to help. But, let me repeat, that absolutely doesn't mean I'm going to be a poster child.

~

"Oh, Mom," Ali says, later that same night, after finishing her homework, after she's told me that what we're doing has become bigger than just her and me. She has leaned her head into the bedroom where I've been lying in the dark, worrying that she's having a bad night. When I tell her to come sit next to me, she says, "Nothing's wrong. I'm fine. I had an idea."

That's my daughter. "You did? I mean, you do?"

"Well, a couple, really." Plopping down on the edge of the bed next to me, Ali says, "I was thinking that in addition to the message board for patients and families on the website, we should really have a NMO newsletter—you know, to give people the latest updates, showing the hopeful possibilities and all."

"That's a fantastic idea!"

"But it should be edited by a patient instead of one of the docs. I mean, we could have medical contributors and pieces from family members and updates about the blood repository and so on."

We talk about how a newsletter would both raise awareness for the general public and get the word out to health care providers, while also providing a source of reassurance to other patients and their families—especially the newly diagnosed.

Sitting there in the dark, strangely, I suddenly don't feel so much in the dark. There is some kind of light trying to streak into the midnight sky. Like an aurora borealis, bursting with electric multicolored possibilities, trying to make its way into my awareness.

Wait a second. Is this the same almost sixteen-and-a-half-year-old Ali who once referred to her diagnosis as That Which Shall Not Be Named? Of course this is the same Ali who earlier in the day had startled me with her comment about the scope of the foundation's undertaking. Now I see that the newsletter idea is not just her acknowledging that the battle is bigger than both of us; it's her going into warrior mode too.

I want to cry, to keep her safe, to prevent her from having to carry the weight of anything bigger than both of us, but at the same time I'm excited to have her in the trenches, to watch her come of age before my eyes.

Excited, I sit up, turn on a lamp at the side of the bed, and ask who'll edit the newsletter.

"Well, I know something about journalism," she says with slight understatement. Ali has been working on the Buckley paper since middle school. "I could volunteer to be managing editor, maybe."

We laugh, hug, high five. Or more of a low five.

"What should we call it?"

"I don't know, Mom. I hadn't thought that far. The GJCF Neuromyelitis Spectrum Disease Newsletter isn't too catchy."

We toss around a few names and settle on *Spectrum*. Sounds like a club, an elite fighting force—*I love it!*

Ali's other idea goes back to a suggestion she made earlier in the year, that instead of simply having a medical symposium in the fall that brings the top NMO docs together with the media and the general public, maybe the foundation also ought to pay to include patients and their families. Who better to provide insights on the course of the disease?

She now wants to make sure that the schedule includes a whole day of activities for patients. "You know," she says with a shrug, "Patient Day."

"Patient Day—that's so perfect. Why didn't I think of that? We can do healing sessions and meditation and bring in alternative therapies.

And you know it would be so great for the doctors to do some meditation . . . "

"No woo-woo stuff, Mom."

I promise no woo-woo, but I can't help smiling as she scoots out the door and back down the hall. Amazing. Ali has the problem-solving gene. Thinking outside the compact!

That energy carries me through the next week, as the final pieces for the Symposium start to come together, all as we get closer to the date. We have about forty doctors from around the world scheduled—very encouraging numbers there. Not so encouraging is that my pledge to find forty patients to come is apparently overly ambitious.

Locating patients has been challenging all along. The real hurdle is convincing some of the orphan disease sufferers that there is genuinely a reason to have hope, to make the trip and not be let down. In some cases, when we start making phone calls, I am talking to NMO patients, many who gave in to despair a long time ago. I relate, totally. But for the most part I'm reaching fellow parents.

So many of the stories I hear are also from fellow 2%ers. I hear of the rare and beautiful charmed life a family might have lived before lightning struck and their beloved, perfectly healthy, gifted athlete son or award-winning daughter suddenly had their world turned upside down from a fluke blood test or an MRI or unprecedented symptom.

I also hear from parents who had a feeling, that instinctual accompanying parental Voice that told them their boy- or girl-next-door child was too golden to always have it easy.

"Hiccups?" one dad says as his voice breaks. How could hiccups be a prelude to an incurable, debilitating disease? How could they? But hiccups are sometimes known to accompany early onset of NMO.

One mother tells me of the anguish she felt after thinking her daughter had gone into remission—with three and a half years of being attack free—and then having her wake up paraplegic.

I'm sorry, I'm so sorry. That's what I say.

Fuck NMO. That's what I want to say.

There is nothing correct to say, however, other than to ask, "How are *you* doing now?" and try to cloak the rattle of fear in my voice.

Another similar story comes from a mom who says that the day her daughter became paralyzed she had woken to experience a series of charley horse spasms. The paralysis never reversed.

What? Did she say charley horse?

No. I didn't hear that. I didn't hear that. Please, tell me I didn't hear that.

Not so sure I ought to be talking to so many parents. But then again, I have to, so I can remember, as Ali said, that this is bigger than just the two of us. And that way I can coat us all in white light and not lose sight of the bigger picture.

There is power in community; there is power in numbers. That much I know. So I keep on working the phones. And guess what?

Instead of the impossible sum of forty patients who will be with us for Patient Day, we are able to include fifty-six, along with members of their families.

Now that's some woo-woo for you.

~

OCTOBER 10, 2009

I don't want to tell Mom *and give her anything else to worry about, but I've begun to see a pattern to the dreams that I've been having lately. This is potentially a good thing, although she might not see it that way.*

The dreams I've been having lately seem to tackle a new theme. They're about journeys, travel, being on the move—all versions of me being prepared for some sort of change. Could it be as simple as, gosh, I don't know, that I'm going to start trying to decide where to go to college in about a year and then before I know it I'll be leaving home? But the bizarre thing is that in these dreams, Mom is encouraging me to hurry up and get going on the journey.

Maybe that's just a daughter's fantasy dressed up in wishful dreaming. The thought of my mother, Victoria Jackson, encouraging me to get going somewhere, anywhere, even college, is much too much of a stretch to even let it enter my dreams.

In fact, I'm so worried about how my leaving will affect Mom, I've actually been avoiding the subject of college. That's why the dreams of us going on a journey might be less about that and more about me just growing up. Even there, I suspect she has mixed emotions about me having to become a warrior.

Mom once told me about a scene in a movie where a knight in full armor is riding along, brings his horse to an abrupt halt, and then takes off his helmet, shaking out his long blond hair. He turns out to be a beautiful girl.

Could that be her suggestion that she sees me as signing up to be a crusader? Because if so, I have to keep reiterating: no St. Joan action for me. At least as long as I have a choice.

There is nothing wrong with change and growing up. It's what's supposed to happen, right? But the reason I don't want to tell Mom about the dreams of change is that she might interpret it as a sign of something worrisome, even something tragic, that's about to happen.

And you know what? Deep down, I might be wondering the same thing.

We never really grow up,
we only learn how to act in public

(ATTRIBUTION UNKNOWN)

~

The double-edged sword of my 2% thinking is that you believe, even with the slimmest chances of something happening, that it could be possible—whether it's finding a miracle cure to a rare disease or being on an airplane that's destined to crash. So naturally, if you believe in both possibilities, miraculous or disastrous, you will invariably opt for situations that you can control.

No mystery there. For me, though, even with all the self-help that I've attempted over the years, I've never figured out why I'm not scared doing certain things that would terrify others who suffer from many of the garden-variety kinds of anxiety—say, public speaking or driving at high speeds. To throw a large conference and organize close to a week's worth of activities for the famous and traumatized alike would be overwhelming to some people. Not to me. That I can do in my sleep.

But the whole fear of travel and not having control of where a journey is taking me—ah, that has been an ongoing challenge. Big understatement there.

Back in those pretherapy days when I diagnosed myself with anxiety disorder, the claustrophobia part was obvious. As time went on, again, I also could see that some of the issues stemmed from agoraphobia. When I first went to the library to do some research about my symptoms and looked up the definition of agoraphobia and read that it meant "fear of the marketplace," I thought, fear of shopping? Not me!

Later, however, a therapist explained agoraphobia, and I could see the cocktail of circumstances that could start anxiety prickles in an instant for me probably came under that heading. At the height of my career as a makeup artist, when the location was far away or somewhere that I'd never been, I was usually okay as long as I drove. Otherwise, the thought of being stuck without a way home could bring on a full-blown anxiety attack. One of the few ways I found to calm myself down on such occasions—or, really, whenever life was especially challenging—was this exercise I developed as a way of that practice of reading my own success story. A pep talk, basically.

With this self-talk, I would sometimes imagine talking to someone inspirational, as if I'd already achieved great success or overcome a major obstacle. These Acting-as-if scenarios might involve seeing myself sitting down with Oprah on her TV show or introducing myself to Gloria Steinem—those two being among the most fearless and iconic women alive—and reporting how exciting everything was turning out.

Ironically, however, the anxiety issues seemed to become more pronounced the more confident, successful, and secure I became in general. Turns out that's common. And the treatment of choice for these issues, from the reading that I did, was therapy with medication.

Drugs were a no-go for me. (I know, I know, this from the Mom who offered medical marijuana to her teen.) For one thing, I'd seen what substance abuse did to relatives when I was growing up. For another, the mere thought of not having use of my full mental faculties only added to a state of anxiety. But in terms of therapy I was open to everything. One technique that seemed promising was doing mental dress rehearsals for situations that might trigger anxiety or panic.

The first time I attempted to fly after using this approach as preparation took place in my midtwenties. During my rehearsal I did feel a flare of anxiety while imagining the countdown to that moment when the cabin doors would close and it would be too late to flee. But the moment passed, and I made it safely and happily to my destination—that is, of course, in my imagination.

In reality, when I boarded the actual plane, I began to tremble the instant we were in the countdown before the announcement of the closing of the cabin doors. Naturally, I mean for me, all my systems had to be on alert for signs—you know, what happens if the Voice sends a negative warning or if there are other gut-check kinds of signs that the plane is going to go down—and then the door closes and I can't get out? Seeing no signs, I began to relax, but at the last minute, the ultimate sign came: the announcement that the flight was going to be late.

Now I knew with certainty that the plane was going to crash. But the door was already closed. I whispered hoarsely to the flight attendant, "I need to get off the plane. I'm not feeling well. I can't fly today."

She took my ticket, pointing at the baggage claim stapled to it, and said loudly, "I'm sorry, Miss, but your luggage has been loaded already. You have to fly with your luggage."

"Are you worried there's something in my luggage?"

Her face contorted and she shot an accusing finger at me. Like an inquisitor, she asked, "What made you say that? Is there something in your luggage?"

"No, no." I defended myself. "You were the one who brought it up!"

In moments flat, security guards were at my side and promptly escorted me off the plane and back to the airport. A bomb-squad had to check out my luggage, delaying the flight for four hours (during which everyone I knew was calling airport authorities to assure them that I wasn't a dangerous person) before I was allowed to go home.

After that, no matter how much I mentally rehearsed getting on an airplane, doing it was impossible. I was incurable. When Victoria Jackson Cosmetics began to boom, I had to come up with the most creative excuses under the sun to avoid out-of-town meetings. By the time we hit a million customers worldwide and the demands for me to travel built up, I ran out of excuses. Finally, when the infomercial marketing company decided to host a luncheon in my honor on the East Coast, I agreed to make the journey.

My close girlfriends like Kathleen Beller and Ali McGraw did all in their power to encourage me.

Kathleen, spending more and more of her time overseas with her British husband, Thomas Dolby, reminded me, "You're not the same fearful Victoria you used to be. You're a businesswoman and a mother and famous. You'll do fine."

Ali, always yogi-serene, gave me meditational secrets to make the trip go easier.

With so much love and encouragement, I opted to take a page out of my own playbook—the same one in which I would imagine that setbacks and challenges were merely a form of reading my own success story that I would report one day to Oprah. Never had my visualization been so strong when I imagined telling her, on the show, about how I overcame my fear of flying.

With every passing day as the departure date approached, I became more confident. A week out, I was joking to everyone about how I couldn't "wait to get on that airplane!"

Then, with only three days to go, I woke up from a horrific dream, gasping for air.

I think that in the dream there was a man with a ski mask.

All day long I wrestled with every worst-case scenario, wishing, hoping, praying for rescue. Nobody could win this for me. I had been fooling myself all along. In the end I put together a twenty-eight-minute video and apologized to everyone, especially my team in customer service who had been working for the company and helping in its success.

"We all have our demons and dragons," I confessed, "and I really wanted to be there with all of you. But I can't right now. I want each of you to know how much I appreciate all that you do and that I'm working so hard on this. And one day I know that I'll find a way to slay the dragon."

That wasn't totally true.

I wasn't going to slay any dragon if I couldn't get on an airplane. And that was just not going to happen. I had given up.

Then, somewhere in the early 1990s, right before Bill and I started dating, my office assistant handed me a message on a small pink square of paper that, according to the note, had come from a TV talk show producer.

Message slip in hand, I went to my desk, dialed the number, and started reviewing mail and other paperwork as the call went through.

"Oprah!" was what I thought the receptionist who answered my call had said. Yeah, right. I must have heard wrong. An audio mirage of some sort.

But no, when the producer came on the line, saying first, "Oh, thank you so much for calling back so fast," she went on to state that she was indeed the booker for Oprah Winfrey's TV show. Warm, energetic, and to the point, she pitched me a show Oprah was going to tape in two weeks about successful women entrepreneurs who "made it against the odds."

"That's wonderful," I interjected, not sure where this was headed. After all the years of imagining how I was going to be reading my success story to Oprah on her show, I didn't yet grasp that the opportunity to live out the reality of that dream was about to be handed to me in all of its 2% glory.

"We wanted to feature you and your story, along with a couple of other terrific women who have built companies from the ground up."

Oh my God. Unbelievable. Should I laugh, cry, pinch myself? I was speechless.

The producer continued, "So we think you would be perfect for our show," and then she started to review the logistics for flying me into Chicago for the taping. Before that date, a camera crew would possibly come to LA to shoot B-roll.

Wait a minute. Let me just rewind that. Had I just heard that I would have to get on an airplane and fly to Chicago to be able to go finally meet Oprah?

The instant I realized that she wasn't coming to me but that I would have to physically go there, the magical almost-dream-come-true evaporated.

The clock struck midnight and my carriage turned into a pumpkin and I had to scurry off that phone call as fast as humanly possible. Telling the producer that I would call back once I checked my schedule, I hung up in time to stave off a mini-panic attack in my office.

For the next twenty-four hours I entertained several extreme scenarios under which, somehow, some way, I could white-knuckle it and get to the Promised Land of Oprah. But in the end, I couldn't.

In later years, amazingly, I would find my path crossing Oprah's on several occasions. We have even sat across from each other over dinner at some memorable black-tie affairs. Never once did I mention my life's great disappointment of not being able to be on her show. Never once did I exchange more than passing greetings with her.

The Oprah disappointment taught me many lessons, not the least of which was the old adage that if you don't grab opportunities when they come along, they may never come again. Deep down, I also recognized that the survival switch that had been turned on during those early experiences, when my life was on the line, now needed to be flipped off.

But how? How to get past just surviving and learn to start living? Even if I wasn't ready to slay the dragon, I wanted to at least try to tame it. And then one day in the time of happily ever after I would join the rest of the fearful flying public. In the meantime I was convinced that there was some knowledge that I needed to find, some cure that always seemed to be out of reach—like looking for a needle in a sea of needles.

What I didn't know in those days was that there is not one AHA breakthrough moment that was going to fix me; instead, a series of moments and factors would all come into play.

And that's the point, that when in search of a Holy Grail for any cure, whether it's for anxiety disorder or a rare autoimmune disease, there are many pieces to the puzzle that have to be fit together, not necessarily in the way that you think they're supposed to fit.

You have to give up the need for control and take a leap of faith and even be willing to fly blind.

October 17, 2009

Sunday dinner back at home. No one says a word other than to comment on the tasty pasta. Ali, eating gluten-free rigatoni, nods somberly in agreement.

We've just returned from a weekend stay at the ranch in Carpinteria where we normally go for fun. Instead, the events of the weekend had mainly to do with saying a last good-bye to Scooby, Ali's beloved cat.

In hindsight, I'm wishing that the NMO doctors didn't so often use cats in their explanation of how autoimmunity works and how the myelin sheath around nerves becomes inflamed and develops hot spots. First it was Ali's main doc, Ben Greenberg, talking about the cats gnawing on the wires. Then it was our lead research advisor, UCLA's Dr. Michael Yeaman, who not long ago was praising the power and plasticity of the immune system when it has started to behave inappropriately, say, like a cat that loves to drink out of the sink in the kitchen.

"If you close the door to the kitchen," he pointed out, "the cat figures out how to drink from the sink in the bathroom."

That's what the immune system does when it figures out how not to be blocked by medications. By introducing an antibody—essentially what the "R" drug is—you redirect the immune system toward a solution. Theoretically, this presents the possibility for a miracle. But translating it to actual therapies that don't create other lasting problems, as far as we know now, still looms in the distant, uncertain future.

Scooby lived in Ali's room. For ten years, other than a few trips to the vet, he never stepped outside those four walls. Even when she left her door wide open, Scooby would cloister himself under the bed or in his ubiquitous pose, curled up underneath her arm chair.

That's where he was when Ali checked on him after dinner on the night of the thirteenth. She stroked him a few times and heard his familiar purr before diving into her books. When she started to get ready for bed and went to pick him up and move him to his blanket, he was dead.

There had been no sign, no clue, no breathing trouble. Nothing. The shock was so much for Ali that she didn't scream, didn't sob or cry out. Not at first. As the initial disbelief began to wear off, though, Ali started to weep, quietly at first and then loud enough for all of us to hear and come running.

None of us had any explanation for Scooby's sudden demise. We planned the funeral, and Ali agreed that burying him at the top of the hill at the meditation spot overlooking the ranch and the ocean beyond—underneath the watchful eye of a serene Buddha—was a final resting place fitting for the likes of the great feline Scooby Doo.

Later I was referred to a healer/psychic known for communicating with sick and deceased animals and was given an interesting explanation for what might have caused Scooby's death.

The psychic mentioned that in some cases in which certain animals like cats or dogs or horses or birds have been close to humans with serious illnesses, the relationship is so symbiotic that the animal takes on the worst of the symptoms and lifts the disease from their loved human counterpart. The idea seemed somewhat far-fetched, even to me.

Needless to say, I wouldn't have breathed a word of the pet psychic's theory to Ali. Strangely, though, as I watched Ali in the days following Scooby's death, she seemed different almost immediately. Maybe it was how stoic she was over the loss that she appeared stronger and oddly healthier than she had been in a long time.

We offered to take care of the arrangements for the funeral, but Ali wanted to be in charge. After selecting the two rough-edged river stones to mark Scooby's grave and the words to engrave on them and the meditation bench to place nearby, she asked that we lay him to rest in the middle of the cluster of native grasses and flowers planted at the high point of the ranch. Ali wanted "nothing fancy" for the stones themselves. One stone was engraved to say, "In memory of our beloved friend," and the other read, "Scooby, May 31, 2000–October 13, 2009."

On the meditation bench Ali asked for the following lines:

Gone yet not forgotten,
Although we are apart
Your spirit lives within me
Forever in my heart

Of course, all of that provides the melancholy subtext of dinner around the table after we return from the funeral. What can we say that hasn't been said?

Ali and I avoid conversation or eye contact, as though it's implied that we'll both lose it all over again. But deep, deep down, I do feel so strangely at peace. Not sure why. Could it be because Ali, far beyond her years, also has let go, accepting everything we can't control, especially everything that mothers and fathers can't control?

I'm wondering if the answer to that lies in the words of the note that sixteen-and-a-half-year-old Ali tearfully wrote and placed in Scooby's kitty coffin:

> I love you my dear my love my only child.
> —*Your Mom*

~

OCTOBER 25, 2009

Look, none of us growing up, living*, or working in the world of Victoria Jackson and Bill Guthy is any good at talking about the* PAST*. We are* NOW *oriented, for better and for worse. I mean,* NOW *is awesome for engaging in the moment and connecting to truth and beauty and music and winning the day and all that great stuff. It's awesome for taking the possibility/opportunity out of the* NOW *and allowing it to let us soar on wings into the future. But* NOW *can be a trap for those of us who don't want to think about anything awful, sad, or bad from the past. A trap of avoidance. I know that. And it's also a trap sometimes for any of us who sees the dark side of* NOW *and can't see anything that provides a pathway to the* FUTURE.

You want to know how I feel right now, twelve days after Scooby left us, right? I miss him, of course. I'll always miss him. Scooby will always be my boy in my heart, and nothing can take that away. But I do remember that after his burial, when it came time to leave the ranch and we drove down the hill, passing the now-familiar painted wooden sign that reads, "LEAVING PARADISE," that I felt more gratitude than sadness knowing that Scooby couldn't have asked for a better resting place. Whenever I start missing him, he'd be right there, and I could remember my past with him in every visit to the mountain, every sunset over the ocean, every sunrise over the avocado groves.

The thing I thought about that evening after the funeral was how inspired I was by my parents, who both started from very limited means and have created a paradise for family, friends, and medical pioneers out of a horse ranch and working farm.

Then in the days afterward I thought about the reality that there comes a time for all of us when we leave paradise and grow up, whatever our circumstances. So that's where I am NOW: *not oblivious to the* PAST *and grateful for the Scooby love that will stay with me and help me be ready, as much as anyone can be, for the* FUTURE.

~

November 1, 2009

With the Fall NMO Roundtable Conference and Patient Day a little over a week away, I am on the phone with doctors Michael Yeaman and Katja Van Herle, reviewing changes to the main sessions and order of events for the three-and-a-half-day Symposium, plus the growing list of attendees.

The reaction from the press and from the medical community at large has been incredible, Katja reports. She and the rest of the planning team are hearing the buzz from others in the research and nonprofit worlds.

Katja says, "No one has ever seen anything like it."

"How so?"

"Well, for starters, the sheer speed at which you've moved."

Michael concurs, reminding me that it was only in June of last year that Ali was diagnosed and that a month later, GJCF was a full-blown, bona fide foundation, preemie on wobbly legs though it was. Last year's Roundtable, it seems, was for everyone in the field of autoimmune research a kind of shot heard round the world, turning traditional funding models upside down. In the past, because research into diseases with the greatest numbers of diagnosed receive the most funding, the hope had always been that the results would reveal findings that might be applicable to the related rare diseases, even when they hadn't been specifically studied. Hand-me-down research doesn't always fit, however. Michael confirmed that by focusing on our "rare approach to a rare disease" and narrowing research into a frame of the actual mechanisms that cause, treat, and cure that disorder specifically, we're making discoveries that could potentially have applications for the diseases impacting larger populations and possibly the entire field of medicine.

Sounds dazzling. But then why can't I breathe?

Sure, we're moving more quickly than other foundations. True, we don't have mere wind beneath our wings; we have jet streams. (Or should I say Guthy-Renker corporate jet streams?)

And yes, I get that we have gone from horse-and-buggy to dune-buggy to moon-buggy in record-breaking time. But now it's time to turbocharge, which is what I say to Katja and Michael, who laugh in agreement.

"Can I say that in public?" I'm joking. My point is that I'm still looking for whatever it is that fires up the imagination of the researchers to recognize the ticking clock that is my daughter's life. Not to follow my hunches but theirs. Ultimately, a doctor needs to believe his or her opinion will lead to the treatment that will best serve the patient; in other words, that he or she is right and everyone else is wrong.

Or perhaps that's me and how I'm finding my wings as a Mom Expert who has been rifling through the literature for a year and a half, following sheer instinct as to what's relevant and what isn't. Around the clock. The difference being that I only have one patient, one daughter. I'm drawing on a lot of doctors' collective experience and a mother's gut. We don't have unlimited resources, and no dollar of funding should go to research that doesn't move us forward—or that is duplicative. That much is clear, as is making sure that everyone has to friggin' talk together and share what they know and have learned.

The other issue is making sense of whatever I decide in regard to my daughter's treatment, at least until she's of age, unless it's illegal or crazy or both—well, they really can't do much to stop me, and might not even try. That doesn't make the rejected treatments wrong or the purveyors of them bad physicians—just the opposite. They know that I'm the mom; I'm the one who will shoulder that burden. They know that the consequences of my decisions are on me, whether it turns out to be Mission Accomplished or Mission Impossible. They know they might not even be in the room when it all comes down.

In a year and half, when Ali turns eighteen, all that will change. Hopefully she'll have her own great hunches and will draw on some of my instincts and some of what I've come to understand about the immune system. Ali is the first to recognize the 95 percent art and 5 percent science balance in the search for a cure as well as why thinking creatively, exploring outside traditional frames, is necessary.

There has never been any second-guessing from our close advisors like Katja and Michael about why I need to read the fine print and teach myself the science. Does it occur to them that part of going on this journey to study the mechanisms is in order to believe that there will be a path out of the maze, to a place where Ali isn't sick anymore? Do they know that part of my compulsion for learning the language that they speak is not in spite of the fact that I never graduated from high school but because of it?

Michael has always believed in the path out of the maze. He comes to his expertise in immunology in a somewhat roundabout but still accelerated way. Originally from Roswell, New Mexico, where he was "dropped off rather than born" (according to his mother), Michael was a prodigy, starting the second grade at age four, going to college at thirteen, and completing undergrad studies at nineteen. He finished all of his doctoral courses and training by twenty-six, focusing on infectious diseases and then changing to immunology. He actually started college focusing on astrophysics. Or as he says, "I went from the telescope to the microscope." Almost unheard of, he became a full Professor of Medicine at

UCLA at the age of thirty-nine, on top of other major accomplishments in the field of music.

Something of a 2% résumé, I'd say.

Michael often speaks of the immune system as operating by a means of wireless communication, which is something I intuitively understand, and therefore he says not to dismiss my nonlinear problem-solving approach.

During our planning phone call, when I give recommendations for which docs should be on which panels, I have to add, "But what do I know?"

Michael answers, "That's something I've thought about, how one of the many impressive aspects about you is your intuition." He goes on to observe that this is an interesting reflection of the immune system because there are things that science doesn't fully understand and that only by having an intuitive grasp can that understanding be reached. "So you already know what medicine is just starting to realize."

Really? I put on my learning hat and ask him to explain.

"Well, you already realize that when the immune system 'sees' a microbe, it's not like it has a video camera that recognizes a big bacterium out there. Instead, we have evolved receptors—a system of microdetectors or scanners—and these detectors can sense patterns. All they look for is patterns. They can't tell where the microbe came from or why it's there, but they can say, 'Aha! I recognize that pattern and that pattern is associated with something bad so I'm going to activate a system of triggers that will turn on the immune response to that pattern.'"

"Right." So far, so good. I do understand the power of pattern recognition.

Katja interjects, "Exactly."

Michael continues, "And because one hundred million years have taught the immune system that the identified pattern is associated with a microbe and it shouldn't be there, the response is clear and strong." Pattern recognition by the immune system, he notes, is a beautiful and even miraculous phenomenon. Which brings us to a simple but powerful understanding: dysfunctions in pattern recognition can result in autoimmune diseases such as NMO.

A failure to communicate? Yeah, I did know that.

"The same wireless connections that enable our immune system to function correctly in terms of pattern recognition and communication, I think, are what you're drawing from, intuitively, in leading the research." Michael means this sincerely.

Katja chimes in, "And that's why we've been able to move as fast as we have."

Michael explains, "You and Ali have a similar kind of wireless connection between you in this undertaking. We could even make the analogy that there is a wireless connection—some inherent, ancient encoded DNA mediated understanding—between you, Ali, and everyone with NMO, and maybe with everyone else who has an autoimmune disease and then everyone else who is a mother who has a daughter who is ill." And so on.

If what he is telling me is possible, then maybe the animal psychic was right about Scooby. Of course, Ali wouldn't in a million years agree with the total nonscience of that. But maybe Scooby and Ali had a wireless connection and he needed to go so she could detach from him and use her detectors to focus on tuning into her other goals. Maybe Scooby's monastic dysfunction provides a clue to solving the mysteries of NMO.

I'm just saying.

~

NOVEMBER 7, 2009

The Saturday night before *all the events for the Fall Roundtable and Patient Day (a.k.a. the Symposium) starts out fine.*

Mom and Dad are hosting an elegant, tented fundraiser in the backyard for the LA County Museum of Art, and I've opted not to come down to do a social/meet and greet. Normally I would, but it's been a long week and there's no pressure to get the added attention—not my thing. So that's not a problem. Instead of partaking of the party food, Jackson and I both put in orders for Jerry's Deli.

At first, I'm in great spirits.

Why? Because I love Jerry's Deli! For me, it's comfort food. And it's a chilly night, ideal for savoring a hearty bowl of chicken soup and then finishing up homework before watching a little TV. Halfway through the meal, though, I'm starting to get horrifically nauseous. Bad food? Nope. Nausea is usually a telltale sign that the antibodies are wreaking havoc. Crap.

But now I don't want to tell Mom because she's got this huge event tonight and the big conference tomorrow. And once I start puking—God, it's so nasty with all that deli food coming up—I can't stop to tell anyone else. This goes on for close to an hour, and I am seriously unable to summon anyone. But my mother's worry radar—her Momdar—must be picking up on it because suddenly she's rushing into my room in her ball gown and heels, asking, "Oh gosh, honey, is everything okay?" and I'm trying to tell her what's going on.

Not necessary though. When I open my mouth to explain, an explosion of partially digested deli food comes out of my mouth like in The Exorcist. *And Mom has a gala going on in the backyard.*

"I'll be okay," I say finally, once the worst has passed.

"Don't worry, honey," she says and makes a joke about how she'd rather hang out with me than with all the hoity-toity art people. She's pushing it, but I appreciate the effort and give her a grateful smile. "No, I'm serious," she insists. "Carl has this one under control."

Carl Perkins is another magical member of the extended family who oversees and coordinates the intricacies of my parents' businesses and the details of travel and scheduling. In our Beverly Hillbilly days Carl arrived just in time to elevate our knowledge of etiquette and how to hob-nob while still staying normal. British born and bred, with dual degrees in hospitality and business management, Carl quickly became a sidekick to both Dad and Mom, something that often requires being in two places at once. He does do that. He has amazing taste and handles multiple details for all of us. After Nanny, he's one of the most knowledgeable people I've ever met. If he doesn't have the inside scoop on it, he'll find out. Kind of like having a British genie.

After almost an hour has gone by, I convince Mom that I'm feeling all better and she should return to the party. She agrees only because Dad will come up and check in on me.

That night definitely sucked for me. But I think being in Mom's shoes would suck even worse. Wouldn't trade with her if you paid me. And she would pay anyone if she could trade with me.

~

Hours before the doctors and medical investigators begin to convene in Los Angeles for their meetings, I'm on the phone talking to Ben Greenberg about a new challenge in fending off NMO attacks. It seems that just as the immune system can misread the appearance of patterns and overreact, there are certain symptoms Ali may experience that will look and feel like real attacks but won't be. Phantom tingling in her extremities, passing numbness, even pain. So how do we know without an MRI to confirm inflammation? We don't. We have to learn not to jump to conclusions.

Who, me? Not jump to conclusions and worst-case scenarios? Well yes, me, who managed to overcome a lifetime of anxiety-based thinking to tackle my fear of flying.

After Ali was born and we were expecting Jackson, I put that goal back on the front burner after having given up. But before I tried to get on an airplane, I took my first baby steps by doing family vacations in the car.

We started out with short distances and then eventually worked up to an adventure planned for the furthest destination yet: Jackson Hole, Wyoming. In my research, I had come across lodging that went by the name of Off the Beaten Track. The name wasn't reassuring, but the brochure described it as a real-life Ponderosa—a dream come true for a gal raised on watching *Bonanza*. We could hike, fish, commune with nature, and ride horses at nearby stables.

The Victoria Jackson–Bill Guthy family set off on our journey with great expectations. The Yukon was crammed with enough stuff to last us indefinitely in the case of some unknown calamity that would make it difficult to return home. No one complained. I notoriously never traveled light. As a matter of fact, I call myself the President of the Overpackers Club. My main concern was that ten-year-old Evan and three-year-old Ali had everything they needed to be entertained on the way there. Because I was pregnant, I brought along Raquel and Mimi, always part of the family, to help out.

By planning out as many of the details in advance, I found that my usual level of dread and discomfort was noticeably diminished. Not perfect, but so what? All in all, when we arrived just outside Jackson Hole city limits late in the evening, I felt victorious. (No pun intended.)

But when we pulled onto the road that led to Off the Beaten Path, our rented *Bonanza*-style ranch house, we discovered that it was literally off the beaten path. The road hadn't been paved, and the dirt we kicked up was thick dust, making visibility even tougher in the dark.

"Wow, this is rustic," I said. "Cool."

"Cool!" the kids echoed.

"It's rustic, alright," Bill remarked as we pulled up in front of a two-story shack-like lonely dwelling out in the middle of nowhere.

My bad! But we had made it this far, and there was no heading back, no trying to relocate in the middle of the night. That was a prescription for an anxiety attack.

We began to unpack and get everyone settled into the right quarters, with Bill good-naturedly doing most of the heavy lifting. At last, some three hours later, everything was put away and everybody either in their PJs or tucked into their beds. Bill went upstairs to hit the hay too. Twenty minutes later, when I hadn't come up to join him, he came down to the main room to find me pacing, trembling, unable to catch my breath.

"Aren't you coming up to bed?"

"We have to go."

He stood there and stared at me, dumbfounded. I didn't need to say that there was a dark and ominous energy in the house and that I couldn't be off the beaten path. Nor did I need to say that this had been a mistake, a terrible mistake.

Bill inhaled. He looked around as if wishing that he could confide in someone else, *Can you believe that we just took three days getting here and three hours unpacking the car and getting everyone settled and now she says we have to go home?*

"We need to get everyone up and just load up the car and go."

"Honey, let's get some sleep and we'll talk about it in the morning."

With that, he went to bed. I stayed up all night, in my own mixed-up logic to stand guard and protect my loved ones from the bad forces. Were the pregnancy hormones amplifying the anxiety? I didn't know. What I did know was that this was no freaking Ponderosa.

At seven the next morning Bill started loading the Yukon and, within an hour, we were out of there. By a stroke of good fortune, we were able to find a lovely home to rent in Park City at the Sundance Institute. We salvaged what was left of our vacation, painful though it was. Evan was probably the most disappointed about not getting to stay in Wyoming, and I felt bad for letting him down, for allowing my fear to cut short our adventure into the unknown.

As for Bill, he understood that when the fires of fear were raging, only I could put them out. His role, as he would later tell me, was just not to add more fuel to it once the fire had begun.

So the trip was a minor breakthrough for me, at least from the standpoint that we had been able to reroute and end up somewhere we hadn't planned on going. And I survived!

The next significant breakthrough came from the realization that I had been combating claustrophobia at its worst on an ongoing basis and, again, had lived to tell.

For years I'd been visiting prisons and working with women inmates, one of the heaviest yet most rewarding things I ever did. I'd started basically doing makeovers with the ladies in jail back in my late twenties and would continue up to my late forties. At the Sybil Brand women's correctional facilities in LA that I visited regularly, I had to take an elevator down several stories into the bowels of the earth and then be led down windowless corridors with gates that would lock behind me at every hallway.

For the extreme claustrophobe, yours truly, this ought to have been a descent straight into hell, but every time I did it, the anxiety became slightly more dulled. I'd joke with the assistant warden and ask, "Could we just leave this door open?" every time they'd get ready to lock us into the next hallway.

The incarcerated women could see that there was something wrong with me at first, and I'd tell them about my anxiety issues and how freaked out I was to be locked in. One of the gals once blurted out, "We know how you feel!"

The years of getting to know the ladies behind bars taught me to get to know myself differently and to think about what mattered in a new way. To them, makeup was war paint. I'd ask the gals things like, "What do you like your makeup to say?"

One woman said, "What do I want my makeup to say? I want it to say, 'Pull over.'"

We all laughed. But then we began to look at ways that makeup shouldn't be about attracting customers but should be a way to honor themselves as women. Less about "pull over" and more about stopping to think about who they were and what they were made of. After that, I was amazed by the courage they had to soften their makeup and show their natural beauty. If they could let go of old ideas, so could I.

As all of this was emboldening me to work up the guts to try flying again, there was something else that happened that added to the push. In 1995 the Pillowcase Rapist, who had finally been caught and locked up in the seventies, was let out on parole, despite warnings from a prison psychiatrist. I was terrified, thinking he would see me on TV and hunt me down. That was until August of 1996, when the news reported that he was in Gary, Indiana, where he had been beaten within an inch of his life after breaking into a woman's apartment and robbing her.

Whatever happened to him after that, I'm not sure. But some part of my psyche stopped having to stand guard all the time, always on alert. Some part of me decided that it was high time to stop being so afraid of being too far from my comfort zone.

On top of all of that, once the children were old enough to accompany Bill on some of his out-of-town trips on the company plane, I hated to think how much I was missing of their formative years. I hated to be AWOL from all those family snapshots of times they had enjoyed without me.

With the incentive of sharing memories with my kids, I found a powerful motivation. The thought of getting on a plane was no less paralyzing than it had been in the past. But then, in the summer of 2001, an opportunity came up that gave me even more of a reason to break my own ban on flying.

By this point I had licensed Victoria Jackson Cosmetics to a new distributor and had designed a brand new, exciting, sexy line of makeup, Lola, that was set to launch in October. Originally, I was supposed to break the line on the West Coast, but when Henri Bendel's proposed a significant purchase in return for having the launch in New York City, I could find no reason to say no.

Every day during the summer I vacillated. Was I going? Yes! Could I go? No! Then came 9/11. All of a sudden, fear of flying was a common affliction. We had taken so much for granted, all of us, for so many years. Now I wasn't alone in not being able to fly. But the launch of my line in New York City was still happening. I had to go. I had to get there. I had to fly through the fire.

What were the odds that I would be flying less than a month after 9/11 when everyone else was scared? Probably a lot less than 2%.

Bill and the kids began to encourage me to consider going on the company plane. I debated. If I was going to bolt, which was very likely, I didn't want to be around my family. And so, with Ann, a friend and therapist, at my side, I boarded a commercial flight to New York City, curled up in a fetal position—with my seat belt on—and stayed like that for the next five and a half hours. The thought of not missing another Oprah opportunity kept me battling the dragons. The image of my kids and Bill cheering for me helped me slay them.

At the other end, the family was there at the airport, waiting with open arms. After the festivities in connection to the launch, I flew home with them. No, I didn't love flying and would continue to have some major anxiety in connection with being out of my comfort zone in the future. But between a few more commercial flights and the ease and security of the company plane, I was liberated.

~

NOVEMBER 11, 2009

The day after my GI upset *during my parents' big soiree, I felt fine and, after an MRI showed no new lesions, I didn't need to have an infusion. By Wednesday I was able to attend Patient Day and witness firsthand how extensive the scope of the Symposium was. Amazing!*

I have to add that when I had first come up with the idea for Patient Day, I had no idea what I was getting myself into—and that's putting it lightly. For one thing, I had to get special permission to miss tennis practice, which was no small feat because we were never allowed to miss practice before a match.

Experiencing a mixed sensation of excitement and anxiety, I made my way toward the large conference room. Outside at check-in tables were both of my beautiful grandmothers. They joked about not needing to see any ID as they waved me on, saying the program was getting ready to begin. My first thought when I walked into the room was OH. MY. GOD. AM I THE ONLY ONE NOT IN A WHEELCHAIR?

My heart immediately sank as all the hope and promise I had been accumulating since my diagnosis vanished in an instant. I have never felt so idiotic. I realized in that moment that I didn't know a thing about this disease. I had no idea what these other patients were going through or what I could do to help.

Nothing had ever made me feel so completely helpless to others. Was there any way to rescue me from drowning in my own ignorance? I faked a weak smile and sat down to listen to my mom's opening speech. I am always amazed when I watch her take the stand. She strides to the podium so gracefully, situating herself and taking her stance with so much poise and confidence, like she's truly in her natural habitat. She opens her mouth, and words flutter out, each one grabbing the audience's rapt attention with their honest potency and heartfelt sentiments. And she's so heartfelt in her grace, with not a word of her remarks scripted. It honestly stuns me.

That day was full of lightning strikes and thunder claps. As if the wheelchairs weren't enough, there was my mother, standing in front of everyone like some speech-giving goddess, and me, sitting there, looking clueless as ever. And to make matters worse, people kept greeting me throughout the event, shaking my hand and commenting on how "inspirational" I was.

My reaction: INSPIRATIONAL?!? HOW ON EARTH AM I INSPIRATIONAL? IT'S MY MOM WHO DOES EVERYTHING! SHE'S THE ONE WHO BROUGHT US ALL TOGETHER AND IS MAKING A REAL DIFFERENCE IN THE WORLD.

Two things happened at that Patient Day that continued with the doctors going up to the stage and forming a panel to answer the questions of patients and family members. The main thing that happened was that my eyes were opened, and I was given a tremendous wake-up call.

Let me take that a step further. That day was my call to duty. Watching my mom speak motivated me to become more involved with the foundation and really embrace my condition, whereas all the comments of my "inspirational" spirit really encouraged me to live up to that title. No Joan of Arc heroics, I promise. The point was that I could still walk and see and do all the things I love. So why should I do anything less than put all those abilities toward helping those who've lost them to the very disease I'm fighting against?

Before this, I had never met any other NMO patients before, with a couple exceptions, and in those cases I had been reluctant to talk to them. But that day began a dialogue with like-affected patients, a bond that inspired me to enter the NMO world more forcefully.

As shocked as I was seeing and experiencing everything I did that first day, I still managed to maintain a calm and understanding expression. I could not control myself, however, when at one point during the question-and-answer panel, one of the patients stood up and began to ask Dr. Ben Greenberg a question about life insurance and how her insurance would cover potential treatment plans. Dr. Greenberg had been advocating as to how patients should join the blood repository so they can be included in future research studies and treatment tests that could possibly cure NMO. The patient asking the question broke down crying in the process, asking if her insurance would pay if she were to die during such potential treatment. That struck a lasting chord with me.

And that was the second thing that changed about me after my visit to Patient Day. For the first time I grasped what "potentially fatal" meant.

Up until then, the idea of dying—or death in general—had seemed a very foreign concept. It doesn't seem real. Even with the death of Scooby at the time, even with writing about it now, dying just doesn't seem real. Realistically, I can say with confidence that at this writing the chances of me dying tomorrow from NMO is probably just as likely as being struck by a proverbial bolt of lightning.

That's what I believe. And yet to hear this woman stand up and ask such a direct question about her death, as if it was imminent, as if she had no chance of surviving NMO, took me by surprise. I had never thought of dying from NMO until she went and said that.

In that moment, as I sat next to my mom, I instinctively looked at her. Whether she knew why I did, I'm not sure, except that she gave me a reassuring, loving glance. The moment of grasping the reality of death that could happen, likely or not, passed, and we continued listening to other questions. Shortly after that comment I got up to leave to head back, just in time for the last hour of tennis practice. Or maybe that was just me making an excuse to get out of there.

Needless to say, I don't like unhappy topics, and I think death is just about the most unhappy you can get! So bottom line, I wanted to get as far away from that place and that question asked by that woman as humanly possible. Oh, but that was foolish because fear and unhappy topics like death can't always be outrun or outmaneuvered, even by a fast-footed girl like me.

6

The Meaning of Fire

The general function of dreams is to try to restore our psychological balance by producing dream material that re-establishes, in a subtle way, the total psychic equilibrium.

—Carl Jung

NOVEMBER 12, 2009

So you know the whole worry gene *that some say is a mom thing in general, but that my mother has had pretty much in excess for most of her life? Turns out that I do my own share of worrying.*

Crap, it's true. I got the worry gene!

Not the "Oh my God, something bad is going to happen to me!" kind of worry. Not the Voice that messes with your head when it comes from fear. Even during my worst attacks—the last of which was back in August—I'm not worrying about me. I'm just going into my own survival mode. Oooh, that August attack was bad. The pain was at about an eight. Mom was trying to get me to eat a pot brownie! I was crying and throwing up, and the nurse hit me too hard with the needle, so blood spurted everywhere.

In the middle of all that, a next-door neighbor at the beach in Carp wanted to come over to say good-bye—she was leaving for college—and I couldn't see her, couldn't do anything but write her a farewell e-mail, not even going into the health issue. But I'm not going to worry about how that makes me look or sit there and let anyone play the worry violin and make the music be about how horrible the attack is or how awful the next one is going to be.

My worry? I'm worried about Mom, Dad, Nanny, Evan, and I really hate to say this, Jackson. And can we please, for the moment, for this discussion, take NMO out of the equation?

I worry that my amazing mother who has done everything to take care of every single one of us—not just covering her bases but everyone else's on the field and in the stands and, if she could, for everyone in the whole world—is not taking care of herself.

Look, I'm no shrink (though I might become one, you never know), but I think Mom needs to have an outlet, like we all have, that lets her just chill at least for an hour or two every day. That must sound lofty coming from me because I'm almost always on the go, but I find a kind of serenity in having a physical outlet that lets my brain be quiet or at least focus on something that is not earth shattering.

I mean, she barely sleeps, and when she's awake, she's like in the Special Forces of Momdom. On the job 24/7.

One thing I worry about a lot is that my parents have been in crisis mode for almost two years and aren't taking time for each other—for the marriage. I suppose that I wouldn't worry so much about that if I hadn't gone to Patient Day and observed the toll on parents and marriages taken by dealing with all the constant uncertainty of NMO. It's normal, it happens. But still, much as I hate to emphasize this fact, you have to talk about it.

Mom would probably agree. Except who does she seek out to discuss her issues with?

A psychic!

Now you know why I worry.

~

In the early days of Ali's diagnosis I stopped reading the stories of mothers who had children stricken with life-threatening diseases and stepped in to become a mom on a mission. Mainly because in most of the stories the children died and that was too unbearable to think about, and partly because of how many of their marriages suffered under the weight of trying to save their children.

Bill and I had never been skilled at finding an emotional meeting ground.

When he went through his cancer, he held fast to his private way of coping. Quiet, introspective. Then with Ali, he's stayed on his same stoic path, not allowing himself to veer from it and not allowing me to force him to veer from it.

Even attending the Symposium had been difficult for Bill. Not because he doesn't care but because he cares so much that it pains him beyond his own ability to mask those emotions. I understand. He understands that I have enough emotion for the two of us—and then some.

But still, especially lately in the sleepless midnights, I've started to get so lonely. After weeks of waking him up every time I turned on the light to read, every time I got up to go walk outside, I started crashing out in the guest room just to give him space.

At any other point in time the idea of sleeping in separate bedrooms would have freaked me out. But it's not like we're fighting or mad at each other. We're not splitting up or anywhere near that point. It's not for lack of love. It's just a crazy time. All bets are off. Our marriage is unsteady from having the rug, the floor, the ground, pulled out from under us. But we will find our way. We always do.

We're just getting by as best we can, whatever that means.

And it's going to get crazier.

Tomorrow's a big match against one of Buckley's rivals, Arlington, and I want to hear Ali's strategy. She's more brilliant, funny, and gorgeous than ever. In the past few days, I swear, my daughter has grown a couple inches. She's statuesque with those slender, long, athletic legs of hers, deceptively powerful, just like the horses she loves to ride.

Lately she's been moody too. Could be hormonal. It's the no-worry worry she's trying to keep at bay.

Since the Symposium Ali's started working on her first piece as editor of the *Spectrum*. And she's been in touch by e-mail with some newly diagnosed patients, many from other countries, just letting them know that she's doing well and answering all kinds of questions. All of this on her own.

~

NOVEMBER 25, 2009

Ever since I became a member *of the Girls Varsity Tennis team at Buckley, I've had an image that has driven and inspired me: a massive white CIF banner that we would win in finals and bring home to hang in our gym as our team's legacy.*

Every time I went to the gym for a rally or gathering or meeting with our athletic director, I'd look up at exactly the place on the wall where it would hang. Even when I wasn't in the gym, I could close my eyes and visualize the banner in all its future glory.

That image was never so strong in my mind as it was when we prepared to face Arlington, our nemesis from the previous year, on November 19, for the CIF semifinals round. This was our second year making it into the CIF semifinals, and everyone was fired up and determined to win the match and move onto finals as payback for the previous year's loss. We knew in preparing for the mental strategy we would need to employ that Arlington was a very good team. But their fans were terrible! Known for yelling, screaming, and making really nasty comments at pivotal moments in a game, their fans could easily become that X-factor in harming our confidence and tenacity.

Because we would be facing them on their home courts, we just assumed we'd be confronting more of the same this year. So to prepare, during our practices leading up to the match, we set up a drill in which we would all yell and scream right before our player on the court was going to serve or return a ball. Simulation! Actually you might even compare this to tolerization in medical research terms.

The point is that we wanted to get used to what it was going to be like so the fans wouldn't throw us.

Compared to our loss the year before that left us with a score of 10 sets to 8 sets, we battled, hung in there, and managed to tie in sets, 9–9. In such cases of a tie, the winner is determined by what's called "counting games." The tally was 80–73 Buckley. We won! We won against Arlington in the semifinal match and were vindicated!

We were one match away from the glorious CIF championship. This was the furthest the Griffins had ever gone in the history of Girls Varsity Tennis at Buckley. Now, on Monday, November 23, at 1 p.m. at the Claremont Club, we would play Viewpoint. The Viewpoint players were mentally tough. We had never beaten them before, although our match had been close earlier in the regular seasons.

Coming off the win in the semifinal round, we weren't lacking in focus or the desire to win. Right before the match, Coach Sherman reminded us of the card she had given to each player at the start of the postseason that read, "Success is determined by how determined you are to succeed."

We hit the courts and all played our hearts out. Unlike the Arlington team who assumed they could intimidate us, Viewpoint took us as a serious threat and played with respect for our abilities. Their confidence came from being exceptional players. As much as I tried, I couldn't be mad at them for their talent.

In the end, we fell short and lost to Viewpoint 8–10.

A loss like that is such a killer, especially when we came so close. But we were CIF finalists, after all. And we had another season to start thinking about. The rivalry with Viewpoint pushed me and the rest of my team to do better, and this would be a meaningful factor in our future contests.

My stats for the season were pretty great too, all things considered. Compared to sophomore year, when I had to miss twenty games or more due to attacks, I had only missed a handful of games this year. My overall individual record was 48–7. And of those games, my CIF individual record was 14–1. The season also brought me the award of Number One Inspirational player for Buckley. Not too shabby.

As soon as the celebration started to simmer down, though, I caught myself thinking back to Patient Day and the memory of a fellow patient talking about her mortality. In my waking hours I wouldn't allow unhappy thoughts to cross my mind without being controlled. But because dreams are in a realm beyond the mental capacity to control them, that was the only place my fears could sneak in.

I remember the time period leading into 2010 as a time when my dreams took a dark and fearful turn. They had come on suddenly, not unlike the earlier dreams about going on a journey and the dreams of fire. If I was going to understand any of them and what they were trying to say to me, I supposed that the place to start was back in the past where the fire dreams began.

Ugh, the past—my least favorite place to visit.

~

At some point it occurs to me why I prefer a psychic to a shrink when it comes to dealing with the obvious. Because therapy is work! A therapist would probably also say I needed to work on myself.

Really? And I pay money to hear what I already have read in a self-help book. Besides, all work and no play makes Victoria a dull girl. And psychics are entertaining. And that's one more reason why I like a good psychic and why I've scheduled a visit with one.

As I head to her office in Beverly Hills, I am humming for no damn reason.

Bev Hills are alive . . . with the sound of psychics! With songs they have sung for a thousand years.

Sometimes when you're tired, depressed, raging, feeling like a bitch and menopausal, you have to laugh and be foolish.

"Deal with the stress because if you don't, you can't breathe. You must have celery juice every day! A big glass. . . . You've been taking everything on your small shoulders—this is huge what you've been carrying. Your husband has his own worries. He loves you, honest to God. He's looking up to you, he knows what you're doing, he knows how stressed you are.

When your daughter gets balance in her health—and I believe that will be soon, I'm not just saying it!—you and your husband should take a vacation and be alone. Trust that, do that, and don't forget the celery juice. You can do this."

How could she be sure?

Because, I have to admit, ours is somewhat of a common story. Because every marriage goes through some version of being tested, though with different results after the exams come in. But in the end, because we're both fighters and will never give up on the other.

~

So I do some research.

Google is no longer my enemy. But still, this isn't like me. Anyway, I look up what dreams of fire are supposed to mean. Turns out there are multiple meanings. Naturally.

Fire is about destruction and transformation. It's about purification and cleansing. Fire can inflict pain and be used to light the way to truth. Whenever you dream about fire, all the websites say, it's a very powerful sign. But it's also very ambivalent as to what it's trying to say powerfully.

Okay then. Fire can mean that a person's emotions are getting out of control and they're a hothead. Nah, I don't really relate.

Carl Jung believed that a mystical interpretation of fire in dreams was a reflection of a psychological transformation. One website noted that fire was what alchemists used to turn lesser metals into gold. Dreaming of fire could mean taking on magical properties. I kind of like that. Maybe my dreams of fire were about coming into my own.

Well, one of the books we have in our den, a dictionary of dreams, says whenever you dream of a house it always represents the self. Dreaming of a house that's on fire means that you have to go through some kind of major change. Recurring dreams of a fire consuming your family's house is supposed to imply that you are resistant to change. Another interpretation is that you are surrounded by love and the passionate support of others. When you dream about escaping a house on fire, the message is that you will eventually overcome difficult obstacles. Makes sense.

One other book I find says that fire in a dream is about a spiritual need to awaken self-knowledge. And then just before closing the book, I see an explanation of a house on fire as meaning, "an actual body fever."

Oh no. No! Could my dreams of fire have been predicting an actual body fever? Was my psyche registering the inflammation in my optic nerve and spinal cord? Is the meaning of fire just a movie trailer for NMO?

I don't like the idea of dreams being capable of telling the future. Too depressing, for one thing.

And for another? WAY too woo-woo.

~

After I arrive back home from the psychic, a new juicer in hand, along with bags of fresh produce—lots of celery—I'm in the kitchen when almost-fourteen–year-old Jackson makes an excited entrance. He wants me to come right away and hear the new song he's written. I do, and it's amazing.

Jackson has this weird genius for music. From the time he was six or seven he's been writing melodies and lyrics, accompanying himself on the piano. He's completely self-taught. I've seen visitors to the house politely beg him to play just to get it over with because they've heard the mom—me—raving about him just like moms rave about their little geniuses.

By the time he was done, their mouths are hanging open. They just can't believe what they've heard and seen.

But Jackson can be a challenge. His mind and body move too fast. He's a truth-teller, though it gets him into trouble. There's no inner censor there. With Jackson, it's the whole truth and nothing but, and he doesn't realize how wounding that can be. I think that comes with the territory of a fourteen-year-old kid who composes soulful eight-minute ballads about love and loss way beyond his years.

He wants to record, go on tour, get out and develop an audience beyond the local gigs he's been playing. For an off-the-charts creative kid, he's also got marketing chops. Bill and I have tried to keep him on the local level, wanting him to have as much normalcy in his development as can be possible for a child growing up in our not-so-normal world. If he keeps up his grades, and if it really is his calling, we've said that he can go into the studio when he's fifteen.

A family friend thought it would be great for Jackson to meet the team at Disney and set this up for him. All the top executives were there, meeting with Jackson, who just took it all in stride. Secretly, I was relieved, although he could turn around and surprise me any time, as he always does. Sometimes if we have guests, he'll pretend he's a butler and serve a perfect dinner, pouring the wine like a sommelier, with a little towel draped over his arm—he won't break character once. He's irresistibly incorrigible.

We're in the middle of Ali's junior year, and still, only one friend knows what's up. She had a close call a few days before I went to the psychic. Ali was sitting in one of her first classes of the day and started to get super nauseous, with that aura, as she describes it, descending over her in a bad cloud.

"It's like having one of those nightmares where you're out in public and you have no clothes on," explained Ali, who has made some references lately to worrisome dreams. Not knowing what to do, she asked her teacher if she could be excused so she could go to the girl's room. There, she vomited for twenty minutes then went to the vice principal's office and called us.

Otherwise, she hasn't had a severe attack for a while, which is starting to be something of a pattern of showing up with less frequency. But this one required a call to the nurse and an IV infusion. Before we went upstairs to get the IV pole ready, Ali quipped, "Hey, Mom! Isn't it great?" Laced in irony.

"What, babe?" Served with tenderness.

"Jackson gets to be the rock star, and I get the fatal rare orphan disease."

This is our reality.

March 19, 2010, The Guthy-Jackson Charitable Foundation Research Summit at the Ranch in Carpinteria

Early on the day of the scheduled arrival of eighteen globally renowned medical investigators and advisors at the first Summit up at our mountaintop ranch, I'm huddling with the troops, namely Dr. Katja Van Herle and Jacinta Behne, whose expertise comes from her years of working with NASA, running programs focused in public outreach and education that required collaboration with laboratory researchers, engineers, and public information experts. Jacinta and our administrative team coordinate every organizational aspect of the work of the foundation, including a NASA-like schedule for making sure events run like clockwork, even with many moving pieces.

Because the schedule during the Symposium conference in the fall is usually oriented more toward reporting results, public education, and interaction with patients, little time is left over for the kind of intense collaboration that our researchers and advisors will hopefully achieve over the next three days. Along the way we'll break from science and enjoy great food and wine at the appropriate times—also important for exchanging potentially life-saving ideas. This is my version of lighting a bonfire and having everyone gather round, sing Kumbaya, or whatever world-leading scientists and healers sing before they go into disease-curing battle. And I feed them lots of guacamole.

Before the whole group arrives, I have a chance to catch up with one of our original Knights of the Round Table, Dr. Lawrence Steinman of Stanford University. I'd met Larry back when I was just starting to think about forming the foundation. The universe definitely appeared to be working in my favor that day when it brought him into my world. While talking to a friend about not knowing how to fund research that could fast-track a cure, she brought up the name Dr. Larry Steinman as a leading light in MS research. Coincidentally, he happens to have a home in Beverly Hills just up the street from our house—where he stays when he's not at Stanford.

From our very first phone conversation, Larry was immediately enthusiastic and helpful. After visiting him at Stanford, I felt as if I had hit the multidisciplinary genius jackpot in Dr. Steinman. Besides being an internationally revered clinician/researcher in autoimmune diseases, he is a professor of neurology and neurological sciences, pediatrics, and genetics. (At Stanford he served as Chair of the University Program in Immunology from 2002 to 2011.) Included among his numerous achievements in the lab are two therapies being used in the treatment of MS and type 1 diabetes. His research had also led to a breakthrough development of a drug being used to treat patients with MS and Crohn's disease.

Like many of the Knights who came aboard in the early stages of the foundation, Larry was excited to join forces with others—foremost names in a handful of different medical disciplines—who were already lining up as advisors and investigators. At the time he told me that he had a feeling this was going to be a high-quality exploration. Later he would say it became that and more.

With the Summit getting ready to start, Dr. Steinman says, "It's already the most amazing scientific adventure I have ever seen."

I remember how patient he was at our first meeting in getting me up to speed on the basic science of NMO. He began with what he called, "The immune system in one minute."

For a mom on a mission, a minute was perfect.

"You have heard of an antibody. Antibody is made from B cells—if I get a vaccination for the flu and then I become infected, the vaccine has already instructed my immune system to quickly make antibodies to neutralize the flu—and thereby prevent or lessen severity of infection. B cells make antibodies and dysfunctional B cells in NMO make antibodies against one water channel, a particular version called aquaporin-4."

Right, that much I knew: AQP-4, to us water channel/protein molecule insiders.

He reminded me that medicine didn't know about water channels until some years back when Peter Agre had discovered them and won a Nobel prize for it. "It would have been difficult to know what the target of the disease was until we knew what that molecule was," Dr. Steinman explained. So the B cells, he continued, make the antibody. But the T cells play a role. "The T cells are fine tuners, T for tuning. T also stands for thymus, the gland below the breastbone above the heart where these cells are developed and educated." So as the explanation went on, I learned that the T cells communicate with the B cells and tell them when and when not to make antibodies. In an autoimmune disease the process is deregulated: the T cell is giving the wrong signal, and the B cell is making antibodies against the wrong entity.

And then Dr. Steinman identified another player in NMO called the granulocyte, one of the more primitive parts of the immune system, and it's there basically to fight off bacteria. "But lo and behold," he said, "you see granulocytes at the site of disease, and they evolve to fight bacteria like a Sherman tank filled with explosives and projectiles. What happens with NMO is the granulocyte closes up without a bacteria to fight and you get what I call a 'sterile explosion': nothing happens. If you have a strep throat, you want your granulocytes to invade your throat where these bacteria grow—as in, you got a sore throat and you fight the infection off."

The question in NMO that can lead to significant answers, then, is what happens when granulocytes explode in your spinal cord or in your optic nerve? He explained that the T cell sends a signal to the granulocytes that there is another invader filled with vicious weaponry. The granulocytes explode when they are not supposed to be doing that; T cells are orchestrating this. The result is this inner battle that agitates and inflames, I assumed, leading to the destruction of the myelin.

As a fellow parent and as the head of pediatric neurology at Stanford, Larry spoke to me on an emotional level too. In his experience as a clinician, he had recognized NMO early in his practice as one of the most alarming and terrible of the many diseases that are similar but distinct from MS.

The majority of his patients with NMO were children and young adults. He told me frankly that over the years he had witnessed how devastating the course of the disease could be and how much more aggressive it is than MS.

One of the reasons that he was excited about an accelerated approach was because he had seen how it can manifest so disastrously. His description of the spectrum disorder was "Absolutely tragic." But the urgency of a mother battling bomb-exploding granulocytes for the life of her daughter, he believed, was exactly the boost in the unraveling that the mystery needed. After hearing that, I needed a friggin' drink! And I knew it would be a while before I would sleep again.

As we moved forward once the foundation was up and running, Larry was incredibly receptive to any and all of my ideas and questions. One in particular that kept me up at night was what the long-term impact of the treatments were going to be that we had found to be effective for intervening in and even preventing attacks. This was an issue for many of the autoimmune-related diseases that are treated effectively with life-saving drugs that also can have really vicious side effects.

Larry had similar concerns, as did all the docs, that giving an adolescent steroids on an ongoing basis could raise other complications, especially because the suppression can affect so many aspects of their developing physiology. Aside from steroids, the more powerful drugs meant for cancer or those used in transplant rejection therapy also come with other sets of problems.

So I asked—my throat closing, tears starting—would we always be looking at choosing the lesser of two evils?

"It's a terrible dilemma that can't be ignored. We need better drugs." He was able to make that statement with less fear and emotion than maybe I was feeling, he said, because (a) he didn't have a child as a patient and (b) he and fellow doctors were actively in search of new, better, less destructive drugs.

Could he really be hopeful we'd get there soon?

"If we didn't have hope we could fight NMO and find life-saving treatments that didn't come at such a huge cost, that I or somebody in the field couldn't solve the condition, then I don't know what we would do." He paused and then added, "What I would do is I would maybe choose another field."

That was the kind of emotional support and energy he brought to our cause, helping me navigate through the maze of doctors, researchers, institutions, and studies to determine what was the best way of advancing toward a cure. His brand of science-based hope had frequently been the remedy that I'd really needed at my lowest points.

After the November 2010 Symposium Larry and I had a debriefing in which he said, "You know, in the forty years I've been doing research, I've never seen a foundation or a government organization as well organized as GJCF." Echoing what doctors Katja Van Herle and Michael Yeaman had been saying about the speed at which we were moving, he went on to put a spotlight on what it was that we were doing, as he suggested, to create a new model for medical/scientific collaboration.

Obviously, our willingness to invest a significant amount of money as incentive for that collaboration had been meaningful, as had the recognition that in order to produce better treatments and cure the disease, we have to understand it better. He pointed out, "You've set a strong precedent of not being in business to be giving out money as an entitlement to laboratories. You've let our investigators know that you want the labs to do highly focused research that will elucidate the basis for the disease and the basis for findings to get a cure."

Larry went so far as to say that the platform we had created could be used for type 1 diabetes and even much more prevalent diseases. He pointed out how far we had come on relatively little resources compared to the billions and billions of dollars being spent by the National Institutes of Health (NIH). I wondered how much they could achieve if they would institute some of the operating procedures in place for the foundation.

The credit for those procedures went in part to being able to learn from what hadn't worked with other nonprofits seeking to fund a cure for a variety of issues. True, we had also put a great amount of thought into spreading our net wide while still keeping the scale from becoming too large. The other balance we struck, Dr. Steinman reminded me, was by having the most extensive network of experts who act as the reviewers, judges, and critics of the requests from potential grant recipients. The rule we set was that if you are a judge, you don't get to receive a grant; if you are a grantee, you don't get to judge. We also require that our grantees don't go longer than four months without a site visit from our experts or without presenting progress reports for the purpose of collaboration at the fall Symposium or the March Summit. Our advisory team is also available to provide answers and guidance 24/7.

So here we are at the ranch, hopeful and eager as we await the arrival of many of the same investigators who we saw five months ago along with some new promising additions. Because we are so selective with our recipients, we can afford to appropriate higher amounts of money than competing funders might. Money matters, no doubt, to make the investment of brain power worthwhile to the researchers. Also, the timing is such that as government funding decreases, everyone in academia has to look for other sources to finance research. But just as important as funding, Larry reminds me, is that NMO—and Ali for that matter—make a very compelling, inspirational scientific problem for the doctor as a medical scientist to say, "I'm going to devote a certain amount of time and resources to try to help solve it."

He goes on to remark that although there have been many moms and dads on missions, few of their efforts have involved their child who is also a patient as an advocate. Ali gives hope to all the docs not only for us but also for all their patients. One more thing that Larry says is making a big difference is that Bill and I have embraced the Knights as part of our family. Where Bill might have more logistical questions, I can ask the gut-check questions of how is this going to cure Ali or improve our current treatment. Larry is flattering in saying he's not sure how someone like me, without medical training (forgetting the high school dropout piece) can grasp the science very quickly. "And you can then come up with amazing insightful criticisms and questions."

All thanks to Fake It Till You Make It, I actually do know some of the science now. Larry says that though some dazzling minds can fool medical panels, nobody can fool me.

Yep, the Voice does serve a purpose in helping me cut through fancy talk, and this is moving the ball forward. And some of my marketing background has come in handy. Just as I had to earn the trust of the investors in the infomercial field to believe in never-been-tried ideas, I have to convince the scientists to go into the garages in their brains and tinker madly on untested theories.

In fact, midway through the Summit, late after our dinner, I turn to Dr. Alan Verkman, the brilliant professor of medicine and physiology from the University of California, San Francisco, and ask him, "If you were to stay up all night, or like for a couple nights, you could solve this, couldn't you?"

Maybe he was my guy because he looks a little like a darker-haired, younger, hipper, handsomer Albert Einstein, so I pegged him for having big theories up his sleeve. He did not look at me like I was crazy. Instead, he smiled and shrugged. I couldn't wait to find out what was going to come next in his work.

The other side of the collaboration is that we often ask our experts to take money out of the equation in dreaming to the limits of their imagination. If we were going to develop a brochure for global distribution, say, that focused on educating physicians and specialists about the difference between MS and NMO, we might ask our Knights how many offices or waiting rooms they could imagine using our brochure. Dr. Brian Weinshenker and the team from the Mayo had been among the first to suggest that the misdiagnosis of NMO as MS was much more widespread than current statistics showed. Many of the patients who attended our first Patient Day had originally been diagnosed with MS.

In March 2010 that awareness was already changing our original high estimate of twenty thousand people in the world with NMO. The guess at the time, picking the biggest number possible, was that as many as thirty-five thousand people worldwide had NMO. So we came up with thirty-five thousand as a target for how many brochures we hoped to distribute.

As we discussed at the Summit, educating the public about the differences between MS and NMO in terms of language and specifics would prove to be difficult because both encompass a spectrum of symptoms, meaning that for most of the rules there are going to be some exceptions. We know, for example, that a positive test for the presence of the NMO-IgG antibody rules out MS. However, not all patients with NMO have the antibody present. For those patients NMO is diagnosed by the MRI of the spinal cord that typically shows long, thin lesions different from the lesions that show up in MRIs of MS patients. But not always. In fact, current imaging technology may not pick up on the lesions of NMO patients and thus allow them to go undiagnosed and untreated.

There was never any controversy over the cruel nature of NMO. One of the docs called it the "crazy cousin" of the autoimmune diseases because, unlike multiple sclerosis and many other afflictions in which myelin is destroyed, NMO isn't considered to be progressive—you can't really track it, predict it, or hold up precedents for it to follow.

You'll never hear a doctor say, "This type of NMO is manageable," or "This is the bad kind of NMO." You'll hear about "milder" forms of lupus or MS, or a certain autoimmune diagnosis that's less deadly than another, but they don't talk about NMO that way. They don't talk about NMO being in remission either.

Some other differences of note are that NMO affects only the optic nerves and spinal cord, whereas MS affects the brain as well. Attacks of NMO tend to be more frequent and severe than in MS, though this is not always the case. With NMO/Devic's, the brain MRI is usually normal, but there are exceptions. In contrast, with MS, the MRI of the brain typically shows many areas of inflammation. Even though our researchers were at the Summit to compare or develop studies of how to prevent or stop attacks, a few recounted patient stories involving the most dangerous and sometimes fatal threat for NMO sufferers—when severe damage occurs that can lead to the inability to breathe on one's own.

At that point I time traveled right back to the Mayo, back to being stuck in the snow globe, and in real time got up to leave the room, tried to breathe, and checked on how preparations were coming along for our last day's lunch. By the time I returned I heard hopeful accounts of patients whose treatment had stabilized their condition and who seemed be doing well over long periods without attacks.

And finally, this is why Bill and I want to expand the breadth of research we'd been doing up until now: because there weren't many studies of NMO in large enough populations, predicting the outcome of cases with any degree of certainty was impossible. Yet another reason our Connecting the Docs and reaching out to patients on a much more massive basis had to happen.

Not long after we brought the Summit to an end, I said good-bye to Larry Steinman, thanking him for everything he had done to guide the process. He told me he thought I was right about the air up here at the ranch, the view, the amazing Shangri-La setting where we had been gathering. A fire had definitely been lit. Something very powerful had taken place.

"Do you think so?" I asked, nervously, hopefully.

He laughed and complimented me a bit more, saying that was something else he wanted to mention, that "besides understanding the science of autoimmunity, you manage to handle being in the valley, still maintaining optimism."

Who, me? Hopeful? Not everyone would agree. But actually I'm very hopeful. I couldn't breathe if I wasn't. I couldn't be the mom I need to be if I wasn't hopeful.

"You know, I understand that you are a parent first and a crusader second," he told me. "And I know there is no night when you go to sleep and you say that the world is perfect. You go to bed worrying that Ali is going to have one of those early signs of an attack and the first thing you think about when you wake up is worrying about Ali. My gut instinct tells me that's where you begin and end, with Ali."

"Thank you" is all I can say for his kindness and care.

And his truth.

For anyone in search of a cure for a rare disease, one of the mightiest challenges is always finding ways to put the word out and engage the scornful media. Compassion overload is not a new phenomenon, but it seems to have gotten much worse in the age of the Internet, when every cause under the sun begs for attention and dulls our natural instincts toward wanting to care and take action.

I knew that and had for a long time. But I also knew that with the right storyteller and perhaps some help from some celebrity voices, we could hold an advantage in at least gaining more attention for the existence of NMO—and reach that many more people potentially impacted by it.

It was a lunch at the Polo Lounge with Bob Dylan's son that brought this effort to the next level for me. Honestly, I never thought of myself as a huge Dylan fan. Once when talking about him, I made a friend mad because I couldn't name any of his songs. But I felt a kinship with Jesse right away, and not only because of his sweet nature and the quiet certainty he had about himself but also because he already had his own "2%" thing going on. If you've got Bob Dylan for a dad, believe me, you qualify for club membership at birth.

But more than that, the arc of Jesse's career struck a chord in me; his last few years seemed weirdly similar to mine. He made his name as a brilliant young director of music videos for artists like Elvis Costello and Tom Waits before taking the logical step toward directing movies. Jesse had made some comedies with big stars that grossed hundreds of millions of dollars. Of course, his agents and managers wanted him to do more.

But what he did instead was to become a dad on a mission. At the time his young son had begun having terrible stomach pains. The doctors couldn't find out what wrong. Jesse and his wife then began that journey into the medical maze, with no relief for their little boy. Jesse spent sleepless nights poring over the Internet while Susan watched over their son. Why couldn't the doctors diagnose him? Why did all the experts seem to have different opinions? It seemed like there was nowhere to go, nothing that could be done. Whatever information was out there was badly designed and user-unfriendly. After three frightening years of feeling helpless, their son writhing on the living room couch in chronic pain, he was finally diagnosed with Chron's Disease, another autoimmune condition.

Our meeting at the Polo Lounge, however, wasn't only to commiserate about our kids or exchange knowledge we'd both gained. I was also there to explore the possibility of Jesse bringing his storytelling gifts to make a little movie about NMO, perhaps with the help of some celebrity friends of ours. If it had worked for makeup, why not try it for raising awareness about NMO?

In pursuing Jesse to work with the foundation, I was having a case of my own Audacity of Hope. As it happened, he was the director of the transformational *Yes We Can* video that became a critical piece of President Obama's campaign. Jesse had also directed a commercial-length video with a message from doctors across America saying that the world of medicine needed to change and that it was time to share information. Needless to say, we were both on the same page. At our meeting he explained that his company was split in two. To pay the bills and keep the lights on, he shot commercials for Nike and American Express. But his true passion was in developing websites and movies that benefited patients and loved ones who were struggling with a dire diagnosis but hadn't been able to find the right information to get help.

Jesse had heard about the foundation and our "rare approach to a rare disease," and he asked, "How can I help?" before I got to the question of how to engage him professionally. When I described my ideas, he told me he'd fly anywhere, anytime, and talk with all the doctors, scientists, and patients he could as well as capture interviews with stars like Dustin Hoffman and Reese Witherspoon, who had already agreed to be on board. Jesse waived all his fees, asking only for expenses to be covered to make an initial four-minute movie. If we wanted to go viral, four minutes was the new normal for documentary-length storytelling.

He didn't come out and say, "I got your back," but that's how I felt when lunch came to an end. Oh, and there was one other takeaway from the meeting. Even after Jesse's son had somewhat stabilized, further questions led to the discovery that he had been misdiagnosed. He didn't have Crohn's; rather, he had celiac disease, another autoimmune condition but, in his son's case, capable of being treated mainly with a careful change of diet. As a result, his son's stomach pain disappeared.

Hearing that part of the story sent me on a new quest to look more closely at the gluten connection to inflammation. Most of our doctors tended to see dietary changes as falling under the heading of "can't hurt." I disagreed and now not only had a new line of investigation to pursue but a new Knight in Jesse Dylan.

~

SPRING 2010

My first newsletter for the SPECTRUM *appeared not long after my seventeenth birthday. Wow!*

My first public statement about having NMO was slightly scary, I admit. But more than anything, I was inspired to join my parents in making a contribution to the extraordinary work they were doing.

One thing I knew from the early stages of my diagnosis, even though I didn't even know the name of the disease at the time, was that there was very little information available about it. The Spectrum, *it seemed to me, was the next logical step in terms of conducting the flow of information.*

My mom and dad were brilliant at running the foundation and fostering life-changing research that could actually alter the current view/understanding of modern medicine. I, however, brought a unique perspective in the midst of that advancement. I knew what was going on behind the scenes with the foundation, and I could supplement that with my knowledge of an NMO patient's needs when navigating this diagnosis. Drawing from both sides, I had a distinct understanding of how the foundation and its different forms of outreach could better address the needs and concerns of NMO patients everywhere. The newsletter came to reflect information that would have been helpful to me at the time of my diagnosis, if I hadn't been so resistant. It included information on what NMO is, current treatment options, resources for support, other patient stories, and what hopeful actions are being done to cure it.

My goal from the start was simply to offer fellow patients the confidence that there were people out there trying to cure this thing, and to relay the message, repeated as often as necessary, "You're not alone."

That was a message that I had to give to myself, believe it or not, even as I became more comfortable and connected to the NMO community we had created.

In the summer between junior and senior year I spent a wonderful—attack-free—several weeks of academic enrichment at the University of California, Santa Barbara, and fell in love with the campus and the sense of diversity that was honored there. Guess where I would end up deciding to enroll in college?

Life was mostly grand. Senior year loomed. I was named co-captain of the tennis team as well as was co-editor in chief of our high school newspaper, the Student Voice. *I couldn't wait to make the most of my last year at Buckley.*

The only shadow that I can recall were the fears that had been seeping into my sleep, haunting my dreams. It was when I woke up from those dreams that I felt the most alone.

~

June 2010

"The celery juice must not be working," quips Carl Perkins in his clipped British accent one afternoon in my office when I'm looking and acting overwhelmed.

He's referring to the tonic prescribed by the Beverly Hills psychic and the fact that I've been especially on edge lately. It's the usual—not enough sleep, too much worry, way too many months of being over-vigilant about mostly everything. The Voice has been out of control with weird dark premonitions not connected to anything.

Carl puts his foot down and talks me into doing something for myself. Studying my calendar, I've got an opening at the end of the month and another in October. That's it. Between a trip I'm making to the Mayo in July and our family vacation to North Carolina in August, that's all that's available. Hmmm. What should I do for me?

Carl reminds me that I'd won a stay at a spa in San Diego. Not hesitating, I book myself a long weekend there in October and invite my dear friend Lisa to go with me.

Feeling better already, I decide—what the hey—why not take advantage of free time at the end of the month and have that second breast reduction I've been meaning to have all these years? No time like the present! Have I lost my mind? Yes, I think I have!

Next thing I know, Bill comes home to grab lunch and drops into my office, just to be sweet. This is my kind of day.

To top everything off, we have a houseguest arriving for the weekend who is one of the most magical presences on the planet. The two of us became BFFs a handful of years earlier when a mutual friend gave her my number.

That afternoon when Carl announced that there was a call for me, and I heard "Gloria Steinem on Line One," I vowed some day to write a memoir with that as my title. I was totally star struck. My first reaction was—*me*? Gloria Steinem wants to talk to *me*? I'm talking about the author of *Revolution Within*, a book that had already changed my life and not only convinced me that it was never too late to have a happy childhood, but also inspired me to embrace myself, low self-esteem and all, and push past self-imposed limitations. Oh yeah, and there was the whole women's empowerment movement and *Ms.* magazine that she had mobilized.

Gloria had called that first time because she was organizing a fundraiser with Jane Fonda to develop the infrastructure for a women's radio network. Gloria was hoping I might consider an investment and possibly host the fundraiser. After saying how delighted I would be to host an event, I invited a group of women who had a few dollars and who loved the idea. From that event on, Gloria and I have been the dearest of friends.

The only hitch in my schedule for the upcoming weekend when she is supposed to visit is that I have already agreed to meet with a vitamin/natural healing-type expert who I was told could really help Ali's condition.

"Victoria, you have got to meet this guy. Right now," our financial advisor insisted. He knew someone whose incurable cancer had been reversed by this fellow.

In all things, in all ways, I continue to remain open-minded. As everyone had observed at the Summit, there could be no bad ideas in the search to understand and treat a rare orphan disease.

Still, my priority was being with Gloria and didn't want to take up her time. When I explained what was going on, she wasn't inconvenienced but eager to hear what this miracle worker had to say.

Who needs celery tonic when you've got Gloria cheering you on?

Soon enough he arrives. Attractive and confident. He talks about his line of vitamins and how they have these remarkable curative powers and amazing abilities. He thinks Vitamin B is the most overlooked among nutrients.

Interestingly enough, I've been reading about Vitamin B. "So are you saying that I just have to give Ali heavy doses of B and she'll be cured?"

He nods.

Most of Ali's doctors are skeptical but don't think trying to add B to her cocktail should hurt. After talking to them the next day, I Google this guy. Turns out he is not known for curing incurable diseases. He is well-known for making high-end, nutritious dog food.

Oh my God, I thought, the doctors are going to think I've lost it!

Sure enough, a couple days later one of the experts calls and asks, "Victoria, did you know this guy makes dog food?"

Embarrassed as I was, I was nonetheless convinced that Vitamin B held promise in keeping Ali stabilized. Gloria agreed. I mean, just because the guy might be questionable doesn't mean his advice was. Right? Dog food has Vitamin B in it too, doesn't it?

July 2010

What was I thinking?

Perhaps I should have known that I was heading for a breakdown and that, maybe, major (albeit elective) surgery was not the best idea at this time. But that would have taken more self-awareness than I had right then. Between fretting about Ali being away for a summer program at UCSB, having little contact with Evan, and Jackson getting ready to go into the studio with a major team of agents and independent producers behind him, I was anxious about the trip to the Mayo to visit the lab and meet with the team there. And then there was the not-sleeping thing.

But I keep visualizing how much lighter I'll feel, so I go ahead with the surgery. Big mistake. Before the stitches can close up and everything can heal properly, I have to get to Rochester, Minnesota, for the planned activities at the Mayo.

Unlike the winter weather of a thousand lifetimes ago when we were first there, I arrive to an oppressive July heat wave. It's humid, sticky, and pretty much miserable. Even though our previous meetings had been in beautiful rooms above ground, for some reason this meeting has to happen in the lower level, where there are no windows, no air.

Battling claustrophobia—no surprise there—I discover during a visit to the ladies room that I'm having an allergic reaction to my stitches. My skin is itching and splotching and probably requires medical attention. Wait. I'm at the Mayo, I think. If the reaction gets worse, I'll have someone look at me. Everything gets worse when, in the middle of being applauded for the work of the foundation, I realize that the dampness I feel under my suit and satin camisole is blood! During my next break and dash to the ladies room, I check to see how bad the bleeding is, and it's out of control.

I realize I don't want our Mayo team to have to deal with this for me. I want them to continue their wizardry and keep pushing the science forward. I can't have them distracted by my tawdry tale of not giving myself enough time to heal.

So I go in search of bandages and find myself in the wig shop where chemo patients are waiting to be fitted for their wigs. Hating to bother the receptionist, I tiptoe over and whisper, "Could I trouble you for a few bandages?" She gives me a strange look and I proceed to give the explanation that my incision isn't healing well and I'm just trying to push the stitches back together to stop the bleeding.

Oh, and I'm sweating and panting from the humidity, kind of laughing at the same time. Somehow I've landed a role in a theater of the absurd play. Like one of those dreams that keep going from scary to hilarious.

What is friggin' up, Universe? That's what I want to ask at the top of my lungs.

Instead, after putting on the bandages, composing myself, and returning to finish the meeting, I realized that this was too much for me. When I prepared to go back to the hotel, I stepped onto one of the people-movers, the long moving sidewalk that is the distance traveling device of choice at the Mayo, and I slowly moved down a dim, humid long basement-level hallway. As I crawled along on this thing, I made up my mind that as a mom, I couldn't do this anymore.

There aren't enough words of gratitude that I feel for Brian Weinshenker, the original Wizard of Us and one of the true healers among the rest of the team at the Mayo. I'm so grateful it's there and grateful for all their superb research. As a funder and layperson sleuth, I could go back anytime. But not as a mom. That was one thing I decided wisely to do for myself—to let members of our advisory team make most of the site visits, wherever they were, from then on.

Oh, and the decision had nothing to do with the breast reduction.

~

AUGUST 2010

For our August vacation *I make time to do all the regular out-of-door activities, from swimming, hiking, boating, fishing, and river rafting to exploring quaint little country villages in the North Carolina hills. In the humid afternoons, instead of pushing myself, I get caught up on the required reading for my AP English. Everything is just normal, fun, delightful. Except for the new bothersome dreams. I haven't told anyone. Mom doesn't need another reason to worry—trust me on that. And Dad isn't the guy to interpret dream speak, I don't think.*

For most of the trip Mom seems to be relatively relaxed. Considering how far she has come from the days when she couldn't travel off the beaten track, it's miraculous that she can be so much at ease in the rustic North Carolina woods.

That is, until the day when we're leaving and packing up the two rental cars. Dad and Jackson are going to meet us at the airport in one car while Mom and I go in the second car. Along with us are Ann, Mom's friend/therapist who is usually along on longer trips, and Carl, who doesn't always travel with us but has this time to keep all the moving pieces organized.

As I'm getting into the car, I notice that Mom has a sort of intense look that ought to have been a tipoff that the ride ahead was going to be anything but normal. But woe unto all of us, I ignore it and hop into my seat, buckling up.

I should have known when my mother gets behind the wheel and starts mentioning this dark-field microscopy thing that we were all in for some major woo-woo.

But I didn't pay attention, and when we really started to go off the beaten path, it was too late.

~

I couldn't help it. During our stay with Bill's brother Rick and his wife, Denise, I kept hearing how much their son Connor, my nephew, had been helped by a doctor who lived in a remote part of North Carolina and specialized in the use of this rare microscope that allowed her to analyze blood against a dark field.

With just a single drop of blood she could determine many things about disease that doctors using conventional tests could not, and she prescribed tinctures and alternative remedies based on that analysis. The use of dark-field microscopy was not well known but was producing promising results. Denise had previously mentioned Ali's condition to this doctor who said that, yes, she could be extremely helpful if she could get that all important one drop of blood.

This sat in my mind the whole time we were in North Carolina. The Voice kept goading me on. But good sense and logic had mostly prevailed. If we had the top scientists in the world looking to cure NMO and Ali, why would I want to travel over miles of back-country roads to visit some doctor with a kooky microscope? But, then again, who knew? You never know what might work, and I am the queen of being willing to try anything and everything. Still, I hadn't pushed the issue. We were on vacation. Couldn't we just leave NMO somewhere else for a change?

But on the morning that we were supposed to leave, I called the doctor. She said she remembered hearing about Ali from Denise. Again, she thought that her approach might really be able to help. One hitch, however. We had to get to her office by 2:00 p.m. when she would be leaving. She repeated, "I leave at 2:00 p.m. sharp."

Overjoyed, because we weren't that far and it was sort of, kind of on the way—and it could save Ali's life—I then had to find a way to tell Ali and not stress her out.

"We're going to make little stop—cool?" I say. Then I tell her about the doctor needing to draw the one drop of blood, and that it's no big deal. "Besides, I think it could be kind of funny."

Ali laughs. Out of the corner of my eye, I also detect the sadness on her face, like, *darn, we can't even get through a vacation without NMO.* But now I'm one step further, and again, you just never know. Even though I recognize the absurdity of thinking, really, that some woman here in North Carolina in the middle of the friggin' nowhere backwoods is going to solve NMO, the other side of my brain keeps thinking, *Crazier things have happened. Let's just go see.*

We haven't gone more than twenty miles when the expedition suddenly turns into Mr. Toad's Wild Ride at Disneyland. But without the fun. What started out as this funny little adventure starts to become fraught with danger and ominous, foreboding signs. For one thing, we're up in the Blue Ridge Mountains back in the hill country of North Carolina, where it's all densely wooded and the August sunshine vanishes as it turns to rain, first in a light downpour, then in a deluge. Before long the skies darken even more and the rain becomes hail.

The mountains are soon shaking with thunder. It's like the universe is throwing all these obstacles in our way. Obviously, this journey is a metaphor for our fragile lives, throwing all these crazy roadblocks and delays in front of us when our very existence depends on us getting there by 2 o'clock.

Well, that's how I feel. Apparently, I'm in a minority of one. Ali is no longer engaged in the potential fun. Ann is advising that we cancel this mission and is a little testy when she says it. Carl is trying to figure out where the hell we are on the GPS at the same time that he's using his phone to try to Google our location.

Why? Because I'm lost! I'm driving through apocalyptic weather by feel. "Carl," I'm yelling at him, "give me a location!"

"I'm trying," he says through gritted teeth. "Google isn't working."

The backwoods have broken Google? That's it, my bad, we're not only hopelessly lost and going to miss out on dark-field microscopy, but we also might never get to a resting place where real civilization abides.

"Mom, just calm down," Ali says.

Read: this is not the end of the world. Ann and Carl both chime in, urging me to reroute and get on our way to the airport.

"No. We have to find it."

So what's started as an almost goofy errand has now morphed into a do or die mission. Because it looks like we're not going to get there on time, I've convinced myself that this doctor holds the key to curing Ali. She might know something, sense something, have the right needle in a stack of needles, but she's leaving at 2 o'clock. If we miss her, we'll miss this chance. Clearly, I am having a weird variety of anxiety. Ann doesn't need to tell me that. Usually, being lost will make me want to turn back and get on the main road. However, these conditions are such that I go in the other direction, driving further into the storm and getting deeper into a state of being lost.

When we hit little towns, we keep stopping to ask people on the streets. No help. The journey just seems endless. With the clock ticking ever more closely to 2, I think we're getting nearer to the destination. No one in the car is speaking to me because of the terror I've been behind the wheel. My own therapist not speaking to me?

Finally, we find the office moments after the cutoff, just as the doctor is shutting her door to leave. I jump out of the car, waving my hands, screaming, "Wait! Wait! Wait! Wait!" as I run toward her.

Ali hops out after me, no longer mad, and so sweet, interjecting, "Hey, hope you don't mind. I know you are getting ready to leave. Do you mind if I use the bathroom?"

The doctor agrees, opens her office back up to let us in, and I take a seat feeling awful for the hell I've just put everyone through. The doctor takes a finger prick of blood, the one drop, and no medical history or other questions.

Bizarre. But then, well, I'm thinking of that magical microscope that will tell her all she needs to know.

Back in the car afterward, it's deathly silent, but it doesn't take long for Ann and Carl to unload. One of the biggest fights we have ever had ensues. Once we get to the airport, we all have to go our separate ways to cool down before we can even get on the plane together.

But Ali takes it all in stride. She might still be mad but just seems to know where my heart was. Besides, it was a little funny, and we did survive.

As for the results, they took forever to arrive. We kept calling, and the doctor insisted they were on the way. Finally, I received them and set a conference call with her and Drs. Michael Yeaman and Ben Greenberg to review her findings. None of what she said made sense or added up to anything. Even me, with my newly made science brain, could tell that it was all gobbledy-gook.

What did we learn? Nothing. Ali would ask from time to time about the findings, and I would make excuses, things like, "She has to rerun some tests." But eventually Ali figured it out. I think actually she was disappointed, although by then other issues that had seriously pushed me to the brink of a nervous breakdown were much more of a concern.

The spa trip in October with my friend Lisa couldn't have come at a better time. The foundation team and I had been planning the 2010 Symposium and Patient Day for weeks, and I'd been on the phone with families of patients, engaged in much longer and more emotional conversations than ever.

For this year's activities for our patients, I had a flashback to my makeup artist/infomercial days as a volunteer at Cedars Sinai. The Look Better/Feel Better program I developed was for women diagnosed with serious illnesses who were getting ready to leave the hospital and responded miraculously to the beauty makeovers that we did. Besides teaching at UCLA, I found that the hospital programs were a way for me to spread the gospel of the intrinsic beauty of all women, so necessary after long periods of being sick and feeling terrible. The fearlessness of the women who were fighting debilitating and often terminal illnesses always inspired me. And the fellow makeup artists who I hired or asked to join me were as moved as I was by the experience. I just loved the tactile expression of putting on the base, blending it, and seeing women enjoy being pampered after constantly having their bodies poked and prodded.

It had occurred to me that doing a day of beauty makeovers for our patients and families at the Symposium would be empowering and add light to our Patient Day activities. A no-brainer for me in my own mascara-to-medicine journey. Ali was over the moon with the idea, and I was in my element planning that part of it.

That being said, I couldn't wait to get to the spa and have a little pampering of my own. First thing I was going to be fearless about was getting away from my cell phone that had been plastered in my hand since Ali's diagnosis. Okay, mild exaggeration. The phone was rarely more than a few inches from me. My ring tone from *Law and Order* was unlike anyone else's, so whenever family was calling, I would jump.

Ironically, once we got to the spa, instead of wanting to turn off the phone, I was concerned about the terrible cell service. This detachment was too radical. For the past almost three years I had kept the phone charged and the car full of gas to be ready to go at a moment's notice, just in case I needed to get right to Ali Rose in an emergency, wherever she might be. Bill was equally wired and at the ready. But what if he had to call me with any questions?

Fighting that worry, I tried to soak in the luxury. The first night there, in these beautiful little cabins Lisa and I had that were right next to each other, all the noise stopped—except the noise in my head. Without the noise and diversions of the house and of Jackson's music, I had time to reflect. And I started to freak out.

Really? Was this happening here in the land of supposed serenity? Yep. And no phone service too. Next thing I knew, the nighttime bugaboos started to come out, and I slept less than I might have at home.

As the sun came up I had to be honest that though I'd learned a lot in life, I had no clue about how to be alone by myself. The battle between the mental T's and B's raged. Did I go home to avoid further anxiety and return to normal stress? Did I leave Lisa? Why was all that inner signaling happening that made me feel that I absolutely had to get home for ominous reasons? This lasted until late in the afternoon, and I knew that another night would make me really nuts. Lisa didn't mind at all. Even though I had driven us, she said not to worry; she was enjoying herself and someone else could come pick her up.

When I pulled up in front of our house that night, I was relieved to be home and not to be greeted by any crisis. When I crawled into bed next to Bill and fell fast asleep almost immediately, I probably slept better than I had in almost three years.

The boom was lowered the next day when a call came in that I would have missed if I hadn't left the spa the night before. The news of the sudden death of my ex-husband, Joe, was so shocking as to be impossible to grasp. He was in the peak of health, training for a triathlon. He had gotten off his bike, no complaints, and collapsed from a massive heart attack.

You hear of lives cut short in those rare, tragic, unforeseen events that never happen to someone you know. The only other time I had ever heard of anything remotely similar was when Bill's ex-wife, five years after their divorce, collapsed from a brain aneurysm while working out in the gym. She was a paragon of fitness and health. How does it happen statistically that both Bill and I had exes who died in statistically rare, similar ways? What do you do with that disbelief and shock and grief?

Joe and I had been divorced for about seventeen years. Even after we broke up, with just different goals and drives, the romance of who we had been together stayed with me.

When Joe and I met, the thought of finding a love interest was the furthest thing from my mind. Back in my makeup artist days, when I was doing so many album covers, I was on my way home from a job, with no makeup on, and I'd come down with a terrible cold, fever and all. Plus, it was raining. I stopped into Cantor's to get myself some chicken soup.

In line at the counter, I noticed the great-looking guy who turned around and made small talk with me. But when I watched him pick up his order ahead of me and venture back out into the rain, I never expected to see him again in my life.

Imagine my surprise when I did see him again a short time later. He was outside of Cantor's, waiting until I'd picked up my soup, so he could ask me out. That was Joe, always so in tune with the moment and with life.

After we split, whenever we saw each other for our traditional once-a-year get-together for Evan's birthday, we maintained enormous respect for one another. He had remarried and built a happy life with his wife, Mardi, and their daughter, Isabella, Evan's sister. As divorced couples go, we had done well, all things considered, to remain connected.

Now I wasn't sure how to grieve or rail against the universe on behalf of Evan. I was painfully struggling myself with the loss of Joe, and I couldn't fix it for my kid. I couldn't fund a search for the cure that would get him back his father. I knew he had to mourn in his own way, in his own time. He asked me to give that to him and know that he would find his way and not to put my fear and anxiety on him.

How could I do that? How could I not worry for his pain?

How? How, in the face and terror of death and loss, does anyone do that?

~

It was very warm in the waiting room—*too warm. Either that or the sweat dripping from my mother's forehead was a mere physical representation of the torment she was experiencing. I looked into her eyes and knew she could feel everything I was feeling.*

We were one heart beating in one rhythm; in unison, we were dying together.

As I try to sort out the details, I'm aware that the hospital bed is not the most comfortable, even with the massive amounts of pain medication and IV fluids running through my body. I still manage to find every inch of it restless and confining. I try to appear calm, stopping myself from squirming so as to appear more untroubled for my family.

These are the last few moments of my life, and I know it. I can feel the life draining out of me, but being the Type A personality I am, I want to make sure everything is in order before I go. I pull my family close, one by one, to make sure they each will be able to cope with my loss but, more importantly, to impart to them my dying wish: I want them to be happy.

I want them to be free from the pain, sorrow, and agony I know fills them now and to live their lives the way I would want them to: positively. I want them to understand that I will not be angered by swiftly moving on from my loss but rather elated by their ability to absorb the true spirit of my presence here on earth. Moving on would mean they have honored my last desire and embraced my personal philosophy of optimism. By moving on, my spirit would live within them—not through their tears and misery but through their pleasure, contentedness, and enjoyment of all of life's pleasures.

I save my mom and dad for last, of course, and hold their hands as they sob helplessly over me. I hold them tightly together and savor every moment of it. This is when the tears stream down my own cheeks, despite my desperate attempts to keep them in. I want to be brave for them, show them I'm not afraid of what is to come, but I can't help myself from crying. I urge them to maintain the foundation, telling them that they can keep my spirit alive by continuing to search for the cure to NMO. My last wish is that they find it.

I tell them how much I love them, over and over again until my eyelids shut in a deep and everlasting sleep.

I wake next to find my pillow bathed in tears that seem to have crossed the barrier from dreamland to reality. It's 4:30 a.m. I know it's a dream, but I'm still shaken deeply to my core. It's just a dream. This is my mantra as I rinse my face with ice-cold water and listen carefully to the beat of my heart to make sure it's still there. It was just a dream.

Even though the days were full of promise and purpose, that dream was the manifestation of the fears that I couldn't extinguish during my sleep, like the flames of the fire in the earlier dreams. After that, however, the dark dreams came to an abrupt end.

What did that mean? I started to think again of the interpretations of dreaming about fire and remembered one that hadn't made sense at the time—the dream of fire as destructive, leading to ashes and the phoenix rising from them.

I guess to be the phoenix, you have to die a metaphoric death. And then you can rise.

7

Defying Gravity

Remember this:
Nothing is written in the stars.
Not these stars, nor any others.
No one controls your destiny.

—GEOFFREY MAGUIRE,
FROM *WICKED*, THE BOOK
FOR THE MUSICAL TIE-IN

October 2010

"His name is Yogi Cameron," says one of my dearest friends in a loving, concerned voice. She worked with him during a rare low point and crisis in her life and thinks highly of him. "You might want to give him a call."

No one has come out and said, "Oh, is that a nervous breakdown you seem to be having there?" No one knows what to say any more than I do. This was as much about Joe dying as it was a feeling of excruciating helplessness for my son, adding to the weight of trying impossibly to banish NMO from our lives. For nearly three years I believed that pushing the boulder up the mountain was something I could do, fearful warrior that I was.

Now it feels as though it's tumbled back on me and rolled us back to the bottom, and I have to start all over and am so weary and unsure. Every day I'm still waking and doing and climbing the mountain and pushing the boulder. And in my mind I am always pushing the boulder, surrounded by a lot of blind and paralyzed people. But getting to the top is starting to become a pipedream. I tell my friend that what I really need in my life is someone who can guide me to feeling that I have summited the mountain, someone who can help me find that serene feeling that we would find at the top, so we can breathe and just enjoy the view.

When I hear that Yogi Cameron has a spiritual focus in his approach and that he emphasizes detachment, I'm open to that. I know that it's time to turn to the higher power and seek surrender. Detachment is not my area of expertise, for sure. But at this point I'm so attached to everything that I take a leap of faith that maybe trying to connect to something outside of all these crazy circumstances that have kept me connected—well, it has to be worth a shot.

Yogi Cameron Alborzian, author of *The Guru in You*, comes to meet with me and asks how he can help. He is an otherworldly combination of worldly and wise. Before he found his teacher in India, for years Cameron was a top fashion model.

How can he help? In tears, I tell him that I'm not sure he can because I'm so tired, depressed, overwhelmed, and struggling to get out of bed.

And then there's the sleeping issue that has been a problem since February 2008. He listens thoughtfully as I tell him that I'm always on alert for Ali's footsteps or going to check if her light is on—usually the sign that she's having an attack. The paranoid mom-on-alert button is stuck and not letting me sleep, with the volume in my head on high since my ex-husband's death and the worry I have for my son.

Cameron says that usually he comes into people's lives when they feel they're at their lowest but also when they're ready for change. I have practiced yoga over the years on my own but have never worked with a teacher.

Being me, figuring that I've got nothing to lose, I surrender to the possibility of surrender. And again, in a situation like this, as I've said, all bets are off. You just keeping trying new things until something sticks.

I'm back in the guest bedroom these days so Bill can sleep. Sometimes I go back and forth, but I hate to wake him with me turning into a vampire at nights, roaming the halls, making up NMO rap songs like "No mo' NMO," and making no sense.

When I tell this to Cameron, it's to make him laugh. But he only nods with concern and offers to be there at night to help me fall asleep. The next thing I know he is camped out on the floor in the back bedroom while I'm in the bed, turning in for the night. The relief I have in knowing that maybe I'm protected and can close my eyes for a minute is like a miracle.

Making up for lost time, I rediscover sleep. Rest. Peace. As this went on for a month or so, during the day I had more energy, more focus, more trust. We practiced yoga, went on walks, worked on quieting my mind.

With the Symposium happening within weeks after Joe's death, I think they all knew that I'd earned the help, however it came. Plus, this detachment thing that Cameron kept reinforcing was so therapeutic in terms of helping me let go of the need to control outcomes of every situation. Something really began to change.

Instead of fighting and being a warrior against the unpredictability, I began to entertain the concept that life didn't have to be a nonstop series of highs and lows but that it could just be what it is—life. Highs, lows, in betweens, scary stuff, miraculous stuff. In the unpredictable maze of NMO, I desperately needed to be in a space where the Voice and the predictions of 2% and all those old survival/guidance tools didn't matter.

Because I was taking care of myself, I could now better deliver the message of self-love and self-care that I wanted to give to my kids and to our growing NMO community of patients, advocates, doctors, and scientists. In this way, our Symposium that fall became the most meaningful and emotionally rewarding of any of our gatherings.

The makeovers and pampering that we did for Patient Day were as transformational for me as I heard they were for the just under one hundred patients who attended as well as for the members of their families. We had come a long way together from those days when many patients and their parents I met over the phone were in so much despair they couldn't see themselves being flown to LA to get their hopes up.

With the sleep, the lessons of detachment, and the joy of belonging to this community that we were building, I felt more present and more connected to this event than had ever been possible before. Of course, a big part of that was having Ali there, as was watching her enjoy having her own makeover and seeing her engage with fellow patients, listening to questions and answering them, discussing ideas for the newsletter. Bill was also on hand for longer periods of time than he had stayed in years past.

Bill and I had done a pretty damn good job at fulfilling our roles of funder and finder to bring together all the resources that were changing and saving lives. We didn't say as much or talk to each other about it in so many words, but at one point I caught him nodding with parental approval at the foundation's growth.

Many of the patients who had attended the year before had grown, much like Ali, through a sense of belonging. Our patients are so scattered around the globe and what they suffer from is so misunderstood that bringing them together in a community in which they could see that there were others like them, others who suffered the same way they did, was clearly empowering.

One of the mothers told me that she had borrowed my Momtra of committing herself toward "making this orphan disease an orphan no more" and that after hearing from our panel, for the first time she had hope for a future for her four-year-old daughter. During the Q&A in this session one of the patients who was in a wheelchair said that she didn't want to ask any questions of the doctors but just needed to thank them and the foundation for giving her "Hope and a home." And she just wanted everyone in the trenches doing the research and working toward better treatments to keep pushing, "because we're counting on you."

A few weeks earlier if I had heard that, I would have honestly felt the comment was being directed at me. But you know what, I didn't anymore. First of all, we had the Knights of the Round Table, who were already starting to talk about drug trials of new therapies. In fact, Dr. Alan Verkman, a.k.a. young Einstein and a specialist in the structure and biophysics of aquaporins, had been listening at the Summit when I had challenged him to stay up for two days and solve NMO. About a week later he came back with a grant proposal that would allow him and his team at the Verkman Lab at UCSF to start screening compounds in search of a combination that could stop the binding of antibody to AQP-4. Eight months later his research was already on its way to giving us promising new insights into molecules that may be candidates for development of new drugs to inhibit NMO-IgG from binding to aquaporin.

Though I'm not crediting all of these positive developments to the power of detachment, Cameron was exactly what the doctor ordered. Maybe we weren't at the top of the mountain yet, but I really was starting to enjoy the view.

~

2010/2011 TENNIS SEASON

Going into the CIF finals for the third time—and my last year on the team—I refuse to allow for the mere possibility of an attack that might slow me or my team down. There had been a couple episodes in the middle of the season, but they hadn't developed into full-fledged attacks . . . knock on wood!

At the start of the season, because I was captain, I finally felt it was necessary to discuss NMO openly with my teammates. They had all noticed, no doubt, my tendency to miss practice at random times in the previous years and my seemingly endless supply of ice for cooling myself down after every drill as well as my inability to perform all the running or overly strenuous tasks that Coach had us complete.

As captain, I wanted to make sure my team knew that I didn't do all these things to be indulgent, and they deserved to know. I'm pretty sure they didn't think I would do any of this without some reason anyway, but I really felt that, as a leader, I needed to be honest with my team. I wasn't concerned that they'd think I had betrayed them or that some of my teammates and friends would be angered that I had not included them in this part of my life sooner.

Nope, that wasn't the hitch. Most of all, I feared their sympathy. I hate pity, no big news there, because this was something I avoided since the very moment of my diagnosis. It's not who I am, and I don't want to be treated any differently because of it. Granted, I do have to do some things differently to be healthy, but that doesn't require any special treatment from my friends and family.

I discussed my concerns with Sherm and eventually was able to confide in my co-captain, Hadleigh, who reacted as I would if the shoe had been on the other foot. She told me how proud she was that I had commanded the mental toughness to play through the attacks. Then she and I were able to devise a plan as to how I would reveal myself to the team.

At the beginning of the season each year Sherm always kicks off with a brief talk about health. She talks about how we as athletes rely on our health and on staying healthy as a priority for each of us.

So that was my cue to interject and open up about my own personal experiences with NMO. I would discuss how staying healthy and dealing with this disease is just as important of a contribution to the team as is practicing my serve. You can't play tennis if you're not healthy. And that is exactly what I did. I was nervous, of course, because this was the first time I had openly and directly discussed NMO with anyone other than my family, my doctors, and a couple friends and teachers.

My voice was hesitant, shaky, and weak, each word seeming to get stuck somehow as it tried to make its way out of my mouth. But I got through, and no one looked shocked, mad, or sorry for me. Phew. Since that day the team never once treated me differently. Getting that off my chest was both a relief and a great starting point for me to be more open when talking about NMO. Call it my big break in public speaking. What better audience than that of my teammates who knew, bottom line, what a competitor I am?

In a word, the season was MAGIC. From where we had started in freshman year, this was our Cinderella story. Every year our uniform changed, but this year's was my favorite as one of the perks of being senior captain was getting to choose the design. My choice was a black on black uniform—a black skirt and matching black tank top with BUCKLEY written in red. Although we were playing in the hot San Fernando Valley heat (and black does attract heat), I saw black as the most intense and intimidating looking of our school colors.

You never know what can give you that edge, and I left no edge unturned. With my sword at my side—a.k.a. my Wilson racket—I knew we were going to have a great season. How far would we go? That was up to each of us and all of us. Yeah, we had some Knights of the Round Table energy going for us too.

Throughout the years at Buckley I loved all my teammates and would stay close to them even after high school. My teammates definitely inspired my leadership style—what I'd call a very supportive approach. I can assert myself and be a leader, but I think it's an important skill to know when it is appropriate to do so. There are times when your team needs you to step up and lead them, but there are also those moments when you really need your team to lead themselves. This last season gave me the chance to find a balance between those two capacities in a way that I think was beneficial to everyone. I tried my best to make sure everyone felt the tennis team was not only a safe and friendly environment but also a family. I wanted everyone to feel together and support one another. By showing everyone how much I cared about the team and every individual on it I hoped to lead by example and inspire my fellow competitors to push themselves and each other to make sure we left everything we had on the court this year.

Without question, my leadership style was also modeled on strengths I learned from Mom and Dad, as different as they are. And then there was Sherm, who had transformed our tennis program in the short time she had been at Buckley as well as being my mentor since freshman year. Her support, teaching, and championing of my growth were directly responsible for many of my successes both on and off the court. Sue Sherman's dedication to the team and her passion for the sport would forever be an inspiration in my life. Without her guiding hand, none of our success as a team or mine as a player would have been possible.

By the time the season wrapped up with the completion of the Liberty League individual tournament, we had a feel of destiny in our ranks, happily qualifying again for the CIF postseason play. And for some serious icing on the cake, we wrapped up league play by defeating our archrival Viewpoint 13–5, making us undefeated in league play and giving us our first league championship.

In adding to my press clippings, Nanny was especially proud when the Daily News *printed the headline, "Guthy Lifts Griffins to First Title Girls' Tennis: Senior Captain Delivers."*

Yes, I was battling an episode of NMO, but I couldn't NOT *play. The adrenaline and the will to win dominated.*

I was so proud of Mom. She could have worried and tried to convince me not to play. But she knew me better and just told me to go out and win! And I think that she and Dad were proud too. Parents of my teammates were coming up and hugging them and saying their daughters were playing for me. Pity I hate. But pride and applause I love!

Mom may worry, but she does so, in a way, to prevent me from having to do so. She had even gotten to become an expert at not appearing to be worried. Maybe it was the detachment or the fact that she was absorbed by plans for the Symposium, but it worked. You can imagine the excitement and the outpouring of love and support from the NMO community. I have to admit that my game felt ever so supercharged after that, as we geared up for the CIF.

Obviously, I in no way wanted to be overly confident. After going all the way to the championship round for the two previous years and then losing, we knew that all the dynamics can change as the field gets winnowed and the best teams either get stronger or get eliminated.

There was an added challenge. We had been bumped up a division at the end of my junior year, from Division 5 to Division 4, meaning we would face higher-ranked and better teams. However, when we met Cajon High School in the quarterfinal round on Tuesday, November 16, we lived up to our intimidating uniform and won decisively. In the semifinals two days later on November 18, we faced Cate School and again sailed to victory.

So now it's four days later, November 22, and we're warming up at the Claremont Club for our finals against Santa Ynez.

I'm ready. The team is ready.

A week earlier Dad, Raquel, and I had driven up to scout the team. Oh yeah, we were SO spying on them! I wanted to watch them play to get a sense of how their team worked so I could better plan our lineup if we ended up playing them. Based on what I saw, on the bus driving to the finals match I make a game-changing decision. I decide to change the lineup according to the information I had gathered by observing who their strongest players were and where they were vulnerable. Our stronger players had to step up to make sure they won their games while sacrificing less experienced players in games that I knew were going to be tough.

Once I've made the decision, no matter how risky, I have to believe it's going to work. As the match continues, I know that it's close and that I won't know if the strategy made the difference until all the sets have been played. Finally, after my last set of the match, I jog over to look at the score.

A reporter (who had been covering our team all season) approaches before I can check and asks, "How does it feel to win a CIF championship?"

Time stands still. For the rest of my life, I will always get chills whenever I think of this moment. But in the meantime I simply can't believe what he is saying. Until I hear it from my coach, I can't believe we've won. I walk over to Sherm, who is standing over on the far side of the court. And as I look at her she raises her arms slowly, proudly thrusting two thumbs up into the air!

The risky strategy worked! We tied in sets, 9–9, but in counting games, the Griffins beat the Pirates, 77–70!

At that moment I knew my dream had really come true. The moment I'd been visualizing since I picked up a tennis racket had finally been realized. I was too stunned to speak.

It was literally the greatest moment of my life.

~

March 2011

Time races. The pace is unstoppable.

Thank God the dire prognosis that we were given hasn't come to pass. Yet Ali, who is always so proud of her tennis statistics, has been living with an altogether darker set of numbers. Since her first attack in February of 2008 to the present day, she has had sixty doctor visits, fifty-six sets of labs, thirty-two MRIs, fifty-two IV treatments, and sixteen full-blown attacks. And counting.

It's truly extraordinary that she was able to accomplish all of those other stats while she was, at the same time, living with these.

While my amazing daughter was winning the CIF championship and bringing the banner home to hang in the gym along with applying to colleges, working as co-editor in chief of the paper, and helping edit the *Spectrum*'s newsletter, not to mention making A's in Honors and AP classes, I was catching up on sleep, downward dog, and detachment.

I finally decided that Yogi Cameron's work was done and it was time for him to let me fly with my own wings. We could still do yoga and get in some hikes together, but the detachment intensive was enough for now. He encouraged me to migrate back to my bedroom, where I found the sleep habit was much better. No more vampire roaming in the night.

Well, not as often.

Bill and I weren't perfect, but we were so much better. The truth is that there is only so much detachment a person can handle. Scratch that. There is only so much detachment I can handle.

In preparing for the foundation's second annual Summit, I want to feel attached to the strides we have made and to celebrate our collective accomplishments. Just in going over our materials for our twenty-four key attendees (up from eighteen that came the year before), I'm getting really excited. Using the analogy of the horse-and-buggy leap to the moon-buggy, Jacinta Behne reminds me how we started from a time when there was close to no information available. Since then the Guthy-Jackson Charitable Foundation has not only become the leading organization funding global NMO research but has also promoted awareness worldwide. Besides developing the first open-source biorepository and international clinical database for NMO research, we have moved the ball forward with opportunities twice a year for researchers and clinicians to share new findings in understanding and treating NMO. We have made the annual Patient Day a central focus of our work so that patients, families, and caregivers come first in being able to interact with clinicians, researchers, and each other. Then there are the tools and resources on- and offline that let the NMO community create and raise awareness, educate each other and the general public, and find support groups both locally and globally.

One of our most effective tools, of course, has come from creating the first online interactive NMO map for Connect the Docs, connecting patients to doctors, advocates, and biosample donation sites. Most recently, as we discuss where we can announce that we're headed next, we have worked to establish partnerships with government agencies, rare disease organizations, and industry leaders, particularly in the pharmaceutical arena.

Reviewing notes from the last site visits that Drs. Katja Van Herle and Michael Yeaman conducted, I'm thrilled with the reports from the thirteen institutions we are currently funding. These include Stanford; the Mayo Clinic in both Rochester and Scottsdale; UCSF; Johns Hopkins; Scripps, UTSW; Harvard Brigham and Women's Hospital; Mass General; University of Colorado, Denver; NYU; UCLA; and St. George's University of Medicine.

Over thirty-five thousand brochures have been distributed to hundreds of doctors and advocates around the world, with more planned. And perhaps the most encouraging news is that in addition to the two drug trials we're hoping to launch in the very near future, we are estimating that an additional three to seven more trials may soon be in the works. With the power of collaborative research, NMO has been transformed in three years from a death sentence to being a treatable though still incurable condition. We have too many more miles to go, but as our research collides with the breakthroughs in science in general, our docs have never been more hopeful.

After a recent presentation I gave to the main brass at the California Institute for Regenerative Medicine (CIRM), where meaningful work in stem cell research is being done, we are now exploring the possibilities of new investigations into stem cells and NMO. In fact, the CIRM people are eager to understand how the GJCF has moved so quickly and perhaps borrow some of the ways we thought outside the compact. Then there is a budding partnership, yet to be finalized, that will let us expand the potential draw sites for our patient biorepository to as many or more than fifteen hundred sites nationwide and eighteen hundred worldwide.

Rumblings from our experts are even beginning to suggest that our last estimate of thirty-five thousand cases of NMO around the world might be much too low. Again, with the ongoing concern of misdiagnoses of MS, I've been hearing new guesses that might go up to five or ten times that number—or more.

What is this orphan trying to tell us about human health in a time of planetary changes? We're looking into that with studies about the linking of diet, stress, environment, and hormonal factors in the inflammatory cascade that impacts all autoimmune conditions. We need focus, but we don't want to miss out on the needle in the other stacks of needles that may be the breakthrough we seek.

Dr. Larry Steinman has said from the start that he believes our research will make NMO the "little disease that could." I'm thinking more like the "little foundation that could." Even earlier in his MS research, he kept his eye on NMO because he thought advancing a cure there might help offer up techniques for a cure for the other autoimmune diseases, particularly MS and myasthenia gravis.

Before the Summit, as he won't be able to attend, Dr. Steinman and I talk on the phone so he can explain to me where his understanding is heading.

With his wonderful way of drawing me in, he begins, "You know this concept is much broader than neurological immune deficiencies. Let's say that you are allergic to rag weeds and you go to an allergist and he will give you an allergy shot and everything works well, you can go out during rag weed season and not sneeze away and develop wheezing and watering eyes?"

Do I!

He goes on to say that there is a new interest in other areas of medicine to use that same idea of tolerance—giving the immune system a tiny bit of what's been setting it off and then training it to become tolerant and not overreact. Nobody has succeeded for any human autoimmune disease and very few people are trying. Actually that's what got him into studying NMO, what he thinks is one of the absolute great examples of where we might be able to develop what he calls "the holy grail of allergen-specific tolerance."

NMO is for the researcher the ideal launchpad to that dream because both the target and the specific antibodies have been identified. "If you could do it for NMO and other autoimmune diseases, you might be able to understand immunology enough so a transplant or even a promising stem cell wouldn't be rejected." Larry says that, at any rate, he believes that NMO is a "very solvable problem" and that its solution would offer tremendous insight into other diseases that are more complex than NMO. Even like type 1 diabetes or MS.

As for developing therapies that don't wipe out Ali's immune system or those of her fellow NMO patients, he believes *that* must be addressed as a priority. After all, he says, it's maddening that we're still using drugs that wipe out huge chunks of the immune system that's only attacking one molecule. "We shouldn't need to tear down the whole immune system to wipe out that one molecule."

My last question, asked with a certain amount of detachment, just to keep it real, is "How soon can we develop a method for using tolerance with NMO?"

"You would be surprised, I know, because it sounds like such a straightforward idea, why isn't everyone in the world working on it? If I touch places on the globe, there are about five people in the world who think this is an approach we can do in 2011 and who think that NMO represents the strongest possibility of producing proof, of showing the proof of a concept of this particular approach!"

So that's why he calls it the little disease that could.

And that's why I call us the little foundation that could, would, and *will.*

~

MAY 15, 2011

My senior year in high school *allowed me to soak up everything that Buckley had to offer. Secure in the sense of how far we'd all come together, I could start focusing on the future.*

The tough decision I faced mainly came down to a choice between University of California, Berkeley and University of California, Santa Barbara. Mom was so good at trying hard not to influence my decision. In the end I just knew that being slightly closer to home—but far enough away to have my independence—was the best choice.

No matter what, I knew that when I left at the end of the summer, it was going to be brutal for Mom. Besides Evan setting off on long-distance trips on his own, either by bike or motorcycle, Jackson was going to be leaving on tour in the fall. The empty nest was a subject none of us dared bring up around Mom.

In the meantime a rite of passage occurred even before graduation when I turned eighteen. I was so thrilled to be able to have all the privileges of a legal adult. (The one foremost on my mind was being able to play the lottery, which at this writing I still have not done!) Never had I even thought that turning eighteen would have such a potent impact on my medical life.

About a week after my birthday Dr. Katja Van Herle asked me to come into her office to go over a few things. I shrugged this off as a no-brainer, assuming a necessary blood draw or even our yearly checkup was in order. When I got to the office, we went through the usual motions of starting an appointment: take my blood pressure, test my reflexes, check my balance, send a piercingly bright light at my eye, and so on. Once the first—and what I think is the last—stage is completed, Katja asks for me to join her in her office. She begins by discussing a very important change that has just occurred: I am not dependent on others but rather can seek advice from my own doctor. No longer is my mom in direct control of my personal medical decisions. I now had the right to decide everything for myself.

In the moment this didn't seem like such a big deal. Oh yeah, I can totally handle that. I loved being treated like an actual adult for the first time, especially with something that matters this much. I was eager to accept the challenge and waited patiently for Katja to finish before I started blurting out all my millions of questions. The one thing we had to decide concretely was what was to be my mom's role in this new medical arrangement? Since birth she has been in control of my medical needs, and since my diagnosis she has gone into overdrive making sure everything was taken care of. That was my job now. When on earth was I going to have time to make all these elaborate decisions?

I don't know many people my age who, once they hit the magic number eighteen, are in charge of dosing of their own medications, communicating with so many different doctors, scheduling monthly blood draws, and various other medical tests. I know NMO is not the only disease that requires all these things, but it sure as heck felt like a lot when it hit me. Why would I not use the resource of my knowledgeable and loving parents?

What's more, let's face it, my mom is Superwoman. She can handle all of this in her sleep. I'm just, well, me! What the heck am I going to do? As the reality began to sink in, another wave of courage swept over me.

WHAT ARE YOU TALKING ABOUT ALI, YOU GOT THIS! But now was time to make the hardest decision of all: really, what about my mom? She has given up so much to take control of this foundation and monitor my personal medical progress. What will she do when that's no longer her job? I don't want to keep her out of the loop entirely, but aren't I entitled to a bit of patient privacy now, and shouldn't I embrace that? I discussed these concerns with Katja, and we decided to take my stance on privacy on a case-by-case basis.

So basically, once a month, when I have my labs drawn, Katja e-mails or calls me about the results. If I have time, I will discuss them with her myself. But no matter what test is done, no matter what decisions are made, it was and still is my personal preference that the doctors speak to me first before sharing information with my mom. I really want to feel that I have total control of my own medication, and although I'm often busy and don't always have time, I still like the idea of someone having to ask my permission to share this information.

Since my diagnosis I have always felt more vulnerable, more on display than ever before. From having to go through the same routines and share my same story with every doctor I meet, even on these pages, I've never been so exposed. I'm better at discussing it now (obviously) than I ever have been before, but this lack of privacy definitely bothered me at first. That is a big reason why I chose to retain so much control when I turned eighteen.

My mom still has complete control of the foundation. The only change now is that she needs to get permission from me to talk to my doctors about my personal medical situation. And this isn't to be mean or anything, but like I said, it's important for me to feel like I'm in complete control over my own life. Call this the tolerance-building test for Mom to accept other big changes in the works.

When all this went down in May 2011, I knew in theory that my mother also really and truly was ready to embrace the concept of my independence. The practical reality of everything that was going on with her as the clock ticked closer to graduation just showed how difficult all these momentous events were on her and the Zen state she had worked so hard to attain.

~

To relax me and make me not stress about graduation and Ali getting ready to fly from the nest, I plan a trip to Mexico to stay with friends in a private, rented home where we're going to do yoga. How lovely will that be? Bill also is heading to Mexico to a resort with some of his guy friends who like to golf. How great is that also?

A group of friends who I really enjoy are all set to fly down together for what can only be a fun, entertaining, memorable getaway. Again we were going to an unfamiliar place, a place far away from home. Yes, that was the point, but it also meant that I started obsessing about being unable to help Ali if anything went wrong. Carl, who has helped me plan this vacation, lets me in on every aspect of the planning, showing me where everything is on the map—as I'm very geographically challenged and travel to new places makes me feel ten years old and terrified.

So here I am, a very strong, capable woman working on curing a disease and trying to understand cutting-edge science, but put me in someplace new with my suitcase and I start to have trouble breathing. Getting myself actually to go to the airport was difficult. I couldn't remember having an attack like this in years. From the moment we landed in Mexico, all I could think about was missing the events leading up to graduation for Ali and, of course, as always, what if Ali has an attack and I'm in Mexico and can't get home.

The fact that she has been attack-free for eight or nine months didn't help at all.

Fuck! I know, I tried to detach from excessive use of the F word. But fuck that!

The point of the trip was to relax, and I couldn't. All I wanted to do was go home.

Yes, I knew the Big Detachment for Letting Go was coming soon. I had to let go. Over the years anxiety had gotten the best of me at times, and when NMO came into my life, that was something I couldn't control. So then I had to focus on controlling the anxiety, the Voice, the dark passenger that I'd been carrying around all this time. And I'd done a mostly good job at banishing the panic and refusing to let it all get to me. Pretty much whatever else had come up, I'd convinced myself that I could handle it.

Put it all on my shoulders. Bring it on.

Now, oddly, as things were starting to get better—with Ali, between Bill and me—I was starting to feel a little off my game without somebody else's life to save, as though having nothing to be anxious about was kind of making me, well, anxious. So, first making my apologies to Bill and my friends in Mexico, I raced back to Los Angeles.

On the plane going home I accepted the reality of anxiety as something that's always going to rear its head but hopefully not as often. I accepted that probably NMO would always just be on my shoulder there—until I find a cure for it. I'm always going to be holding that phone in my hand, afraid that it's going to ring with news of concern for any one of my children.

Maybe I can't be saved from being a mom. My consolation is knowing that I'm not so alone in my incurable condition.

~

JUNE 8, 2011

Final Day Assembly is held *in the afternoon so that family members can attend. As it approached, I did have some question in my mind about who might be chosen for having their jersey retired, if anyone. In fact, earlier in the day we had been discussing an article for the newspaper, tossing out ideas for covering such a story, just in case. That's when the idea hit me for the first time. Was this a 2%, never happens to anybody, just like winning the championship? Nah. There were too many factors counting against it. My parents had left for Mexico in the morning and surely they would have stayed for the assembly had they known I was to receive the award. Plus, I've looked at those names on the gym wall before, all forceful players who graduated to play their sport in college, but there wasn't one jersey of the roughly twenty or so on the gym wall that were from a tennis team, men or women.*

All that skepticism vanishes when I enter the gym for the assembly and wonder if something maybe is up. Why were Raquel and both of my grandmas in the stands? Wait, I'm looking there and, OMG, could that be my mom? No, she's in Mexico, right? When I look again, I don't see her. But I'm not even sure.

I take my seat in the newly designated senior section. For this day we are moved from our usual place in the bleachers to a temporary arrangement of fold-out chairs on the floor. We go through the usual motions of the assembly until we come to sports. Coach Milic, the head of the athletics department at Buckley, takes the stage and begins to announce the senior athletes moving on to play their sports in college.

Then comes time for the retirement of jerseys. He begins to describe a girl who played volleyball all through middle school and high school, and the crowd erupts into cheer as Emily's (volleyball captain and club player) name rings out.

I stand and clap as well, figuring that is the last of the awards for the evening. Wrong. Next Milic begins to describe another girl, played all through middle school. He begins reading the freshman scores of this supposedly groundbreaking athlete, and I'm hung on the numbers he's reading out. I know it's me. Wait, this is crazy. This isn't happening.

My throat becomes dry and my eyes begin to dart around the room; everywhere they turn, they are met with smiles staring back in congratulations. Until he finishes reading scores, I still think—no, it can't be me! Milic stops and then makes a very dramatic opening to my total score. Overall, I've earned 165 wins to 22 losses.

When he announced that score, a massive "wooooaaaahhhhh" rang out from the crowd. Cheering and clapping ensued when my name was announced. Mom, apparently having transported telekinetically from Mexico, was jumping up and down.

A big frame masked in white cloth is brought out, and Coach Sherman then revealed what was hiding: a shiny casing of my senior tennis uniform with the name GUTHY featured prominently and proudly across the back.

I'm sure a few tears crossed my eyes as I hugged Sherm, Milic, Raquel, and my grandmothers. Mom and I hugged the longest in absolute jubilation. I had never been so happy in my entire life! (Well, maybe when we won the championship!)

All those years since the sixth grade, when I'd walked into the gym for the first time, looked up at all the names on those jerseys decorating the walls, and I dreamt of being one of them . . . at this moment, I felt such a wonderful sense of accomplishment and pride.

I was overjoyed, I was shocked, and, suddenly, without warning, I was overwhelmingly depressed. Where was that coming from? In a microsecond I realized that the story I'd been writing for myself to outrun and outmaneuver challenges had come to an end.

The last journals of my growing-up years had no more stories to tell. But now what? Suddenly, and powerfully, I was struck by a feeling of anxiety. What if this is it? What if I move onto college and nothing can compare to the joy I feel at this very moment? What if I've reached my peak in high school, and the climax of my success will remain encapsulated by this hanging frame on the gym wall?

Looking back, I know those were the most foolish things to think. Even at the time I knew they were in no way, shape, or form accurate. But I felt them nonetheless. I made my way offstage, still stunned, and I did what I do best: I found the silver lining.

BE HAPPY FOR WHAT YOU'VE ACCOMPLISHED TODAY, I reminded myself, AND BE GRATEFUL, HOPEFUL, AND POSITIVE ABOUT THE THINGS YOU WILL DO TOMORROW.

~

Every day is a miracle.

That I do know, even though I forget it sometimes.

Isn't that kind of the point of 2%? It's like by throwing a rare light show or random nightmare storm in our direction, the universe is just trying to get our attention so we don't take anything for granted and just appreciate our days and the hours and minutes that make them up.

That's what's on my mind as I talk to a mom who has just lost her son, Ali's age, to NMO. She sounds so strong. For all these years I've been waging war with the image of Ali having to be wheeled across the stage at her graduation, maybe not even getting there. Maybe that's why I'm looking for ways to delay the ceremony. And here is a mother whose son didn't make it. Not only that, incredibly, she's calling not to talk about her loss but to thank us for the work of the foundation that gave him longer than they had expected. She lets me know that friends and family have sent in donations for the foundation to be used in his memory. Her voice is clear and resolute as she tells me to call on her for anything she can do to help raise awareness in the ongoing search for a cure.

When I get off the phone, sad and mad that we couldn't do more, I fight a flood of fearful thoughts and just try to be in the moment to appreciate where we are. The truth is that every worst fear that I could and did imagine for Ali—none of it has happened. The dire prognosis that we were given hasn't come to pass.

It's true that I have lived too often with the subliminal concern that special events and usual rites of passage may be her last. The irony, of course, is that she prefers low key. But my impulse was always to give all the kids happy memories and make all the details so memorable that they'll be able to relish them long into the years to come.

Even thinking that there could be a cap on the years to come for Ali is so sacrilegious, not even something I allow myself to think about, that I compensate by making every milestone the ultimate.

Senior prom, of course, had to be the absolute best in the world because (a) it's prom, (b) there might not be another event like it, and (c) I never went to prom and refuse to let her miss out on anything that life has to offer.

The logic and the love were really uppermost in my mind. But then again, finding the most amazing dress and then having it altered—I went a little crazy, almost going so far as to tell the tailor that it has to be perfect because only God knew how much time she had left.

Evan once told me that you have to try to just have faith in the world. That's the lullaby I kept trying to sing to myself now. He has always said that to me. Still, I looked around at other moms at the pre-prom party and realized that probably no other mother was thinking of her daughter in her very special dress the same way I was thinking of Ali.

~

About my Mom and prom?

Being the loving yet, often, as we have seen, Smother Mother that she is, she clearly wanted to make my event the best that anyone's experience could ever be. And add to that she also clearly wanted to make up for her lack of prom by making mine even more special.

Weirdly, this wasn't her normal Mom MO. Usually in such instances she lets me run the show for myself. It's not that she doesn't care; it's more that she wants to give me my own space to flourish, and she doesn't want to interfere in the areas where I've been asserting my independence. My mother is the original "be all you can be" woman. But the one thing she has never been is someone's prom date.

So in a nutshell, my prom was her chance to experience vicariously the one she never had at the same time that it was my chance to share it with her. She picked out my dress, had it tailored for me, did my makeup, attended the pre-prom party with me—the whole shebang.

I loved seeing her have so much fun. Gloria Steinem really must be right that it's never too late to have a happy childhood.

~

Having faith in the world was still a leap. But having faith in the Knights of the Round Table was never a question.

Probably the first time I began to feel that we were getting off the drawing board and actually starting to test drive some of the ideas for a cure had been during the March Summit at the ranch. To accommodate our growing numbers, we had rented a vintage two-story mansion—Victorian style, what else?—from the owners of an adjacent property. In a spacious wood-paneled back room that looked like it was from the time of Devic, a most impressive array of doctors and scientists from all corners of the earth sat around a room-sized conference table. Even though most of what they were talking about was more or less Greek to me, I followed along well enough to see that whatever was being discussed was causing eyebrows to raise, heads to nod, and slight smiles to appear on faces. Dr. Brian Weinshenker, our original Wizard and Knight, looked up from his notes and gave me a thumbs up. Dr. Ben Greenberg, sitting a few seats away from him, then stood and walked over to Michael Yeaman's board and added a diagram of his own.

Everyone reacted excitedly.

Something big was happening, and whatever was supposed to be on the agenda, I didn't want to lose this energy, this momentum. Katja and I stepped into the hall, and she agreed. The time had come to get the group to decide together which top three ideas held the most promise for stopping the devastation of NMO.

No sooner had I gone in to say that to the group when I turned around to see a television producer entering from the back with a camera crew in tow. They had originally planned to film later but had arrived early.

Just about then I realized that in my haste to make this meeting, I hadn't put on any makeup and my hair was kind of wild and all over the place. My female Einstein look.

After I spoke and stepped out of the meeting, I knew that Katja and Michael had things well in hand. The day hadn't gone according to schedule, and that turned out to be a great thing. A few months later Dr. Alan Verkman was able to announce that with his foundation-supported research he had indeed uncovered a molecule that can bind to aquaporin-4, neutralizing the ability of the NMO-IgG antibody to bind to it. This strategy serves as a kind of doorman at the spinal cord, throwing his hand up to antibody invaders and saying "you're not welcome here." If such an approach were to be proven effective, next steps would include clinical trials and the work to bring this kind of drug to market quickly. Yes, these are ambitious goals, but time is ticking and lives are at stake; this work is critical to helping patients in halting progress of the disease both for those who have suffered as well as for those who have just been diagnosed.

Looking back, I can see how far we really have come. Our repository contributed directly from NMO sufferers and their families, doctors, and researchers includes not only patients' clinical records but also specimens the foundation has collected of their blood and spinal fluid. Blush for Blood and our traveling nurse, Martha, are responsible for helping us build the Fort Knox of samples so we can actually do further testing. Once the new drug is ready to be tested, along with the other novel therapies that are going to be up next, we'll have the patients ready. Rarely does one foundation coordinate these different phases, especially for an orphan disease.

The way the foundation has approached NMO is multidimensional, and in my opinion, that's a key to success. Visualizing the disease as a multidimensional problem means that treating it has to come from that same multidimensional approach, which is why the next two years are full of even more hope and promise. We are actively working to facilitate industry-sponsored clinical trials—connecting an eager patient population to help us test a drug that may help them—as well as expanding a talented pool of researchers dedicated to this cause. But we know that we're not going to stop there. Is there another blood test we can use, one that is even more sensitive? Perhaps there is a second antibody we might look for. That'll be good for the next couple months.

The real hope that I've found is from the connections to other moms, dads, and patients, from the community that we've created. One of the most memorable exchanges came from a mother who wanted some advice on how to be more of an advocate for her daughter who had NMO but had first been misdiagnosed with MS. She said, "Victoria, I'm not like you. I'm just a small voice in Tennessee. You're a big voice in LA."

And at that moment I realized, *no, if my job is anything, it's that I've got to make everybody's voice big*. That's what I said to her. "You can have a big voice in Tennessee or anywhere." I don't have any magic. If there's anything that I feel I need to give to people, it's the encouragement so that they can have the big voice—all the patients and families for themselves.

NMO had no voice until Ali was diagnosed. We saw early on that there was no conversation around it, so Bill as a funder and I as a finder, bringing together different elements, had to create a conversation and turn up the volume, and now I need to take everyone who thinks they have a small voice and make it a big voice for them. Kind of a throwback to my makeup days when I wanted everyone to know that the key to looking better and feeling better about yourself is in your own hands, I believe that everybody has their own big voice. And if I can get one, so can they. Right now, as I tell everybody on Patient Day, it's like they've got to own this and have the big voice, ask their doctors the questions, be Proactiv (for sure), and play a part in the cure.

That's our hope. Not that it rests in me or even in Ali but in all of us saving each other. A lot of the credit for that realization, by the way, goes to the mom from Tennessee and her big voice.

On the eve of Ali's graduation I sort of feel like I'm graduating from my version of college, ready for the next challenges.

Late blooming is just fine by me.

~

JUNE 2011

I'm in "the dungeon" *(that's what we call the journalism room) when Jordan, my co-editor in chief for the* STUDENT VOICE, *and I get a message to go to the principal's office.*

I'm honestly quite clueless as to what the note could be for until someone else in the room says it's probably about graduation awards. Me? Really?

I'm nervous as we walk over to his office; I've never been summoned to the principal's office before, other than going to ask a question or to talk—never without knowing why I was there.

When we get there, we see him one at a time. When I'm in his office, he leans over and begins to talk to me about graduation. Smiling, he announces that I have been awarded the Head of School Award for my demonstration of "leadership, academic achievement, character, and service on behalf of the school and the community," to be presented at graduation.

I'm honored and barely able to speak other than to stammer my thanks and run out of there. Before I know it, the day arrives.

In the movie version of your life, graduation is a day you tell yourself will never come. But then the day arrives, what are you supposed to make of it? After fifteen years at Buckley, how was I supposed to feel? Fifteen years! I've spent fifteen years of my life in one place, and in one fleeting ceremony it will be over.

The fleeting, fragile nature of life was brought home to everyone in the Buckley community earlier in the year when we tragically lost a member of our graduating class to a skateboarding accident. He was a great person with a contagious smile and zest for life that will forever be a part of all of us. Without question, the loss of one of our own was being felt even more poignantly now that our momentous rite of passage was upon us.

Momentous doesn't even begin to describe other feelings I was having. Graduation not only marked the end of my high school education but also a departure from my second home, my place of comfort and security, my little bubble, as it is commonly known. The bubble is not a good place to spend one's entire life, but there is a feeling of loss, sorrow, and uncertainty when forced to face the reality that, no matter how you look at it, life is about to change.

The setting for our graduation was at the magnificent Disney Hall. It was the most beautiful ceremony I could ever imagine.

We rehearsed for days before the event, and when it was finally put together, everything turned out PERFECT, *and that's saying a lot with my standards. But I also felt like this wasn't really happening. That was running through my head the whole time along with the disbelief that my life had flown by in an instant. It seemed like just yesterday I was going to my first day at school, or attending grandparent's day, or going to my first tennis practice freshman year. It all seemed like yesterday, and now I was being given the Head of School Award and about to receive my diploma.*

I couldn't see the members of my family, but I knew they were there, tearful and joyful. Maybe they were thinking the same thing that I was: WHERE DID THE TIME GO?

That's the question that most everyone asks at some point or another, but for me it hit right as I was walking across the stage.

I didn't need to look out to see my mom at this moment to know what she was thinking. As the story goes, there was a time when she couldn't see me walking across the stage on my own to be handed my diploma. She never told me that, exactly, but there may have been some doubt as to whether or not this could ever happen. But here I am, and there she is.

We did it—defying the odds, defying gravity, saving each other.

~

In December 2011 when Ali came home for Christmas break and went to have an MRI with Katja, she kept me out of the loop initially. We were exceedingly grateful in any event that the combination of drugs, diet, exercise, vitamins, and birth control pills had helped her remain attack-free for over thirteen months.

When Ali asked me to come with her to hear the results, we both braced ourselves not necessarily for the worst but, given the unpredictability, we didn't know what to expect.

That first MRI we had of Ali's spine in June of 2008, after her attack in New York, was awful to see. On it Katja had pointed out that from the top of her spine—T2 is the way doctors identify it when they speak with each other—all the way down to the bottom, or T11, Ali's thoracic spinal cord had a major long, thin lesion.

That was the incident when the radiologist reviewed the initial MRI and said to Katja, "This patient is in a wheelchair, right?"

To which Katja replied, "No. She's actually in the waiting room about to go play in a tennis match."

The shock of seeing that image was scarring. One of the ways that Katja explained what the lesion was came from comparing it to falling off your bike, skinning your knee, and getting a "big, red, yucky scab."

During her review of the new MRI she told Ali and me, "That's kind of what happens to the spinal cord when these antibodies, these proteins from this autoimmune disease, when they go in and they start skinning the knee of the cord if you will, they make this long lesion. It's kind of like if you were to fall and skin your spinal cord. Yikes. It hurts, it's inflamed, and this is how the spinal cord shows us that on an MRI image."

When we looked at the MRI that December afternoon, it appeared completely different from how I remembered from almost four years earlier. I stared at it for a while, and so did Ali. When we looked up from it, Katja was beaming that beautiful smile of hers.

"Ali, your spinal cord is clean," Katja said.

Clean? I looked at Ali and she looked back at me. Then recognition spread over her face and she was beaming too.

"Clean? As in, the lesion is gone?" Ali asked.

"There is no evidence of that inflammation," Katja said. There was no explanation for this rare occurrence. Was it a miracle? Medically, scientifically, it was possible. Maybe there was still inflammation and proof of NMO activity that the imaging technology wasn't strong enough to capture. Ali was still in a state of having her immune system suppressed, still having to take twenty-plus pills a day.

But in the meantime I was going with what Katja had said to me after we had looked at the MRI back in 2008 and marveled that she was up and around and walking—that Ali is a miracle.

We knew for sure that this was a sign that there are some good medicines out there that can calm down the immune system. We could learn from all of this and from Ali, who said, "We want to make it so that every NMO sufferer, not just the lucky ones, can have a moment just like this."

Coming from my extraordinary daughter, there was nothing surprising about her making that statement. What did take me by surprise not many weeks later was an observation she made during a family weekend get-together at the ranch. As Ali and I were getting caught up, suddenly out of nowhere she said, "Isn't life perfect?"

With everything that had been put on her shoulders, with all the uncertainties we pray none of our children will ever have to face, and the loss of innocence, the fact that she could say that made me realize that I could too. In terms of my own healing, growth, and the potential for a reversal of damage, that awareness marked my version of a clean MRI.

All of my panic-driven thinking that once led me to believe I couldn't survive if the worst happened had been wrong. Instead of being taken down for the count when the worst really did happen, I chose to take action. Instead of being diminished, I had been empowered.

At the end of this leg of the journey, my version of a clean MRI also includes the age-old discovery that you never know what you can accomplish until you must. Miraculously, I came to see that life doesn't have to control us anymore than NMO can be allowed to have the final say. We always have a choice in how we respond, no matter what life serves up to us. The question we get to answer is to ourselves: *Well, so, what are you going to do? Will you fall apart or will you get up? Will you find a path to the other side and persevere?*

This was where the journey of *Saving Each Other* has led me—to being healthier than I'd ever been and to having real faith in the world. Ali had helped show me to myself. The miracle is this: what we can all do when we love from a place that's so deep and so powerful, we can—by sheer force of will and empowered by that love—transcend.

Epilogue

Changing the Narrative

NOVEMBER 2011
GUTHY-JACKSON CHARITABLE FOUNDATION ANNUAL SYMPOSIUM

When I opened the *general session for the 2011 Symposium, I had already been at college for almost two months. You're probably wondering how that separation was for me and my mom, right? Well, it was really rough! Big understatement there. But we survived.*

Back during the summer after graduation, Dad and I were on guard, anticipating the separation anxiety to kick in at some point. Because I was sticking close to home for my last summer, we thought it would be fun to plan a father-daughter trip to Europe in the weeks before I would have to leave in the fall. We had postponed other trips out of fear of attacks, but this was going to be short and not a big deal.

The hopeful part was that Mom was deeply immersed in the growth and expansion of the foundation. We were all hopeful. She, incidentally, is the miracle worker.

What's the secret? If you ask me, the truth is that my mom is like glue—she holds them together. The foundation itself would be nothing without her. She's the sun, the moon, and the stars in terms of leading this world-class organization. Her confidence when she is in her element makes her someone not to be messed with. Although the personal incentive to find a cure for me may be the strongest underlying reason for her drive, that reasoning should not in any way diminish the impact her work has had on all patients with NMO, and other autoimmune conditions as well. The way my mom has structured the foundation is so revolutionary that I have no doubt it will impact the medical field greatly in years to come. Her emphasis on a cooperative versus a competitive spirit among researchers has been imperative in opening the flow of communication more effectively. In order for researchers to obtain grants, they must vow to share their findings with the organization as a whole and work together with other scientists for the common purpose of finding a cure. The importance of this communal aspect as well cannot be overstated. By eliminating the usual competition for grant money and the resistances some researchers may have to sharing because of wanting exclusive rights to finding the cure, my mom has broken down some very strong obstacles that often hinder rapid scientific advancement. I think the massive growth and expansion of the foundation, even in the few short years it has been in operation, is a testament to the success of my mom's visions and planning that draws from her business background.

It's unfortunate, in fact, that the medical field is too often reduced to being a business, and I haven't been more certain of that reality since I've been diagnosed with NMO. The for-profit element that tends to fuel greed and ego doesn't seem conducive to serving patients and promoting medical advancement. The work my mom has done should provide the medical community and other funders of private foundations for research with a template for righting these wrongs.

The great news during the summer of 2011 as Dad and I planned our father-daughter trip, letting Mom know about the details, was that she was so busy with the preparations for the Fourth Annual Symposium, she seemed to handle the news well. Well, that was until the last minute, and then she had a full-blown anxiety attack. Seeing her inability to control it was scary. Not to mention the fact that Dad and I were kind of bummed not to go. But in a weird way, after that she was so much better at handling the separation when the day came to move me into my dorm at UCSB. For her birthday I had given her what I called, THE BOOK OF MORE-MOM: A DAUGHTER'S GUIDE TO HELP HER MOTHER COPE WITH THE FACT THAT SHE'S GOING TO COLLEGE, *by Ali Guthy. I think it really helped.*

We talked once a week, texted, and e-mailed. Before we knew it, I was arriving at the hotel on the eve of the general session for the Doctor's Panel for Patient Day and thinking about what I was going to say. Mom was excited by the fact that we were in the biggest ballroom yet—not bad for a rare orphan disease.

This year was by far the most heavily involved I had been with NMO and the foundation. From opening the Symposium to talking with the patients and even getting my picture taken constantly, I definitely began to embrace my role as a "poster child" for NMO. At times I've felt that the appearance of good health that I have sometimes lessens the appearance of the severity of the disease. That's misleading. However, I don't feel that NMO has prevented me from living a normal life. I have still been able to do all the things I've wanted to do and more, whereas so many other NMO patients are forced to face the reality of their circumstance daily.

I'm not like everyone else—I'm very upbeat and don't let things like attacks or medical ordeals stop me from moving on—but I also have a lot of reasons for that to be true, including access to amazing care. All of that being said, I'm proud to represent us, the NMO community, although there are so many other patients who have overcome their challenges better than I have. But this is the position that came my way, for better or for worse, and although I don't feel I deserve it, I have come to embrace it and try my best to use this newfound title for the betterment of all patients.

All of that was in my head for what would be my first real attempt to embrace my role publicly and communicate my message to other patients. The night before, I was in the hotel room, thinking. I had made some public speeches before, but nothing like this! I didn't really know what to say or how to say it. I outlined a few ideas I wanted to highlight and mulled them over in my head. Of course, I asked my mom for her opinion, and she gave her signature advice whenever I'm about to present something: speak from the heart. This method had always served her well, so why not me?

I retired my outline for the night and slept, hoping that some words of genius would strike me in my sleep. I woke the next day, had a light breakfast, and made my way down to the conference room. When I stepped inside, that's when the reality of what I was about to do just hit me. Inside were so many patients, more than I had ever seen in years' prior, and it dawned on me what I was about to speak for. I wasn't just speaking to open the Symposium or to thank the doctors for all their hard work. I was speaking for—no—TO the patients. I was about to address a group of people in search of answers and support. I remember being in their shoes, after my diagnosis, so desperate to get answers but too scared to hear what they were. I had the luxury of leaving all the hard stuff to my mom, but these people didn't. They all had to face NMO despite their growing fears and uncertainty. It was my job now to help ease their worries and get them through this difficult time. I had been there before, so this should be easy, right? I made my way to the stage, as it was time to start, still unsure as to exactly what I was going to say.

My heart stopped when I reached the podium. Oh boy.

I looked out into the sea of people, all of their eyes trained on me. It was now or never. Thank God I could hide myself behind the podium. I began by welcoming everyone and, of course, by thanking my mom and all the doctors for all of their hard work. Then came the challenging part: addressing the patients. For me, the most important thing about Patient Day is creating a sense of community. The realm of NMO is so small that I feel it's crucial that, when we're all together, we see that we're not alone. I know from my first Symposium, although I was very taken aback by the whole thing, one sense that really struck me was the empowerment of knowing I'm not alone. This is what I wanted to impart to my fellow patients, and that's exactly what I did. I talked about family—that's the exact word I wanted to use. We are a family. I wanted everyone to be able to expel their fears and worries and doubts for just a moment, to recognize the NMO family they have before them. None of us have to go through this alone—and none of us will. We are one, big, loving, and supportive NMO family, and together, we will find a cure.

When I finished, my speech was met with a swell of applause, which allowed me to hope my message had been received. I don't consider myself to be a great speaker. (Often, I feel that my voice when giving a speech sounds much more artificial than I intend.) But the patients' response suggested they accepted me anyway. I was so thrilled. I had done it! It didn't all hit me until I was making my way back to my seat. I was walking around the outside, as not to disturb anyone, when a patient (or she may have been a caregiver) reached out to stop me. She asked how old I was, and when I told her eighteen, she was shocked. She told me how poised I was and how grateful she is for all that my mom and I are doing.

When I returned to the table in the back where I was sitting with my parents, my grandmothers, and my brothers, they were mostly wiping their eyes—Dad maybe more than Mom. Evan and Jackson had come to help for the day, and both of them said they could have never pulled that off.

The outpouring of thanks and praise was almost too much. But that probably goes back to my resistance to being a poster child. On the other hand, if it's the one thing I can do that is best for the betterment of the patients and the NMO community as a whole, then I will happily proceed. Regardless of my title or the perception of my role in the realm of NMO, I was proud to represent. Everyone—doctor, caregiver, and patient—are so loving, open, and accepting. If I had to be diagnosed with a rare orphan condition and had to be the poster child, I'm glad it's for this one.

Acknowledgments

From Victoria Jackson

The book-writing experience that started off a few lifetimes ago (even though it's only been a little more than four years) really has been a transformational journey. As I've traveled this road—over a period in which the book evolved into something much more ambitious and collaborative than I could have dreamt—I've remained grateful to each of my guides and supporters who stepped in at different stages along the way. Wherever each of you left the process or joined in, I know for a fact that we couldn't have gotten to where we are today without you.

The first person I would like to thank who has been with me every step of the way is Dr. Katja Van Herle. I didn't feel as alone knowing you were at my side.

Special thanks goes to writer Bruce Wagner who was there in the very early, dark, scary days, and who helped me develop a framework for telling our unfolding story, even if only as an outlet for dealing with what was going on. Thank you, Bruce, for helping me find my voice. I'm also thankful for writer Lisa Dickey who stepped in to help focus the story and point me in the right direction. Heartfelt thanks go to Laura Barrett, my assistant during the book's development, who was steadfast in encouraging me.

My eternal gratitude goes to a handful of great publishing professionals who have been the best partners on this journey that we could have ever imagined. Special thanks to attorney Wendy Bleiman for helping us navigate the paperwork and providing your expertise. Major acknowledgments are due to agent Elizabeth Kaplan—for believing in the book and us, even when our prospects looked challenging, also for turning over all stones on our behalf, and for opening doors at Vanguard. Thank you to the Vanguard publishing team not just for stepping up but also for being extraordinary in every way. Publisher Roger Cooper, from the moment we met, I knew that we had found our publishing home and that NMO was going to be an orphan disease no mo'. Thanks to publishing manager Melanie Mitzman and the rest of the team at Vanguard, for passion and precision. Editor Francine LaSala, thank you for your gifts of structure, for hitting the right notes in the narrative, and for getting us through the process with such ease and grace. Thank you to Lori Hobkirk at the Book Factory for editorial production and to designer Cynthia Young at Sagecraft. Big thanks to our PR team at February Partners, along with social media maven Fauzia Burke, for all you've done to elevate awareness of the book and the issues it focuses on.

I will forever be indebted to the amazing Mim Eichler Rivas without whom the book definitely would not have been written or finished. You are an extraordinary writer and woman. Mim, thank you for helping to shape the writing and balancing my voice with Ali's, for taking our words and understanding what was in our hearts and then turning all that into music on the page. Thank you for taking your own leap of faith and being on a journey that honestly wouldn't have been possible without you.

When it comes to the 2% Rule that continually allows me to have rarity in my life, I have to collectively acknowledge the brilliance of our medical/scientific teams who have helped write the story of *Saving Each Other* by giving us hope where there was none at the start. My deepest gratitude goes to our core group of advisors as well as our investigators. Thank you to all partners of the Guthy-Jackson Charitable Foundation, with special acknowledgments to each member of the staff who do all the heavy lifting. Valerie, Derek, Megan, and Dan, you do so much without enough fanfare, thank you for everything. Sincere thanks to

Jacinta Behne for all you do and for helping us hunt down statistics and materials for the book. Thank you to Jesse Dylan for your contribution to the website. I also want to acknowledge our partners at the Accelerated Cure Project and at Labcorps—with huge gratitude for helping us expand the bio-repository so that life-saving research can be done. And big thanks go to traveling nurse Martha, who is so critical to the growth of the blood-bank.

These acknowledgments wouldn't be complete if I didn't individually thank some of the Knights of the Round Table who gave so generously of their time in interviews for *Saving Each Other*, also reviewing drafts for us, and contributing some of their own writing. Thank you with all my heart to doctors Katja Van Herle, Michael Yeaman, Larry Steinman, and Brian Weinshenker for being a part of the book's evolution in deed and word. Thank you to the doctors in the trenches: Ben Greenberg and the team at UTSW; Claudia Lucchinetti, Sean Pittock, and the rest of the Mayo team; Alan Verkman and everybody at the lab at UCSF; Vijay Kuchroo at Harvard; and all our teams who dare to think outside the compact. My infinite gratitude extends as well to some key advisors who have helped the foundation move at warp-speed and informed this book: doctors Amit Bar-Or, Terrence Blaschke, Terry Smith, Michael Sofroniew, Andre Van Herle, and Howard Weiner. To all our medical/scientific searchers and healers—without your guidance and your focus on unraveling the medical mysteries of NMO and other related diseases, there would be no science in this book to write about. We feel so blessed to have you and your passion, your brilliant minds, and your hearts committed to our cause.

I want to offer a collective thanks to our NMO community—our patients, doctors, nurses, caregivers, advocates, and loved ones—and acknowledge the growing, loving, supportive family we have become. Your struggles and your hopes fuel our determination.

My sincere gratitude belongs forever to our most esteemed group of colleagues and friends who contributed quotes about *Saving Each Other* to the back of the book: Gloria Steinem, Reese Witherspoon, Kathy Freston, Tony Robbins, Sherry Lansing, Rob Lowe, Dustin Hoffman, Garry Marshall, and, again, Dr. Larry Steinman. Thank you, again,

Dr. Brian Weinshenker of the Mayo Clinic, for writing the book's powerful afterword.

Acknowledgments are overdue to my personal sisterhood, my group of dearest friends Ellen, Portia, Gloria, Lisa, Kathy, Robin, Julie, Janice, Sherry, and the rest of the gang. Thank you for giving me all of your shoulders to cry on and for reminding me to find reasons to laugh. Ditto to Barbara, Gerard, and all my friends who are there in every season.

I'm also very grateful to Cameron for helping to quiet my mind . . . no easy task.

A special heartfelt thanks has to go to Dr. Anne La Borde for traveling with me and being with me continuously over the long haul of the journey. Thank you for everything.

I have always been a believer that the universe sends us just who we need to give us guidance and support when and how it's most needed. That would be true in the case of Carl Perkins who has been there in lockstep with me from the start, making my personal and professional lives run so much more smoothly than I could have alone—especially during the most difficult times. Further thanks as well to assistant Bryan DiNallo who handled overflow in tough stretches. Much gratitude to my assistant, Jen Harris, who jumped in during the later stages of work on the book, and who has been a godsend in every respect—keeping drafts sorted out and being the best cheerleader we could have ever asked for.

Thank you, Joe, for always being a guiding light from above for me. You will forever and always be in my heart.

Thank you to my mom. I love you more than anything. Thank you for your Momtras that have served me so well, for being there for me in every way, and for your strength. Loving thanks to my mother-in-law, Elaine, for your faith and support.

Gratitude goes to all of the members of our close and extended family: my sister, Audrey; my niece, Nicole, and siblings, Andrea and Danny; to all the Guthys we love so much in North Carolina; and to Raquel and Mimi who have allowed me to focus on the work of the foundation and this book, knowing all matters of the household were in their capable hands. Thank you so, so much to Greg and Stacey Renker,

Ben and Laura Van de Bunt, and Kevin and Joan Knee—for all of your support for our family.

Thank you to my loving husband, Bill—for always being there, for standing by me no matter what, and for your support, partnership, and being on this journey with me. Thank you for the toast you made when we got married—to all of our adventures together. You have been on this book adventure from the start, always with the belief in Ali and in me.

Finally, to my three beloved kids—I know I can drive you crazy, but I love you and thank you for being in my life every day. You are my inspiration, my reason for being, the lights of my life. Yes you are.

Dearest Ali, how can I acknowledge everything miraculous that you are? You are my soul mate, my teacher, my role model. Thank you for your courage, the light that shines through you, the lessons you've taught me. I read your guide to surviving and thriving challenges all the time. *Saving Each Other* is the story we've lived together, and now we close the book on this chapter as you prepare to write the next. I could never thank you enough for your gift of sharing this extraordinary experience with me. I love you to bits, boodles, and beyond.

FROM ALI GUTHY

Thank you to all the people at Vanguard*, without whom this book would never have been published; with a special thanks to Roger Cooper, Melanie Mitzman, and Francine La Sala.*

Thank you to Mim Rivas, whose writing helped our story transcend from reality to paper; and Elizabeth Kaplan, the most dedicated and encouraging agent.

An extra special thanks to Katja Van Herle and Benjamin Greenberg, whose superior medical knowledge, advice, and never-ending support has guided (and continues to guide) me through this difficult diagnosis. More love and thanks to all the researchers currently working on finding a cure for NMO; your dedication, passion, and commitment to solving this rare disorder has strongly impacted my life, and is changing the lives of so many patients as well.

Thank you Buckley Girls' Tennis and coach Sue Sherman for four amazing years of laughs, love, and unforgettable memories. Also, a special thanks to the entire Buckley school, in particular—Dina Figueroa and Brooke Yoshino, for being my second home for fifteen years.

To all my friends, thank you for your never-ending support, your unconditional love, and for being with me every step of the way. Extra hugs and kisses to Sarah, Celine, Catherine, Madeline, Isabelle, Suz, Samantha, and Matthew.

Last, but certainly not least, thank you to my family—Raquel, Mimi, Nanny, Grandma, Evan, Jackson, and Dad—my life would not be the same without you, and no words can express how much I love you. Mom, you are my soul mate, the wind beneath my wings, the light of my life, and my best friend. I love you with all my heart and more, and I can't wait for the years ahead as we continue on this journey together. I love you always.

Resources

From Victoria Jackson—What You Need to Know

I wanted to share a few more thoughts with the moms, dads, spouses, partners, best friends, and caretakers of loved ones who may be struggling through your family's version of NMO. My heartfelt hope is that the steps of our journey may offer you some guidance and reassurance during what may be your fearful days and sleepless nights.

If your child or loved one or anyone you know has symptoms that could be associated with NMO/Devic's Disease, MS, or other autoimmune diseases, please visit our website at www.guthyjacksonfoundation.org to learn what resources are available to you. In addition to discovering vital information about how to get tested (it's as easy as a blood test), where to find clinicians who treat NMO, and how to connect with our blood draw sites, you will also find answers to urgent questions you and your physicians may have. We can't emphasize enough how important early diagnosis and treatment are in preventing the damage attacks cause. We also want to reinforce the importance of seeking out the appropriate drug therapies through doctors who are treating your loved one. Although we've fine-tuned the right combination of medications, supplements, and a gluten-free/low-gluten diet for Ali, we have to stress that because something works for one patient, that doesn't mean it may work for others. There are also treatments we haven't tried that may hold great promise for others.

As the little foundation that could, we've grown from a handful of people to a team of people all over the world dedicated not only to finding a cure for NMO but also understanding this disease and what we can learn and do in terms of treating and curing so many other related disorders and diseases. When you join our NMO Advocacy Network, you can be a part of making a difference in the world of medicine.

~

FROM ALI GUTHY, A THRIVER'S GUIDE TO NMO AND OTHER CHALLENGES

Yes, it's true. *The 2% deal of the cards is not always fair, especially when it comes to being given a rare orphan disease. But as I learned, those same low odds can be overturned. How? Well, the following five steps have certainly worked for me and for others who've given them a try. Hopefully they'll provide you with a starting place, if not a roadmap to thriving, to how you might create your own map. The steps are: (1) Discovery, (2) Throw a Fit, (3) (In the words of my mom) "Put on Your Makeup and Get Out There!," (4) Don't Be a Victim, and (5) Remember: The Sun Will Come Out Tomorrow!*

STEP 1: DISCOVERY

Know what you have! Ignorance can be bliss, but it's also a means of avoiding the situation. Take your time, but confront your enemy, face the music, and then, in your own way, learn how to deal with the facts presented.

STEP 2: THROW A FIT

Don't bottle your feelings, but don't allow them to take over your life. Stick to a normal routine, but allow yourself to balance that normalcy with the realities of your unusual/unique circumstances. When someone says or does something that's insensitive—even if it's the most minute comment—if it makes you feel upset, be upset! Allow yourself to have bursts of anger or fits of depression, as long as those moments don't start to encroach upon or ruin your normal life.

STEP 3: (IN THE WORDS OF MY MOM) "PUT ON YOUR MAKEUP AND GET OUT THERE!"

Don't let the reality of your situation or the every-so-often fits of depression stop you from living. Lead a normal life and pursue activities or goals that are both enjoyable and alleviate you from the stress, anger, and confusion that surround your health challenges.

STEP 4: DON'T BE A VICTIM

Self-pity, self-judgment, and all other forms of internalizing a diagnosis like NMO are not the answer. Don't be the helpless Cinderella waiting for the magical Prince Charming (commonly known as the cure) to come sweep you off your feet. As much as it pains me to say it, in the realm of NMO and other dire diagnoses, there is no time for the magic of fairy tales. You can't indulge in "if only" thinking anymore than you should allow for "what-if" thinking. Don't be a patient; be an advocate. Be your own Prince Charming, and be a part of the search for the cure. Donate blood to the repository or be part of research efforts, talk to your doctors and other patients, and spread the word about NMO or other little-understood diseases by educating those around you.

STEP 5: REMEMBER: THE SUN WILL COME OUT TOMORROW

Stay positive! Always try to find the silver lining. I know, sometimes it just doesn't want to be found. If you can remember that everything you are going through is going to empower others to overcome their odds, that might help you remember that you are being part of the solution—and that's a very powerful force to be.

And finally:

Never, never, never give up.

—Winston Churchill

Afterword

by

Brian Weinshenker, MD
Professor of Neurology,
Mayo Clinic, Rochester, MN

AS someone with a long-standing interest in neuromyelitis optica and who has cared for hundreds of patients with this condition, I found reading the juxtaposed perspectives of Victoria Jackson—entrepreneur and cofounder of the Guthy-Jackson Foundation dedicated to curing neuromyelitis optica—and of her daughter Ali Guthy, a victim of the disease, to be particularly poignant. I had not been attracted to study this disease by any personal connection, but because of the clues that I suspected it held to the more common disease multiple sclerosis with which it is commonly confused and which has been the basis of my medical practice. Attacks of neuromyelitis optica are very reminiscent of attacks of multiple sclerosis; initially, most patients with neuromyelitis optica are diagnosed as having multiple sclerosis. Why does neuromyelitis optica selectively target the optic nerves and spinal cord? Why are its attacks so severe and its course so aggressive with frequent clusters of attacks? Could this tell us something about how targeting of the brain occurs in multiple sclerosis and what determines the severity of attacks? Fortunately, there have been major strides over the past decade, beginning with the appreciation that this disease was likely much broader than previously recognized, and shortly thereafter, by the discovery of the first specific biomarker for neuromyelitis optica that rapidly led to identification of the target of the immune system, a recently discovered water channel protein, aquaporin-4. We are starting to be able to answer these questions, and the answers are offering potential hints at target-specific treatments, which we don't have for any autoimmune disease at this time.

However, the story told by Victoria and Ali is not a scientific story, but one that provided me insight into the human side of this tragic disease. Neuromyelitis optica causes its victims to experience blindness or paralysis with lightning speed, and leaves them wondering whether they will recover . . . or not. Even after recovering from the episode, patients are left wondering when the next event will hit, and usually it is without warning. So often, as physicians, we deal with people thrown into situations over which they have no control and no means to fight back. Ali, a young teen, was similarly victimized by this disease. However, she is the daughter of two strong and committed parents whose personal backgrounds and means gave them not only the skills to fight, but the capacity to win. Their story of taking back control when it was slipping out of their grip, and giving hope to other victims by leading the charge against their tormentor, should be inspirational to all. Most of all, it is a story of how a rare disease is being defeated by the power of love between a daughter and her parents, by harnessing a scientific team armed by a new and recent discovery that has facilitated rapid scientific progress.

Victoria and Bill's philanthropy and team-building skills serve as a road map for how health professionals have to reorganize and seek funding to defeat rare "orphan diseases" that neither government nor industry are immediately interested in studying, particularly in an era of constrained governmental support for research.

NMO Defined

—from the GJCF website

NMO is an uncommon disease syndrome of the central nervous system that typically affects the optic nerves and spinal cord. NMO is rare and is thus termed an "orphan disease." Individuals diagnosed with NMO can develop inflammation of the optic nerve or "optic neuritis," which often results in eye pain, blurred vision, and/or loss of color or overall vision. NMO can also cause inflammation in the spinal cord or "transverse myelitis," which can lead to weakness, numbness or tingling, loss of bowel or bladder control, and sometimes paralysis of the arms or legs. NMO can also result in a loss of myelin, which is a fatty substance that insulates nerve fibers and helps nerve signals travel efficiently from nerve to nerve and to the muscles and tissues that they activate. The syndrome can also damage nerve fibers and cause injury or inflammation of surrounding tissues. In the disease process of NMO—for reasons that are not yet clear—certain immune system cells and special proteins called antibodies attack and injure cells in the spinal cord and optic nerves, including astrocytes and their companion neurons. In turn, progressive damage or dysfunction of these cells leads to NMO symptoms.

Historically, NMO was diagnosed in patients who experienced a rapid onset of blindness in one or both eyes, followed within days or weeks by varying degrees of neurological symptoms (weakness, tingling, numbness, paralysis) in the arms or legs. In many cases however, the time period between optic neuritis and possible transverse myelitis can be much longer—perhaps years—and in some cases there is only one episode of symptoms. Additionally, some patients suffer primarily from optic neuritis only while for others it is primarily transverse myelitis. Physicians and scientists are trying to determine why each patient has their own individual pattern of NMO signs and symptoms.

After the initial episode, NMO can follow an unpredictable course. Some individuals experience clusters of attacks that can occur months or even years apart, followed by partial recovery during periods of remission. This type of pattern is called relapsing NMO, and it can affect females more commonly than males. Interestingly, the female-to-male ratio often observed in NMO is greater than 4:1. In another form of NMO, an individual suffers a single, severe attack and then no further attacks. This form of the disease is called monophasic NMO, which may be a distinct type of disease that affects males and females with equal frequency. The range in age of NMO onset can vary from childhood through adulthood, with two time periods of potentially higher occurrence: in young people less that than twenty years of age, and in adults in their forties and fifties. Unfortunately, NMO can occur at almost any age. The potential susceptibility to the disease, including environmental factors and possible genetic links, is being studied, but thus far no clear associations have been established.

In the past, NMO was considered to be a severe type of multiple sclerosis (MS) because both NMO and MS can cause optic neuritis and myeltis and both occur more commonly in females. However, recent discoveries suggest that these are separate diseases. NMO is often different from MS in the severity of attacks, and its tendency to strike the optic nerve(s) and/or the spinal cord at the onset of the disease. Symptoms other than those targeting the optic nerves and spinal cord are rare, although certain symptoms, including uncontrollable vomiting or a prolonged duration of hiccups may occur prior to the first episode of NMO, or prior to a relapse, due to involvement of brainstem tissues. The recent discovery of an antibody in the blood of individuals with NMO gives doctors a reliable biomarker, and when present can further distinguish NMO from MS. This antibody, which is an immune system protein known as NMO-IgG, seems to be present in about 70 percent of patients diagnosed with NMO, and is usually not commonly found in patients with MS. This antibody can be measured by a simple blood test.

This review provides only a general summary of basic information regarding NMO. Research in this field is moving quickly, and such information may change rapidly. Of course anyone experiencing symptoms such as those described above should contact their physician or neurologist immediately for appropriate evaluation.

You can find us on the Internet at:

www.guthyjacksonfoundation.org
http://spectrum.guthyjacksonfoundation.org

GUTHY JACKSON®
Charitable Foundation